The *Hot Rod* Reader

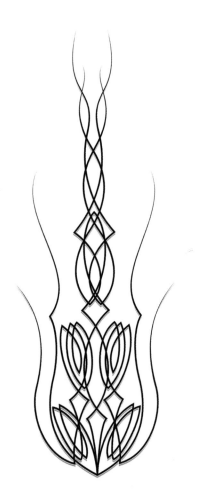

The
Hot Rod
Reader

Edited by
Melinda Keefe and
Peter Schletty

First published in 2011 by Motorbooks, an imprint of MBI Publishing Company, 400 First Avenue North, Suite 300, Minneapolis, MN 55401 USA

The information in this book is true and complete to the best of our knowledge. All recommendations are made without any guarantee on the part of the author or Publisher, who also disclaims any liability incurred in connection with the use of this data or specific details.

We recognize, further, that some words, model names, and designations mentioned herein are the property of the trademark holder. We use them for identification purposes only. This is not an official publication.

Motorbooks titles are also available at discounts in bulk quantity for industrial or sales-promotional use. For details write to Special Sales Manager at MBI Publishing Company, 400 First Avenue North, Suite 300, Minneapolis, MN 55401 USA.

To find out more about our books, visit us online at www.motorbooks.com.

ISBN-13: 978-0-7603-3968-8

Library of Congress Cataloging-in-Publication Data
The hot rod reader / edited by Melinda Keefe and Peter Schletty.
      p. cm.
ISBN 978-0-7603-3968-8 (plc)
1. Hot rods. I. Keefe, Melinda, 1982- II. Schletty, Peter, 1978-
TL236.3.H6833 2011
629.2286--dc22
                    2010039720

Editors: Melinda Keefe and Peter Schletty
Design Manager: Brenda C. Canales
Designed by: Diana Boger
Cover designed by: John Bell
On the front cover and title page: © John Bell

Printed in China

Photo Credits

Contents

Chapter 2: How to Build the Perfect Rod

Chapter 3: History of the Hop-Up Movement

Chapter 4: Dragging and Driving

Chapter 5: Long Haul in a Hot Rod

Introduction

I once had an English professor who told me, "Editors are born and not made." He believed some people had a built-in passion or perspective that made them understand the language and helped them recognize when something was wrong simply because it looked or sounded wrong. In the automotive world, some people just have similar innate tendencies. They can't help themselves! That passion can show itself in a number of ways, but as an in-born, driving force, it's hard to turn off.

Hot rodders have been described in many different terms, especially early hot rodders, who were often the villains of quiet suburban life. Boys

who raced souped-up roadsters down lonely highways were dangerous, radical, and anti-society. They threatened the social order of a stable community. To be fair, there were a few so-called "shot rodders" who deserved the public outrage.

That rebel image has softened in the last 50 years through the efforts of car clubs, timing associations, the NHRA, and all the great hot rod builders and racers who have come since the early days. But even though the image may have changed, hot rodders today remain much the same (at their core) as their pioneer brethren. They have the same passion for speed, the same enthusiasm for building and rebuilding, and the same satisfaction with a fast, good-looking car.

Those who work to improve the performance of their cars, to create art from machinery, embody the "innovation, rebellion, freedom, speed, desire, and passion" that photographer Peter Vincent says is the art of the hot rod. Whether hot rodding represents innovation or obsession (or both) in your life, or if you come to car-building and racing for some other reason, the stories in this book are sure to feed your auto-lust.

Stories from Ed "Big Daddy" Roth, Robert Williams, Von Dutch, and other artists will show you how other hot rod devotees have expressed their fascination, while pieces by Barney Navarro, Robert E. Petersen, Dean Moon, Tom Senter, and other masters of hot rodding pass on the tools and instruction you need to achieve the performance you crave. You'll find articles by great hot rod writers past and present, such as Dean Batchelor, Ken Gross, Jay Leno, Spencer Murray, and Gray Baskerville, as well as words of wisdom from legends like Wally Parks, Jim Jacobs, and Bob Hirohata. And, of course, you can read the stories that inspired thousands of young kids to take up wrenching on cars as a hobby, with excerpts from Tom Wolfe's *The Kandy-Kolored Tangerine-Flake Streamline Baby* and Henry Gregor Felsen's *Hot Rod*.

As you read these works from hot rodders just like you, you may find yourself remembering your first high-speed trip down a side road, your first look at a chopped top, your first trophy at a local meet, or maybe just the first hot rod you pined for. And if you find yourself itching for speed, know that it's not really your fault. Maybe you were just born that way.

—Melinda Keefe

1

The Art of Hot Rodding

The Psychological Components of the Hot Rodder

Unravelling the Hot Rod Puzzle

By Peter E. Siegle, consulting psychologist
for Maremont Automotive Products

※

Hot Rod Magazine, August 1952

Like all social institutions, the hot rod movement in America has its roots in the social and psychological conditions surrounding the development of the movement itself and the satisfactions inherent in the particular activity as related to the manner in which it meets the needs of both the individual and the group. Therefore, the question as analyzed in this study is: "Of what value, if any, is the hot rod to the furtherance of American cultural ideals and to American individuals?"

There are three basic categories of analysis pertaining to the answer to the above:

1. Relationship of the hot rod to basic American attitudes.
2. Present day psychological components of the hot rodder.
3. Sociological and psychological components of the hot rodder.

Hot Rods and Basic American Culture

Let us examine some of the basic American attitudes with a particular eye to the hot rod in the culture.

Americans admire initiative, gumption, stick-to-it-iveness, all of which are basic attributes of the hot rodder. Americans believe in the value of righteous, friendly competition between equals. Competition is essential in the hot rod movement. The American notion of FREEDOM is embodied in the "free enterprise" system and the opportunity to make more and better *things*. The ideal dream is that of a man alone with his raw materials, using his ingenuity and "know-how" along with his industriousness to produce a better THING. "Build a better mouse trap and the world will beat a path to your door." This is the vision which gives a quasi-religious overtone to the phrase, "private enterprise." There is an almost mystic quality to the picture of the young American boy working from scratch in the shop, hoping to build a better hot rod. It fits in with the American shibboleth of recognition for the ability to pull one's self up by the bootstraps. Hard work and luck are key ideas in the American success story.

Americans have a genuine admiration for ability to break records and the creation of things "bigger and better." The genius of Americans has not always been the ability to create basic inventions but rather the ability to translate a basic invention into improved performance, industrial adaptation, and diffusion throughout the population. The hot rod is an excellent example of this in that it demonstrates what this American genius can do to a Ford V8.

Psychological Components of the Hot Rodder

The serious hot rodder is compulsive . . . which may mean that he is attempting to bring some order into his life by organizing and manipulating gadgets . . . an action which is, for him, easier than trying to manipulate people or his common daily activities. He needs this activity to keep himself on an even keel.

Hot rod addiction is a SUBSTITUTE action for reducing the tensions of frustration resulting from an otherwise difficult attempt to achieve status in the ordinary Veblen "conspicuous consumption" sense. Since all motivation and response is modified in some way by the cultural milieu, it is only natural that in a mechanistic culture, young people tend toward mechanistic pursuits. In this culture status is achieved through money, sex, or the acquisition of physical status symbols. The hot rodder gains recognition (negative or positive) by building the noisier, faster, flashier vehicle which he otherwise could not afford.

If Adler's concept is acceptable, this might well be an obvious example of "The will-to-power." The man who purchases a 190 hp stock car manifests it just as the hot rod builder does. The difference may well lie in the ability or desire to make the purchase and, therefore, prove himself wealthy enough or, being less well-heeled, gaining the same end at a cheaper price. It is better to have the will-to-power controlled as in the hot rod competitions . . . with its emphasis on safety . . . than to permit individuals with the same basic power drives to get behind the wheel of a Lincoln and with less intensive regard for safety and the consequences, to power-drive himself . . . and others . . . into accidents.

There are positive socially preventive values inherent in the hot rod movement. Accident proneness is considerably related to emotional instability, whether driving a jalopy or a Cadillac. It has two different general bases: Aggressive desire to hurt others (displaced or free-floating aggression) and the refusal to face reality, causing fantasy and/ or daydreaming while driving. The genuine hot rodder is probably less likely to be involved in the kind of personality struggle leading to accident proneness because he has channeled these drives into more constructive pursuits. Hobbies are useful because they concentrate efforts outside the self. Hot rodding may be of greater value than others' hobbies in that it contains a definite outlet for the power element, not present in many other hobbies. It takes on the value of athletics and competitive sport and has the additional advantage of competition with one's previous performance or with a generalized performance of a nonspecific person. This ties in with the need to let off steam as in the case of the free-floating aggression our culture fosters.

The American social system places many obstacles or frustrations in the path of individuals. This leads to a frustration and subsequent aggression toward the society as a whole. The aggression may not necessarily direct itself toward a particular frustrating agency, but nevertheless requires some compensatory response. The hot rod provides American males with an additional opportunity to achieve mastery (in this case, over machines) which serves as a constructive outlet for these deep-seated aggressions produced by the competitive problems of everyday life. American culture is so inhibitive that a creative sublimation of the need for mastery is essential. We can't all be poets, painters, and lovers, musicians and successful salesmen, owners of Cadillacs or other status symbols. The hot rod provides an opportunity for certain individuals to achieve status through action.

A key advantage in this kind of outlet is the opportunity to work on something which will provide one with a certain element of distinction without confining him to the pressures of potential failure inherent in the more "legitimate" and more "bourgeois" activities of daily competitive economic life. Giving young men such opportunity can relieve pressures and tensions within them and hence take the pressure off the public at large which occurs when the aggressive response to daily frustration leads to so-called delinquent (or at least destructive) behavior.

Postwar frustrations have led to an increase in teen-age delinquency... sex clubs ... teen-age scandals. The intense activity of the hot rod addict leaves him little time for such delinquency, and there has been an increase in serious tinkering with autos and radio.

The hot rod is a mature projection of the development of the child.

The hot rod movement is a "great equalizer," running the gamut of social and economic class, bringing young men from all walks of life into wholesome contact with each other in a common aim. It is American and democratic.

The changing American family, with all its attendant loss of integration as a place where the family unit builds, works, and improves, can benefit from the opportunity the hot rod provides for expansion of mechanical expression (which is really the heartbeat of the American socio-economic system). It's good for today's youth to have a place, either at home or in the community at large where he can learn to build and use the ingenuity prized by Americans.

The hot rod is a mature projection of the development of the child from the educational toy upwards. Holgate, tinker-toys, erector set, model airplanes, model cars, model ships and home car building and repair is the usual progression. The advantage to the hot rod is that it is not only educational, but practical and UTILITARIAN. Hot rods are built by groups and they represent the integration of large numbers of individuals with regional, local, family, and group pride in the results no matter what the goals—be they for racing, sport, or aesthetic purposes; hence strong in-group feelings.

We cannot legislate against the hot rod unless it proves itself a public nuisance in violation of the zoning codes or as a safety hazard. Theoretically, the same safety checks can be applied to the hot rod as those which affect all other vehicles. More careful checks on licensing of motor vehicles would probably delight the serious hot rodder. At the same time stifling the tendency to experiment would be a violation of the American ideals of individual initiative and free enterprise.

The hot rod movement is closely related to the basic American superiority in handling all phases of machinery production and control as pointed out by the experts during the last war. In comparing the French,

British, and American military and their relationship to machinery, it can be said that the Frenchman rhapsodizes; the Briton compromises; the American improvises. To maintain this mechanical advantage, any encouragement toward the mechanical improvisation required in the hot rod movement, while still consistent with basic American ideals of free enterprise, has its value in American culture. The hot rodder is to automotive pursuits what the "ham" is to radio. The motivation is toward expert craftsmanship and performance.

Hot rodding is SPORT in the American tradition. It fits in with the fundamental sporting element apparent in American business and in the great American game of poker. As sport, it has its value in the constructive forces that can be corralled for the production for cold and hot wars necessary in these times. Perhaps the "playing fields of Eton" theme can be applied in some respect to the mechanical superiority inherent in the competitive exercises on the flats at Bonneville.

The continued development of the hot rod movement is beneficial to individuals and society because the activity surrounding the hot rod culture is: CREATIVE, EDUCATIVE, COMPETITIVE, CONSTRUCTIVE, MASCULINE, all of which are desirable elements in furthering the best in the American way of life.

Defining the
Hot Rod Genre

By Peter Vincent

※

Hot Rod: The Photography
of Peter Vincent, 2004

I had a long conversation with Mark Morton, editor and publisher of *Hop Up* magazine, a couple of years ago about the visceral, or just plain "gut level," nature of hot rods, thinking it would be easy to write a few lines about these inherent, sensual qualities. What seemed simple on the surface quickly became complex. This is at least my third attempt.

Trying to pin down, in words, exactly what defines the visceral and instinctual nature of a hot rod is an exercise in contrast and contradiction. Part of the problem is the wide-open nature of hot rods and customs, which fosters continuous innovation. Another aspect that defies definition is the very real sensory reaction that comes from being inside the culture as a participant. This perspective is considerably different than that of an outsider or spectator.

Fortunately, I feel connected to both viewpoints. As a photographer, I relate first to almost everything I see by mentally transferring it into two-dimensional photographic images. However, this process forms only part of the overall equation. Hot rods are felt in a way that awakens all of our senses. This reaction can be overanalyzed to death by saying that real hot rods are the sum of their parts, such as Halibrand quick-change rear ends, big and little tire and wheel combinations with the "right" wheels, or the "correct" engine with the "correct" engine dressing and accessories. Every detail can be formally planned and designed in much the same way the major car companies and high-end car builders work. There is intellectual and real value in applying design, proportioning, and advanced engineering, bringing everything together to create a final cohesive unit. But with hot rods, inspiration also comes from the gut. Real hot rods are built in an instinctual and visceral way that involves heightening all of our senses to create an added dimension. Pete Eastwood told me about a quote he had remembered from Kid Rock that actually makes a lot of sense: "If it looks good you'll see it; if it sounds good you'll hear it; if it's packaged right, you'll buy it; but if it's real, you'll feel it."

In this way, definition comes from experience and history. For example, many of us grew up with hot rodding as part of our everyday experience. We have developed an aesthetic that comes from the roots

Hot rods as a form of expression are here to stay.

of hot rodding, but it also includes a combination of all our physical senses and what we have experienced at intimate levels. The emotional understanding that is derived from sweat, blood, and instinct differentiates one from another much the same way that fine art separates from mere decoration. We all have a tendency to intellectualize, and everyone has an opinion, including me, as to what turns us on and makes our clock tick. But there does seem to be a universal understanding that when all parts are in the right place, you know in your gut that what has been created is an authentic hot rod, and is, as such, "good art."

The true and ultimate knowledge, though, comes from the ride. Here again, it is more than the difference between inside and outside. The view through a chopped windshield is both heaven and hell, especially if it is over a hood punched full of louvers (it's especially beautiful in that pure and visual "hot rod" sense). The difference between riding in a family car and a bare-to-the-bones hot rod is like the difference between listening to Barry Manilow and early Joe Cocker. A hot rod offers a visceral avenue into all the senses. Inside you sense power, fury, fantasy, and the meaning of hot rod. It is a ride down the black line on the salt of Bonneville, or it is kicking up a dusty rooster tail on the dry lakes of El Mirage or Muroc. But it also is a quarter-mile acceleration dash down the local drag strip, or just a late night cruise on the boulevard, listening to the sound of the engine and exhaust reverberating off the surrounding buildings.

A hot rod is memory, and it is a dream. It is you, the car, and a lonely desert highway at sunset. No distractions. It is the aesthetic ideal when the driver becomes one with the ride, with the freedom of the road accentuating life, awakening all the senses. There is an earthy and instinctual connection between pleasure and pride when driving something cool and customized that you made yourself. The hot rod makes a statement.

It is innovation, rebellion, freedom, speed, desire, and passion. It is the ultimate ride.

I have posed five basic questions to many well-known people who are hot rodders or racers at heart. . . . I am still trying to find all the connecting links to why the culture was so important to so many, why they personally became involved in it, and what their influences were. Is the hot rod a cultural icon that relates to "my" generation and the times we grew up in—and by that I mean the 1930s through the 1960s? How do those early decades relate to the 1970s through today? What are today's influences and what does the future hold for hot rodding? Does the hot rod, in its surrounding popular culture, have historical importance? I believe it does . . . . The five questions were:

1. When did the hot rod become part of your personal life?
2. What was it that influenced you at that time (i.e., cars, people, etc.)?
3. Is it still important and if so, why?
4. What influences you now or, what is important to you now about the hot rod culture?
5. What do you think the future holds for hot rodding?

In the 1970s, numerous innovators revised the traditional view of the hot rod by creating new designs that pushed both technical and cultural interpretations of the concept of returning to the roots of hot rodding. First, it was Pete Chapouris' *California Kid* and Jake's coupe that gave new direction and new aesthetic sensibility for me. Then Pete Eastwood's *Barakat & Eastwood* red oxide-primered '32 drag racing Tudor sedan was featured on the cover of *Hot Rod* magazine. Or maybe it was Dick Page's black-primered, blown and chopped '32 sedan cruising in the Seattle/Tacoma area.

I later met Dennis and Debbie Kyle at Bonneville with their orange and much louvered '32 highboy. From there, I met Billy Vinther with his straight-on orange hot rod '34; Cal Tanaka with his flamed, ground-scraping '33; Paul Bos with his '34 McCoy flamed coupe; and Don Small's right-on-the-money black '32 highboy with the tall "sugar donut" tires.

Each hot rod enabled me to re-examine concepts of originality and indi-
viduality through the realization of their fantasies, their creations.

Stepping back, as it were, to see both an inside and outside perspective confirmed the importance of participation, of building it yourself.
It is the touch and feel of each of the automotive parts that informs the
larger truth—the truth in materials. Manipulation of the parts becomes
synonymous with the manipulation of ideas to find aesthetic truth in
this form of expression. Each one of these cars strikes a visceral chord,
as it makes its individual statement. Although many of same parts
and similar ideas were used, they were combined to create a distinctive finished form. Each of these hot rods established a unique, visual
direction that achieves technological and cultural significance, but most
importantly, they all get driven.

The idea that hot rods are part of the environment and the environment is part of the hot rod is often misunderstood by outside observers.
The "in your face" attitude doesn't come off in a fairground venue,
especially when you have a car surrounded by lawn chairs. However, I
constantly find innovative cars in perfect harmony with the environment
at the dry lakes and Bonneville, where Vern Tardel and the extended
group of hot rodders out of the San Francisco Bay Area gather to race
and swap stories. The reliability runs, such as the River City Reliability
Run in November–December, also showcase the symbolic relationship between the hot rod and the environment. Additionally, a sharp,
straight, relationship between object, place, and time comes into focus
on the dry lakes, creating and recreating the hot rod culture's myths
and mores. Midnight races and desert drives down the lonely two-lane
blacktop are ultimately cool and fitting.

Hot rods as a form of expression are here to stay, but because of
their inherent nature, they will continue to evolve. There has been a
movement involving a group of young hot rodders in their 20s and 30s
who are pushing changes based on their own experiences and aesthetic
interpretations of the hot rod. This very positive, energetic direction is
more than retrofit style, because it reflects the experiences, sensibili-
ties, and technologies of a new generation. Where they fit culturally is
open to debate. Some, no doubt, will springboard traditional building

practices to create a new truth within the culture, just as the hot rod pioneers did, to create an authentic experience.

I've heard it said that we are moving back through the decades of influence, i.e., the 1960s, back through the 1930s, and even possibly the 1920s. I agree, but I also think that the traditional builds, in the long run, will continue to stand up through time. As we have seen recently, they are the ones being collected. They have the pedigree of tradition and authenticity. I know many hot rodders in their 40s, 50s, and 60s who agree with this traditional style and have only built traditional cars. But I also believe the high-tech cars will continue to evolve, and we will see new additions and fads. I do have to wonder what culture they really fit in. Some of them probably should be placed in an "exotic" realm, next to custom-built cars, rather than in the hot rod genre. However, this is a personal aesthetic and interpretation of what a hot rod is, by my definition.

How to Think
Like a Hot Rodder

The Missing Link to Your
Overwhelming Need for Speed!

By the *HRM* Staff

✍

Hot Rod Magazine, January 2000

How do we explain what we are? It's so easy to shrug it off and say "either you have it or you don't." But it's not that simple. We all got to where we are somehow. How? Is it instinctive, or is it learned? Nature or nurture? Or some combination of both. Such conversations may be best left for the sociology department of your local college, yet this is precisely what we seek to tackle here. Four voices (Baskerville, Koch, Magnante, McGean) come up with four approaches on how to do it, but the under- lying theme is a simple one: Ya gotta love cars. Everything after that is just fine-tuning.

Steve Magnante

In my eyes, the term "hot rodder" can only be loosely defined as a person obsessed with the act of modifying mechanical devices in an effort to attain increased levels of performance. It doesn't matter whether it's a can opener or a Boss 429. If you alter it for increased performance, you've engaged in an act of hot rodding. Practice the art regularly, and you'll become a hot rodder. The essential ingredient is that exclusively human desire to massage and perfect, to take things to the next level. So how does one think like a hot rodder? Because each of us perceives his surrounding world in a uniquely personal way, there is no single "correct" answer or process, but there are some universally applicable suggestions worth sharing.

Find a Mentor

None of us was born with a complete knowledge of how mechanical things work. Somebody has to show us the way. As a high school student in the late '70s, I used to ride my bicycle 8 miles (one way) to the next town almost every day. I was on a quest to learn more about a bright red Dodge Dart I'd spotted in a secluded backyard. On my third trip, I finally worked up the nerve to ring the doorbell and ask for a closer look. I wasn't looking (or able) to buy it. The owner, instead of telling me to get lost, graciously allowed me to check it out. When he opened the hood I saw my very first 426 Hemi. I was in awe. Whether he liked it or not, Bob Hardy, the car's owner, had just made a new friend. Bob suffered my frequent visits and endless questions like a concerned father, and his patience served as an example of how important it is to get to know people who know more than you do. Listen, learn, and never be afraid to ask questions.

Get an Education

More than a few hot rodders have made the mistake of trading a good education for a fast car. It's great to have the quickest car in the high school parking lot, but not if it eats up money you could have used to attend college or a vocational school. In my case, a stern father forbade me from having my own wheels in high school, but he was totally supportive of my hot rodding efforts the minute after I got my college diploma. Sure, I had to wait several years to burn rubber, but Dad was right; It may sound time-worn, but you'll never regret getting an education—and fear not, your hot rodding urges will not fade away, they'll only grow stronger. I had to wait until I was 21 before I could finally dig in and get my hands dirty with my first, a street and strip 440 buildup. That was 15 years ago, and I've had grease under my fingernails ever since.

Build Model Cars

There has always been a misconception that model cars are for kids, a silly pastime akin to basket weaving or pottery. Forget that. Short of actually working on real cars, there is no better way to learn about automotive engineering than to assemble as many car model kits as you can. Painted and detailed or just tossed together straight from the box, the construction process is much like that of a real car. And as you begin modifying and customizing, you'll be exposed to the basics of engine swapping, axle narrowing, the critical impact of wheel and tire selection, not to mention body and paint work. For me, the old IMC Little Red Wagon kit (recently re-released by Lindberg) is a revelation. With opening doors and a detailed recreation of the ingenious engine and suspension cradle used on the real truck, this kit is a shining example of how model cars are an indispensable educational tool, regardless of how old that calendar on the wall says you are.

Gray Baskerville

"Why is it," my father would ask, "That you spend so much time and money on that old Ford?"

"Because it's fun," I answered, realizing that messing around with old Fords didn't make sense to most adults. To my folks' generation, old Fords were just *old Fords*. They were considered piles of poop, best suited for scrap drives, beasts of burden, farmers, and Okies and sub-Okies fleeing poverty. I thought differently.

Old Fords were none of the above. Old Fords were words I didn't know, like "bitchin'," "way cool," or "far out." They were simply zooty. So to think like a hot rodder is to know what's zooty and to use neat terms (Deuce roadster) or the hundreds of other descriptions in the vernacular that non-rodders couldn't ever fathom—"I popped the clutch in my gow job and blew low." If you think like a rodder, you'll know what I said. If not, you lose, pal!

Thinking like a hot rodder is walking through a junkyard knowing you're in heaven. I remember spending a day with John Buttera darting (Lil' doesn't walk, he darts) around piles of pieces while he mentally cataloged, classified, and consigned each part for a future project. Thinking like a hot rodder is realizing one man's junk is another's jewel.

Thinking like a rodder is what I call "blessed excess," which is usually defined by numbers—speed, elapsed time, horsepower, and a woman's bust size. Blessed excess is four engines when one will suffice. Blessed excess is top fuel-two mags, 16 plugs, two fuel pumps, 34 nozzles, 60 gallons of nitro per minute, and still not enough power. Blessed excess is 400-mph streamliners, 300-mph passenger cars, and 290-mph roadsters aimed by guys that don't get paid. Blessed excess is driving a 200-mph hot rod from Anaheim to Detroit. Hot rodders think that more is better.

Thinking like a hot rodder is knowing what's right. Gary Case stepped into a swap meet and knew that Pontiac Safari was right. Right is forever like the Greer-Black & Prudhomme fueler, the Pierson Bros. coupe, and the Hirohata Merc. We won't dwell on wrong, because rodders think wrong the instant it happens.

Thinking like a hot rodder goes against the establishment. Rodders don't think it's bad to have greasy hands, broken fingernails, dirty jeans, unkempt hair, and a garage full of unrelated parts. Who else but a hot rodder would think that it's totally cool to drive a four-wheel walnut-red primer, uneven sheetmetal, missing grille—powered by a gleaming, multi-carbureted, ground-shaking motor—on his first date.

Thinking like a hot rodder is to not take hot rodding seriously. Serious is losing a street race to a Honda or being caught driving a four-door Essex or riding on a Vespa. If you have to ride a scooter, try a Cushman or step up to a Whizzer or a Marmon twin. Thinking like a hot rodder is being the eternal optimist—this new cam is going to kill them, so are these new wheels; this flame job is going to set them on fire. No rodder thinks of self. The thought process is always predicated on what others think—will my buds approve of this body style and new louvered hood? How do my pipes sound? Rat rodders are great on approval, and much of their time is spent thinking hard-core '40s or '50s.

No doubt about it, hot rodders think a lot. It's just that other people remain clueless to our thought process. When our thinking was discovered by the Smithsonian Institution, they declared hot rodding a national treasure. Now everyone is thinking about burning rubber while stabbing and steering in a chopped Deuce coupe.

Jeff Koch

There are people who own fast cars who are not hot rodders. There are hot rodders who own miserable slugs that they keep working on to improve and personalize. So who is truly the hot rodder—the one with the speed and no interest, or the one with interest and no speed? Hot rodding is not a class you can take at the local community college; you can't teach someone this stuff. It's instinctive. Rather than delve deep into my own disturbed psyche for this section, I'd like to tell you the story of Rick Pfeiffer. He owns the yellow '77 Chevelle SS phantom elsewhere in this issue, and for my money he thinks more like a hot rodder than anyone else I've met lately. Rick's actions followed his thoughts, and Rick thinks like a hot rodder. It is people like him who are the backbone of this hobby.

Rick Pfeiffer, Hot Rodder

Why did Rick choose a '77 Chevelle? Maybe because it was a Chevy. Maybe because it was a car he didn't see every day. Does it matter? Rick likes it. Even friends who crinkled their noses and asked "What're you building that for?" held no sway, and our man Pfeiffer took steps to do it precisely the way he wanted to. It doesn't matter whether you like Chevelles or Mustangs or Volares or VW Rabbits: it's the passion to do it, the enthusiasm, which is the most important thing.

Thanks to his passion, Rick rebuilds transmissions for a living at his shop, Dr. Trans. Cash doesn't always flow as freely as any of us would like, and hot rodders don't always need it to get by. They innovate, they barter, they borrow. They know what they have, they know what they need and don't need, and they work out deals to swap their parts and abilities for those of others. Deals are important. Deals get things done. Rick has a skill/bargaining chip, and he used it. The rebuilt frontend, from bushings to ball joints, was done in exchange for a rebuilt tranny. Rear suspension and a complete exhaust system (since replaced) were done in exchange for another.

Doing much of the big 'Velle himself was a bonus, but doing it on weekends when the car was the family's only reliable piece of transportation put the pressure on. Anything he was doing had to be wrapped up within 48 hours. Soon, all the extra money went toward a replacement vehicle just so he could keep playing for more than two days at a clip. Despite 12 years of thrashing, Rick's energy and forward motion never ceased.

Then there is blessed excess. Hot rodding is at its core about excess, but sometimes it comes out in ways other than the obvious (like horsepower). Rick bought a running '71 Caprice just for the big-block. He bought a '74 Monte Carlo—less driveline—just for its Rally dash and tilt steering column. The man spent 2 1/2 years phoning one guy while chasing down rear quarter-window louvers. If that's not persistence, then we don't know what is. And there were items that simply weren't available. Rather than settle, he used creativity and ingenuity and back issues of *Hot Rod* for reference, and designed his own anti-hop suspension system utilizing 1-inch steel and a couple of Heim-jointed third hitches meant for use on tractors. It exists simply because he wanted it badly enough and was willing to try something new.

And all the while, he's supporting his wife, Laura, two kids, and a house. The Pfeiffer pfamily has gone without a number of niceties, including Rick's presence for long hours, just so he could build his dream ride. If a rodder gets lucky, he has someone whom, if they don't completely understand, at least supports him. Laura has been making noises about needing a new kitchen for a few years now, and Rick has in fact promised that a new Meal Preparation Center is next on the family agenda.

And now Rick is driving. He's showed at two Maple Grove Power Fests and has done several legs of the East Coast Power Tour—went with us all the way to Gaithersburg in '98 and '99. So here's how you think like a hot rodder: Wanna build your dream car? Let nothing stop you. Can't pay for parts? Barter. Parts don't exist? Make them yourself. Be excessive, be clever, have fun. If you're reading *Hot Rod*, chances are you already think like a hot rodder. You either have it or you don't. Rick Pfeiffer does.

Terry McGean

For many of us, thinking like a hot rodder came naturally; the phenomenon grew from within us, whether we wanted it or not. This desire to mess with things mechanical just seems to get inside certain people and consume the better part of their thoughts. Indeed, it is a passion, and like anything that involves strong emotion, it can sometimes impair judgment. Like an adolescent who suddenly sees cheerleaders in a whole new way, the burgeoning car freak can quickly play the fool.

I mention this because I think most "mature" hot rodders have established their thought processes and their opinions, though even the oldest among us continue learning. But the younger set, the up-and-coming generation, these are the ones who can benefit the most from those who have been there and done that. The following are a few guidelines I'd offer in the hopes that rookie rodders will avoid doing some of the stupid things I did before I knew better.

Open Your Mind

Most of us started with cars when we were in high school, and there is no other time when the pressure to conform to the thoughts and ideas of our peers is greater. Get past the fear of not being hip and look for what you like. It isn't only about Mustangs and Camaros, especially in recent years, as unusual models and body styles are becoming more accepted. You'd be amazed how cool it is to be different.

Get Educated

If you want to have a bitchin' car, don't expect someone else to build it for you. You'll soon learn how frustrating it can be to rely on others for their wrenching skills and then figure out that they screwed up your car anyway. Besides, if you're really a hot rodder, you'll have the desire to do it yourself. Take shop classes. Get a job in a shop, read, talk to experts, get comfortable with it. And don't get all your knowledge from one source; a variety of input makes for a wealth of knowledge.

Keep Your Emotions in Check

I bought my first car at 15. I made a big mistake. The problem wasn't that I was too young to drive, but that I fell in love with a turd. It was a '72 Chevelle 55, and it had headers, M/T valve covers, and a manual trans on the floor. That was all I needed to see. I selectively overlooked the fact that the only original body panel was the roof. That the small-block sounded like a Slant-Six and the frame was in need of a chiropractor went unnoticed until it was way too late. You can't beat an original vehicle, especially if it's bone-stock. Worry about the trick stuff later.

Keep It on the Road

So many of us tear into our cars, removing and dismantling key components, or maybe even the whole car, with the intent of making it truly bitchin', only to waste valuable weeks/months/years of cruise time. Projects always take longer than you anticipated, and the bigger the project, the more inaccurate your estimate will be. Take it in steps, and enjoy your hot rod whenever possible. That's what they're for.

You and Your Monster

By Henry Gregor Felsen

To My Son, the Teen-Age Driver, 1964

As a seasoned veteran of movie and TV horror shows, you do not need my help in order to identify Dr. Frankenstein or his monster. You know them and their story well. But are you aware that you might be another Dr. Frankenstein?

Even now your monster—potentially much more terrible than his-sleeps in our garage, awaiting only a transmission, a clutch, a charged battery, and gasoline to bring it to life.

Soon, according to your plans, your monster will descend from its jack stands, sputter into life, and, with a roar, lurch from its cluttered lair to stalk among the local villagers.

Your monster has controls which you intend to operate. But the day your machine comes to life, will you control it or will it, as it already does in so many ways, control you? Who, I wonder, will enslave whom?

It is rather ironic that although the automobile is the greatest single threat to your physical survival, it is not physically that it is the greatest threat to your life. It is more dangerous to you morally, mentally, financially, and vocationally.

What is there about the *idea* of a car that not only appeals to boys, but charms them out of their senses? That blinds them to the true nature of themselves and the world as effectively as though their eyes had been poked out with hot irons?

It is something near, rather than something new.

Boys have always been the easy natural prey of daydreams, especially those that combine a life of adventure with all a fellow can eat. The vehicles of these daydreams change with the times, but the needs they satisfy remain the same.

Sixty years ago your grandfather left the farm to seek adventure and his fortune working on the railroad. Other boys of his time went to sea, or headed west to find excitement that paid wages, but willing to settle for work on the same terms.

When I was in high school, I reluctantly inhaled chalk dust and dreamed of an open biplane in which I, dressed in a long leather coat, breeches, boots, helmet and goggles, would barnstorm around the nation's pastures. I planned to attract crowds with spectacular stunt flying, then earn my fortune carrying the impressed country people aloft on short flights over their farms. What need for Latin or algebra in the life I planned, eh?

What I did about it was to run away from home and school with a knife in my boot and thirty-seven cents in my pocket. It was my plan, as soon as I became a barnstormer and had the necessary costume, to return and buzz the school building in my plane, discomfiting the teachers, astounding the other boys, and thrilling the girls with my feats of skill and daring.

For two weeks I hitchhiked, rode freight trains, slept in missions, and learned how long a teen-age boy could go without food and still live. Finally, not wanting to better my record in this area, I staggered into a police station and gave myself up for being a young fool.

You are the same kind of boy your grandfather was and that I was, but you don't have to run away to find your dream. The Aladdin's lamp that can make your dream come true is in our garage.

Without physically leaving home or school, it is possible for you, here and now, to board your sailing ship, ride your range, drive your train, or barnstorm in your old biplane. The automobile offers you, here and now, freedom, action, thrills, adventure, status, danger, and equality. With it, you can discomfit adults, astound other boys, and impress girls.

But that is not all.

The automobile also offers you an opportunity to earn your living in any one of a hundred ways. The automobile promises not only to be a romantic sweetheart, but a wife who can cook. What more could anyone ask? Why look further? Why waste time on the meaningless, non-automotive boredom of schoolwork? Why bother to investigate other careers?

You do attend classes, but the problems of working on your old car are much more important to you than the problems of your history or chemistry classes. Without leaving home or missing a day of school, you can run away from reality as definitely as I did when I stuck a knife in my boot and hopped a southbound freight.

I know you take a dim view of high school marriages. You think a boy is crazy to tie himself down for the rest of his life on the strength of an adolescent passion. Yet, you are willing to give up unlimited future vocational freedoms and opportunities because of an adolescent infatuation with the automobile. You are giving away the time, the opportunity, and the freedom to change your mind in the future.

What if, in a year or two, you change as you have so often changed in the past? What if you then cast off this spell, look at your coveralls and shrug, and are ready to give away your tools? What if, in a couple of years, you decide you have had enough of cars and want to go to college? What then?

What then, when you discover that the idea of the car has stolen not three weeks of your life, or three months, but enough of your youthful years and brains to keep you out of college and to force you back into coveralls, whether you like it or not. What then?

You assure me that you will always love, honor, and cherish automotive work, and I ask you this: Are you willing to bet your life on a teen-age crush?

You may not believe me after what I have just said, but I have nothing against the automobile as a hobby now or as a career later on. In fact, I think working on a car is one of the finest hobbies a boy can have at your age.

The hours you spend doing meaningful, constructive work on your car are hours that you are not wasting by standing around on street corners looking for something to do. Your car has given you an immediate, purposeful activity in life, a goal to work toward, and valuable experience in budgeting your time and your hard-earned money.

Work on your car has taught you more than a knowledge of mechanics and automobile construction. It has taught you patience, and has challenged your ingenuity and imagination. It has allowed you to dream creatively, then work to make that dream come true.

The time you spend under your car in our garage is good time. Knowing you are safe, happy, and constructive, I often bless the battered old car that "sits" for you so well.

I also think the work you do on your car will help make you a better driver. The more you understand your machine, the better you will be able to control it. The more of your sweat and effort that goes into building it up, the less likely you will be to abuse it, or break it down.

I suppose my argument hasn't been against the car itself, but against your going overboard about the idea of it. Because it really doesn't matter what sews your mind in a sack and dumps it in the corner. Whatever does, hurts you.

What I have said about the danger of an excessive interest in cars applies to any other interest that becomes an obsession and that tends to stunt your growth as a well-rounded human being. With others it could be girls, surfing, amateur radio, team sports, writing poetry, or even classroom work in school that engulfs too much of their young lives. With you, it happens to be cars. You are young and you are human, and what the car has done to others it can do to you. And this is what it has done and is doing to too many boys.

How They've Made Hot Rods Safe

Choppers in Pomona, Calif. have helped slash city's traffic toll.
Yet they have more races than ever—thanks to a hot-rodding cop.

By Andrew R. Boone

Popular Science, September 1952

The hot-rodders of Pomona, Calif., are largely responsible for a drop in Pomona's traffic death toll from 16 persons killed in 1949 to two in 1951.

If you're used to hearing all kinds of accidents ascribed to hot shots, this news may lift your eyebrows. Yet the plain truth is that in Pomona (population 45,000), the boys in the souped-up jalopies have helped cut the auto death toll by seven-eighths.

And the Pomona hot-rodders have done all this without giving up either speed or the opportunity to win drags (the hot-rod word for races) and other contests—two big reasons for being a hot-rodder in the first place.

Three years ago, Pomona's traffic fatalities—like those of so many U.S. cities today—were leaping. So were hot-rod drivers, leaping all over the city streets, leaping out at pedestrians at dark corners at night. The hot-rodders were not, of course, responsible for the whole death toll. But they were involved in accidents, some fatal. They got a lot of blame.

Motorcycle police repeatedly broke up the hot-rodders' drags along Pomona streets. More than once, judges helped the cops make wholesale arrests. California was alarmed and the state legislature passed laws against the hot shots.

Pomona's hot-rodders reacted. They greeted cops with boos and catcalls, moved sullenly, and, when a race was broken up by cops, would congregate on another dark street somewhere and set up another race.

Ralph Parker, the city's police chief, handed this headache to a young officer, E.J. (Bud) Coons, now 28 and a sergeant. Parker's instructions sounded strange indeed from a police chief:

"If you can't control 'em," he said to Coons, "join 'em. Then we'll see what happens."

Coons, in uniform, spoke to a meeting of a hot-rod club called the Choppers. His reception was cool. Coons wasn't controlling 'em.

Coons, out of uniform and in a T shirt and blue jeans, went to a later meeting and astonished the Choppers with a speech as unorthodox as had been his own instructions from Chief Parker.

He Made It

"Listen," he said. "I'm a cop. But I'm a hot-rodder, too. We're not trying to throw the book at you guys. I want to join you. Together we can save lives, run fast on Sundays, have some fun in get-togethers."

To join the Choppers you have to be voted in. Members drop marbles in a cigar box to vote. Three black marbles keep you out. Coons was elected an honorary member. He had joined 'em.

He offered to Choppers a program designed both to give them more than ever from hot rodding and to help cut Pomona's traffic toll. It took a while to get everything into effect. But the program included:

- **Races each Sunday** on the paved parking area of the Los Angeles County Fair Grounds. It cost the city $5,378 to add a quarter-mile black top for racing, with the hot-rodders to pay back the money from entry fees and admissions. Today as many as 165 hot-rodders bring their cars each Sunday for time trials and races on the black-top strip. Thousands of spectators are attracted. They see plenty: a modified roadster recently did 127.32 miles an hour on the strip. The loan is being paid off on schedule.
- **Insurance at the meets.** "We carry $300,000 in public liability and $50,000 in property-damage insurance," Bud Coons explains. Nobody is in danger financially. Nor are life and limbs risked they way they were in the old days. Every car gets a thorough going-over once a month. Brakes and steering gear are checked before every run.
- **Timed runs**, a kind of economy drive in miniature. It takes driving skill to win one of these. Using public roads and highways, hot rodders take off at five-second intervals to compete for the best time within strict speed restrictions over a selected route. The route is marked on a road map given each driver. The speed restrictions: All cars must keep down to 17 m.p.h. in a 25-mile zone, to 23 in a 35-mile zone, and so on. Checkers record times. Too fast or too slow loses the race.
- **An achievement plaque.** The winner is determined by point total. The boy who attends a timed run or other event gets one

point. The winner gets extra points. The boy who manages a run gets five points. But any rabbit who gets a ticket for speeding or running a stop sign or another traffic violation is docked 10 points, and besides he has to stand up in a meeting of the Choppers and confess. The plaque holder keeps it for six months. There is a similar award for the best hot-rodder each month.

- **Poker runs**, or hunts for the best poker hand. The winner depends on pure luck. In this one, a driver follows splashes of lime on the pavement till he comes to a lime circle on the road. Then he knows there's a can of playing cards, each card in a sealed envelope, within 30 feet. The driver picks up an envelope, continues till he has made five stops. At the end of the run, all drivers gather, envelopes are opened, and the man with the best poker hand wins. No double parking at stops is permitted. Speed has nothing whatever to do with deciding the winner.

Joining the Choppers worked for Bud Coons, as Chief Parker hoped it would. By the fall of 1952, summonses given to the Choppers had dwindled to fewer than six a year.

One boy, who formerly was hauled in regularly by Coons for loud pipes, speeding or circling on screaming tires, had not had a ticket in two years.

The energies of the Choppers and other hot-shot groups were going into programs like Coon's. Such programs included more opportunities to win, more chances to display driving skill, more fun, and more chances for speed records on Sunday than hot-rodders had ever had before.

Speed with Safety

And as the traffic death toll plummeted, the Pomona Lions Club gave the Choppers a trophy in appreciation of their work.

"Don't get them wrong," Bud Coons says today. "They're still hot-rodders. I'm just as much of a hot shot as these guys. We've just learned to control ourselves on the streets and take our speed on the strips where the public won't get hurt."

Probably one reason Coons is so effective in teaching safety is that he has a personal interest. He had a jagged scar on his forehead. "Got that," he tells you, "on a cycle."

As the Choppers' program thrived, the club grew so large it could no longer meet in members' homes. How radically things in Pomona had changed was shown then. The Choppers, who in 1949 booed a cop on sight, selected as their permanent meeting place the basement of the Pomona police station.

Safety Tips From the Pomona Choppers

Make sure body is well fastened to frame. Tighten all bolts. Make door latches secure.

If you alter or hand-make a new body, install plenty of inside bracing. That's for protection in case of a roll-over. Chrome-moly tubing is best—it's tough and light.

Inspect steering knuckles for any slack. Kingpins are the main feature. Replace the mechanism if it's worn.

Use aircraft-type tubular shocks. They're available at parts stores in kits, complete with brackets.

Hydraulic brakes are a must. All newer cars have them, but they'll have to be installed on all models of earlier vintage than '35.

Use tires of a good grade, for your life depends upon your rubber. Get racing types for high-speed runs. No recaps, please.

Check the hubs, and make sure they're properly installed and secure.

Keylock all nuts where possible. Be certain no threads are even partly stripped.

Wear safety belt and crash helmet in all contests.

Stay under legal speed limits. Your car may be safe at 100 miles an hour, but only on a supervised and patrolled course.

Ed Roth

By Tom Wolfe

❦

The Kandy-Kolored Tangerine-Flake
Streamline Baby, 1963

I've mentioned Ed Roth several times in the course of this without really telling you about him. And I want to, because he, more than any other of the customizers, has kept alive the spirit of alienation and rebellion that is so important to the teen-age ethos that customizing grew up in. He's also the most colorful, and the most intellectual, and the most capricious. Also the most cynical. He's the Salvador Dali of the movement—a surrealist in his designs, a showman by temperament, a prankster. Roth is really too bright to stay within the ethos, but he stays in it with a spirit of luxurious obstinacy. Any style of life is going to produce its celebrities if it sticks to its rigid standards, but in the East a talented guy would most likely be drawn into the Establishment in one way or another. That's not so inevitable in California.

I had been told that Roth was a surly guy who never bathed and was hard to get along with, but from the moment I first talked to him on the telephone he was an easy guy and very articulate. His studio—and he calls it a studio, by the way—is out in Maywood, on the other side of the city from North Hollywood, in what looked to me like a much older and more run-down section. When I walked up, Roth was out on the apron of his place doing complicated drawings and lettering on somebody's ice-cream truck with an airbrush. I knew right away it was Roth from pictures I had seen of him; he has a beatnik-style beard. "Ed Roth?" I said. He said yeah and we started talking and so forth. A little while later we were sitting in a diner having a couple of sandwiches and Roth, who was wearing a short-sleeved T shirt, pointed to this huge tattoo on his left arm that says "Roth" in the lettering style with big serifs that he uses as his signature. "I had that done a couple of years ago because guys keep coming up to me saying, 'Are you Ed Roth?'"

Roth is a big, powerful guy, about six feet four, two hundred seventy pounds, thirty-one years old. He has a constant sort of court attendant named Dirty Doug, a skinny little guy who blew in from out of nowhere; sort of like Ronny Camp over at Barris'. Dirty Doug has a job sweeping up in a steel mill, but what he obviously lives for is the work he does around Roth's. Roth seems to have a lot of sympathy for the Ronny Camp–Dirty Doug syndrome and keeps him around as a permanent fixture. At Roth's behest, apparently, Dirty Doug has dropped his last name, Kinney, altogether, and refers to himself as Dirty Doug—not Doug. The relationship between Roth and Dirty Doug—which is sort of Quixote and Sancho Panza, Holmes and Watson, Lone Ranger and Tonto, Raffles and Bunny—is part of the folklore of the hot-rod and custom-car kids. It even crops up in the hot-rod comic books, which are an interesting phenomenon in themselves. Dirty Doug, in this folklore, is every rejected outcast little kid in the alien netherworld, and Roth is the understanding, if rather overly prank-sterish, protective giant or Robin Hood—you know, a good-bad giant, not part of the Establishment.

Dirty Doug drove up in one of his two Cadillacs one Saturday afternoon while I was at Roth's, and he had just gone through another experience of rejection. The police had hounded him out of Newport. He has two Cadillacs, he said, because one is always in the shop. Dirty Doug's cars, like most customizers', are always in the process of becoming. The streaks of "primer" paint on the Cadillac he was driving at the time had led to his rejection in Newport. He had driven to Newport for the weekend. "All the cops have to do is see paint like that and already you're 'one of those hot-rodders,'" he said. "They practically followed me down the street and gave me a ticket every twenty-five feet. I was going to stay the whole weekend, but I came on back."

At custom-car shows, kids are always asking Roth, "Where's Dirty Doug?", and if Dirty Doug couldn't make it for some reason, Roth will recruit any kid around who knows the pitch and install him as Dirty Doug, just to keep the fans happy.

Thus Roth protects the image of Dirty Doug even when the guy's not around, and I think it becomes a very important piece of mythology. The thing is, Roth is not buying the act of the National Hot Rod Association, which for its own reasons, not necessarily the kid's reasons, is trying to assimilate the hot-rod ethos into conventional America. It wants to make all the kids look like candidates for the Peace Corps or something.

The heart of the contretemps between the NHRA Establishment and Roth can be illustrated in their slightly different approach to drag racing on the streets. The Establishment tries to eliminate the practice altogether and restricts drag racing to certified drag strips and, furthermore, lets the people know about that. They encourage the hot-rod clubs to help out little old ladies whose cars are stuck in the snow and then hand them a card reading something like, "You have just been assisted by a member of the Blue Bolt Hot Rod Club, an organization of car enthusiasts dedicated to promoting safety on our highways."

Roth's motto is: "Hell, if a guy wants to go, let him *go*."

Roth's designs are utterly baroque. His air car—the Rotar—is not nearly as good a piece of design as Barris', but his beatnik Bandit is one of the great *objets* of customizing. It's a very Rabelaisian *tour de force*—a twenty-first century version of a '32 Ford hot-rod roadster. And Roth's new car, the Mysterion, which he was working on when I was out there, is another *tour de force*, this time in the hottest new concept in customizing, asymmetrical design. Asymmetrical design, I gather, has grown out of the fact that the driver sits on one side of the car, not in the middle, thereby giving a car an eccentric motif to begin with. In Roth's Mysterion—a bubbletop coupe powered by two 406-horsepower Thunderbird motors—a thick metal arm sweeps up to the left from the front bumper level, as from the six to the three on a clock, and at the top of it is an elliptical shape housing a bank of three headlights. No headlights on the right side at all; just a small clearance light to orient the oncoming driver. This big arm, by the way, comes up in a spherical geometrical arc, not a flat plane. Balancing this, as far as the design goes, is an arm that comes up over the back of the bubbletop on the right side, like from the nine to the twelve on a clock, also in a spherical arc, if you can picture all this. Anyway, this car takes the streamline and the abstract curve and baroque curvilinear one step further, and I wouldn't be surprised to see it inspiring Detroit designs in the years to come.

Roth is a brilliant designer, but as I was saying, his conduct and his attitude dilutes the Halazone with which the Establishment is trying to transfuse the whole field. For one thing, Roth, a rather thorough-going bohemian, kept turning up at the car shows in a T shirt. That was what he wore at the big National Show at the New York Coliseum, for example. Roth also insists on sleeping in a car or station wagon while on the road, even though he is making a lot of money now and could travel first class. Things came to a head early this year when Roth was out in Terre Haute, Indiana, for a show. At night Roth would just drive his car out in a cornfield, lie back on the front seat, stick his feet out the window and go to sleep. One morning some kid came by and saw him and took a picture while Roth was still sleeping and sent it to the model company Roth has a contract with, Revel, with a note saying, "Dear Sirs: Here is a picture of the man you say on your boxes is the King of the Customizers." The way Roth tells it, it must have been an extraordinarily good camera, because he says, with considerable pride, "There were a bunch of flies flying around my feet, and this picture showed all of them."

Revel asked Roth if he wouldn't sort of spruce up a little bit for the image and all that, and so Roth entered into a kind of reverse rebellion. He bought a full set of tails, silk hat, boiled shirt, cuff links, studs, the whole apparatus, for $215, also a monocle, and now he comes to all the shows like that. "I bow and kiss all the girls' hands," he told me. "The guys get pretty teed off about that, but what can they do? I'm being a perfect gentleman."

To keep things going at the shows, where he gets $1000 to $2000 per appearance—he's that much of a drawing card—Roth creates and builds one new car a year. This is the Dali pattern, too. Dali usually turns out one huge and (if that's possible any more) shocking painting each year or so and ships it on over to New York, where they install it in Carstairs or hire a hall if the thing is too big, and Dali books in at the St. Regis and appears on television wearing a rhinoceros horn on his forehead. The new car each year also keeps Roth's model-car deal going. But most of Roth's income right now is the heavy business he does in Weirdo and Monster shirts. Roth is very handy with the airbrush—has a very sure hand—and one day at a car show he got the idea of drawing a grotesque cartoon on some guy's sweat shirt with the airbrush, and that started the Weirdo shirts. The typical Weirdo shirt is in a vein of draftsmanship you might call Mad Magazine Bosch, very slickly done for something so grotesque, and will show a guy who looks like Frankenstein, the big square steam-shovel jaw and all, only he has a wacky leer on his face, at the wheel of a hot-rod roadster, and usually he has a round object up in the air in his right hand that looks like it is attached to the dashboard by a cord. This, it turns out, is the gearshift. It doesn't look like a gearshift to me, but every kid knows immediately what it is.

"Kids *love* dragging a car," Roth told me. "I mean they really love it. And what they love the most is when they shift from low to second. They get so they can practically *feel* the r.p.m.'s. They can shift without hardly hitting the clutch at all."

These shirts always have a big caption, and usually something rebellious or at least alienated, something like "MOTHER IS WRONG" or "BORN TO LOSE."

"A teen-ager always has resentment to adult authority," Roth told me. "These shirts are like a tattoo, only it's a tattoo they can take off if they want to."

I gather Roth doesn't look back on his own childhood with any great relish. Apparently his father was pretty strict and never took any abiding interest in Roth's creative flights, which were mostly in the direction of cars, like Barris'.

"You've got to be real careful when you raise a kid," Roth told me several times. "You've got to spend time with him. If he's working on something, building something, you've got to work with him." Roth's early career was almost exactly like Barris', the hot rods, the drive-ins, the drag racing, the college (East Los Angeles Junior College and UCLA), taking mechanical drawing, the chopped and channeled '32 Ford (a big favorite with all the hot-rodders), purple paint, finally the first custom shop, one stall in a ten-stall body shop.

"They threw me out of there," Roth said, "because I painted a can of Lucky Lager beer on the wall with an airbrush. I mean, it was a perfect can of Lucky Lager beer, all the details, the highlights, the seals, the small print, the whole thing. Somehow this can of Lucky Lager beer really bugged the guy who owned the place. Here was this can of Lucky Lager beer on *his* wall."

The Establishment can't take this side of Roth, just as no Establishment could accommodate Dadaists for very long. Beatniks more easily than Dadaists. The trick has always been to absorb them somehow. So far Roth has resisted absorption.

"We were the real gangsters of the hot-rod field," Roth said. "They keep telling us we have a rotten attitude. We have a different attitude, but that doesn't make us rotten."

Several times, though, Roth would chuckle over something, usually some particularly good gesture he had made, like the Lucky Lager, and say, "I am a real rotten guy."

Roth pointed out, with some insight, I think, that the kids have a revealing vocabulary. They use the words "rotten," "bad" and "tough" in a very fey, ironic way. Often a particularly baroque and sleek custom car will be called a "big, bad Merc" (for Mercury) or something like that. In this case "bad" means "good," but it also retains some of the original meaning of "bad." The kids know that to adults, like their own parents, this car is going to look sinister and somehow like an assault on their style of life. Which it is. It's rebellion, which the parents don't go for—"bad," which the kids *do* go for, "bad" meaning "good."

Roth said that Detroit is beginning to understand that there are just a hell of a lot of these bad kids in the United States and that they are growing up. "And they want a better car. They don't want an old man's car."

Roth has had pretty much the same experience as Barris with the motor companies. He has been taken to Detroit and feted and offered a job as a designer and a consultant. But he never took it seriously.

"I met a lot of the young designers," said Roth. "They were nice guys and they know a lot about design, but none of them has actually done a car. They're just up there working away on those clay models."

I think this was more than the craftsman's scorn of the designer who never actually does the work, like some of the conventional sculptors today who have never chiseled a piece of stone or cast anything. I think it was more that the young Detroit stylists came to the automobile strictly from art school and the abstract world of design—rather than via the teen-age mystique of the automobile and the teen-age ethos of rebellion. This status-group feeling is very important to Roth, and to Barris, for that matter, because it was only because of the existence of this status group—and this style of life—that custom-car sculpture developed at all.

With the Custom Car Caravan on the road—it has already reached Freedomland—the manufacturers may be well on the way to routinizing the charisma, as Max Weber used to say, which is to say, bringing the whole field into a nice, safe, vinyl-glamorous marketable ball of polyethylene. It's probably already happening. The customizers will end up like those poor bastards in Haiti, the artists, who got too much, too soon, from Selden Rodman and the other folk-doters on the subject of primitive genius, so they're all down there at this moment carving African masks out of mahogany—what I mean is, they never *had* an African mask in Haiti before Selden Rodman got there.

"They keep telling us we have a rotten attitude. We have a different attitude, but that doesn't make us rotten."

I think Roth has a premonition that something like that is liable to happen, although it will happen to him last, if at all. I couldn't help but get a kick out of what Roth told me about his new house. We had been talking about how much money he was making, and he told me how his taxable income was only about $6200 in 1959, but might hit $15,000 this year, maybe more, and he mentioned he was building a new house for his wife and five kids down at Newport, near the beach. I immediately asked him for details, hoping to hear about an utterly baroque piece of streamlined architecture.

"No, this is going to be my wife's house, the way she wants it, nothing way out; I mean, she has to do the home scene." He has also given her a huge white Cadillac, by the way, unadorned except for his signature—"Roth"—with those big serifs, on the side. I saw the thing, it's huge, and in the back seat were his children, very sweet-looking kids, all drawing away on drawing pads.

But I think Roth was a little embarrassed that he had disappointed me on the house, because he told me his idea of the perfect house—which turned out to be a kind of ironic parable:

"This house would have this big, round living room with a dome over it, you know? Right in the middle of the living room would be a huge television set on a swivel so you could turn it and see it from wherever you are in the room. And you have this huge easy chair for yourself, you know the kind that you can lean back to about ninety-three different positions and it vibrates and massages your back and all that, and this chair is on tracks, like a railroad yard.

"You can take one track into the kitchen, which just shoots off one side of the living room, and you can ride backward if you want to and watch the television all the time, and of course in the meantime you've pressed a lot of buttons so your TV dinner is cooking in the kitchen and all you have to do is go and take it out of the oven.

"Then you can roll right back into the living room, and if somebody rings the doorbell you don't move at all. You just press a button on this big automatic console you have by your chair and the front door opens, and you just yell for the guy to come in, and you can keep watching television.

"At night, if you want to go to bed, you take another track into the bedroom, which shoots off on another side, and you just kind of roll out of the chair into the sack. On the ceiling above your bed you have another TV set, so you can watch all night."

Roth is given, apparently, to spinning out long Jean Shepherd stories like this with a very straight face, and he told me all of this very seriously. I guess I didn't look like I was taking it very seriously, because he said, "I have a TV set over the bed in my house right now—you can ask my wife."

I met his wife, but I didn't ask her. The funny thing is, I did find myself taking the story seriously. To me it was a sort of parable of the Bad Guys, and the Custom Sculpture. The Bad Guys built themselves a little world and got onto something good and then the Establishment, all sorts of Establishments, began closing in, with a lot of cajolery, thievery and hypnosis, and in the end, thrown into a vinyl Petri dish, the only way left to tell the whole bunch of them where to head in was to draw them a huge asinine picture of themselves, which they were sure to like. After all, Roth's dream house is nothing more than his set of boiled shirt and tails expanded into a whole universe. And he is not really very hopeful about that either.

Beatnik Bandit

By Ed "Big Daddy" Roth
and Tony Thacker

⁂

Hot Rods by Ed "Big Daddy" Roth, 1995

The "Beatnik Bandit" started out as a project car for *Rod & Custom*. Joe Henning was one o' these crazy sorts like myself & he had this idea to build a ground-up future rod. So we planned a series of articles where we'd do some drawings & get some reaction from the readers. I needed a project & started building it. I soon found out the pictures Joe was drawin' & the actual facts didn't jive so we made a lotta changes during construction. Every time I'd make a change Joe'd make a different drawing.

That's when Doug Kinney walked into the shop. Doug had this tuxedo that he'd gotten married in & he'd wear it to work. He was always neat & clean so the name "Dirty Doug" stuck to him. Doug became the official sander & painter. He worked for me from about 1960 to 1969. Doug's this really shy guy that is a crackup whenever he decides to cut loose. Him & Ed Fuller kept all the employees in stitches. Ya gotta realize that in between the fiberglass & plaster I was crankin' out T-shirts like the "Rat Fink", "Wild Child" & "Mother's Worry." A lotta you baby boomers got shirts from my place with fiberglass dust on 'em I'm sure!

A little known fact about Dirty Doug is that when Bob Hirohata died his now famous Merc custom fell into unscrupulous hands & really got wasted. Well, Doug was this car nut that had his whole yard full of really stupid cars like Honda 600's & '57 Cad Brougham's & Berkeleys & so he goes & buys the Hirohata Merc for like, 200 bucks. Remember, in them days, nobody really cared about wasted customs. So he salts it away in this garage & for many years just takes his close buds over to see it. It was in primer & had this giant dent in the hood like some demented dude had whopped it for spite with a sledge hammer. He finally sold it many years later when the garage owner threatened him with extinction.

Doug's yard was like a museum. His mom did not appreciate all the cars (The whole yard was full) so she reports him to the local fuzz! Get this! They comes down & make him clean up the yard! Can ya dig it!?!

By the time the Beatnik Bandit came along in '60 I had a set of wrenches & put a down payment on a "buzzbox" welder. Shop? Can ya dig the yard? Me & Dirty Doug worked under this corrugated roof shed (lucky that the sun shines most of the time in L.A.) that Dick Cook erected in the back of the shirt building. Then about the same time I erected this single car garage & we moved into that. It was tight quarters. Clean floor? Ha! Ha! Why clean it? It just got grossed out the next day. So we cleaned the floor after we finished the car. I use'ta find screwdrivers & all sorts o' real neat junk in the sweepings—especially screwdrivers. Lotsa fiberglass dust too. I loved to see them guys with the suits: FBI, Tom Wolfe, etc., come to this back room and freak out. Fiberglass dust is worse'n itching powder. Me & Doug wuz pretty use to it.

Most tourists that came to the Slauson Avenue shop were not hip to the strange way that me & Doug worked. It all seemed like one big plaster mess to outsiders, but we had method to our madness. Actually I don't know why me & DD are still alive. We've inhaled tons o' plaster & fiberglass fumes. DD use'ta take one of the Rat Fink T-shirts & slip it over his head, tie the sleeves behind his head & peep thru the neck hole. Underneath that he'd have this Mickey Mouse (sorry Mr. Disney) air breather. He'd look more like a UFO pilot than a leadsled jockey. He'd grind hour after hour on the bodies getting them shaped the way I wanted them. Every time we'd walk in the dust it'd be like this big puff of white powder. Yech! Yech!

In the back, under the Dick Cook awning, we had this pile of plaster & cardboard. People'd see it & back off real quick. My kids knew what it was. The dreaded "mistake pile." It was a collection of all the trials we'd make on the cars & didn't like. Y'see building the cars outta plaster was cheap & easy so me & DD would try insane stuff & if it didn't look right we'd take a carpenters saw, one o' my dad's big buck ones, & cut off the offending piece & toss it onto the mistake pile. Then I'd take coat hangers (I used them for welding also) & split 'em in two & poke 'em into the plaster & mix a new batch o' plaster & try somethin' different. That's how the insanity of the "Mysterion" nose piece happened. The mistake pile grew a lot in the old days. Then just before we'd paint the car we'd haul off the mistake pile to the dump to get rid of most of the dust. Then there was the scrap metal pile!

The scrap metal pile was just metal, but with all of the dust flyin' around it looked like it was plaster too. But if I kicked the metal pile with a good swift one I'd be able to see what kinda metal I had. It wasn't one o' those neat kinda piles. It had old lamps & electrical conduit & all kinds o' goodies that I could use for makin' new stuff. Sittin' here in this clean room at this word processor & thinkin' about all those years I'm havin' a spazz attack like I use'ta whenever I wuz dealin' with those two grossed out piles. I've got the same two piles gain' nowadays but I keep 'em clean. My plaster piles are almost nonexistent 'cause I work out the designs in my head first. Saves a lotta hackin' up o' those big lungers. My steel piles are mostly new metal. That's one o' the advantages o' bein' a retired (gimme a break!) genius.

The Bandit was a 1955 Olds chassis & engine that I chopped & slammed. The body was built with my plaster & fiberglass method. The idea for the bubble top came from Bobby Darrin's "Mac the Knife" dream car. I called Detroit to find out what a bubble top'd cost & they'd tell me thousands o' bucks so that I got this idea from Louie Aguirre to put some regular plastic in a pizza oven & then blow it up like a balloon while it was still hot. It was a hot idea. (Get it?) It never failed. First time, every time. Plastic was still in its baby stages & the plastic'd break real easy so we really hadda be careful to bolt it to the lifting frame, I used rubber sink washers.

I was always real hip to what wuz comin' down at the drag strips. I use ta go & set up my T-shirt booth on Saturday nights at Lions in Long Beach. I made my kids stay at the booth while I made my way through the pit area. I watched what guys wuz usin' to make their rides go faster. Blowers & multi carb manifolds, usually hopped-up 97's, and slick racing tires were the hot setup on race cars & dragsters so I used the same basic stuff on the Bandit. I had sent it all to the chrome plater & when I put it all together I couldn't get the sucker to crank over & ignite. So I calls this

Sometimes I wonder if the "Beatnik Bandit" would be as popular as it is if I'd named it "Litmus Paper."

same Fritz Voigt & he brings his screwdrivers & wrenches & in like, 10 minutes he had that mill eatin' right outa his hands. There was plaster dust & exhaust smoke all over that garage. We all scattered like rats! Dirty Doug went outside hackin' his lungs out & Fritz split back to his shop mumblin' somethin' about us car customizin' guys that wasn't nice at all.

My car show commitments got bigger & bigger. And Revell was hittin' me up for more cars to make models of. The east coast car show promoters was callin' me beggin' for new show cars for their shows. The Bandit was the first non practical show car I built. I had this one center stick that controlled the steering, speed, & shifting of the whole car. It also became the first show car that I hauled on a trailer 100 percent of the time. It ran, but it was a tricky handler.

Paintin' cars wasn't my favorite trick. If ya don't stay on top of the latest technology the results can be disastrous. Well in the old days, '59 or so, I painted my own stuff. It was simple. I painted the Outlaw white & then got some clear & put in a spoonful of this yechy white pearl essence stuff we got from the local taxidermist that came from boiled fish scales. Mixed into the clear lacquer it looked like a loogey highball. Squirted on top of the white it became known as a "Pearl Job." (Taxidermists used it on mounted fish.) Then I'd put the scallops on top of that. In the case of the Outlaw I used a combination of green & blue toners & painted the scallops over a silver base. I have had people tell me that the covers of *Car Craft* make the colors look like they're purple. Optical illusion I'm sure! But after the Beatnik Bandit I knew that I couldn't stay up with what was goin' on so I got hold o' Larry Watson.

Watson had this shop on Lakewood Boulevard & he started out with me & Dutch & Jeffries pinstriping cars. Watson had this really tough '49 Chevy that he'd painted with this outrageous candy purple over silver & whenever ya'd scope it out in the sun it'd almost knock out your eyeballs 'cause it was so bright. The effect came from painting this mixture of clear lacquer & purple toner on top of a silver base. About 20 coats of paint were necessary. The end result was awesome.

Watson had a sales gimmick that he thought up to sell those paint jobs o' his. He had this four foot by four foot plywood board with about a hunnert light bulbs screwed into these porcelain bases. Each light bulb was painted a different candy color. Wow! Customers couldn't refuse one o' those high tech, high dollar jobs after seeing those light bulbs. I was the same way. My problem was I didn't have the kinda bucks Watson was chargin' so I made a deal with him that he could take all the time he needed, usually a month, & I'd trade him Rat Fink T-Shirts for his work. He went for it! I always thought his best job was on the Mysterion where he painted candy yellow over a silver base. I always tried to give him credit on

RAT FINK® DECALS © ROTH '90

my signs at the shows & now through this record it remains a fact.

I hauled the Bandit with a Cad hearse. I ate & slept in that hearse. It's been to a lotta cities at a lotta car shows in the '60s. By 1970 the Bandit had been painted & changed a lot on account o' the many dents & scratches it got travelin' in trailers & bein' shoved around at the shows & so I sold it to Jim Brucker for 50 bucks. He then traded it to Harrah's in Reno in about 1973. Harrah's restored it in 1985 to its original shape. Today (1994) it's on permanent display at the National Automobile Museum in Reno, Nevada.

Originally I wuz naming my cars after western cowboys, so's "Bandit" was the original name. Then I went to Kansas City for a show & while I wuz cruisin' thru town, tryin' to catch me some grub, I picks up on this newspaper that's tellin' about this bearded dude that robbed a convenience store so the reporter called him the "Beatnik Bandit." I picked up on it & changed the name.

Naming my cars has always been a mind boggling experience to say the least. I realized a long time ago that a good car name is just like a good nickname for a pinstriper. When us guys wuz buildin' rods at Bell High School we never gave 'em names. I think it was Norm Grabowski who started that bit with the show cars. He had this real radical T roadster &

there was this TV program named *77 Sunset Strip* that was photographed at Dino's (Dean Martin's) nightclub on Sunset Boulevard. Turns out that the parking attendant was a dude named "Kookie" who was a real savvy, hair combin' hipster & the producers of the program needed a car for Kookie to drive around in. Norm's T was perfect. So Norm went to the car shows with "Kookie's Car."

By the time 1958 rolled around almost everyone was puttin' names on their cars. Me too. Sometimes I wonder if the "Beatnik Bandit" would be as popular as it is if I'd named it "Litmus Paper" or sumpthin' like that. I'm lucky! I know Robert Williams. Robert worked for me like, four years in the 60's. He became famous as an underground artist later on but at that time I found out that he had this uncanny way of thinkin' up stuff. He's named "Captain Pepi's Motorcycle & Zeppelin Repair," the "Conastoga Star" & "Druid Princess" & helped with other stuff I've had problems with.

Working the shows, we all got to know each other. We did a lotta hollerin' back & forth & with Mouse, if he was really far away, I'd get kids to take notes like, "You stink" & he'd send back stuff like, "I hate rats" or, "You're [*sic*] armpits smell." The kids transporting these notes got a kick outta this, & it added life to the show.

Some years later Mattel calls me & wants to make this new series called "Hot Wheels" & they wanna start it with the Beatnik Bandit. We agree on a royalty fee (I think it added up to about 800 bucks) & it was very very good to them. In 1992 the head honcho calls me & axes me if they can re issue it to which I replies, "Not interested," 'cause they wuz gonna repeat the original mistake and make 'em in red & blue, etc., when the original car was pearl & candy red.

Next thing I know guys're bringin' 'em to me at car shows to autograph. No way man! I wasn't gonna sign any unauthorized models & some o' my fans really got excited & angry at me. All's I can say is, "Call Mattel & complain to them." Maybe they'll tell ya the same thing they told me, "Well, what'cha gonna do about it?" So do me a favor & don't bring those unauthorized models to my booth. They wanted to settle outta court by givin' me 500 of the models. Who wuz they kiddin'?

From Douche Bags to High Dollars

Hot Rods in the Abstract

By Robt. Williams with Mike LaVella

⁓

The Hot Rod World of Robt. Williams, 2006

Let's see if I can give a description of hot rods in the abstract. Now the thing about a '32 or a '34 Ford is that they are new cars for two years, they're used cars for eight years, and they're hot rods for sixty years. So what is the true personality of the car? It's a hot rod. Now, I have always been intrigued by the nostalgia and the history of old cars, and realizing that it was at one time a new car. It went from a domestic passenger car to a semithoroughbred action vehicle. I find very few people have that same sentiment today. They would just get them, cut them up, and move on to the next thing. Then in the late '50s and early '60s, after the '55 Chevy came out, you had a whole new breed of hot rodders who were only interested in the speed factor of the new cars, especially Chevrolets. The inspiration was Zora Arkus-Duntov, and he had no interest whatsoever in the romance and dash of hot rods. And I saw a tremendous amount of historic glory in hot rods.

If you look at the American cowboy, you realize that cowboys were hired hands who worked on cattle ranches and who picked up some style, especially hats, from Mexican caballeros. Later, this thing evolved, especially through the publication of dime novels. By the 1890s, cowboys were a really big thing east of the Mississippi; a lot of bandits were actually Yankees who migrated west from the 1830s to 1890. That's an interesting change from rough frontier life—fur trappers and the like to people who domesticated the land and raised cattle and whatnot. But then in the 1890s, because of dime novels, it became like an adventure thing, it started taking on a mythology.

By the turn of the century, one of the greatest national and international heroes was Buffalo Bill. He had some interesting exploits, but a lot of his background was blown up bigger than life. He started a circus and was very well received in Europe, where he'd have a whole bunch of cowboys have a "shootout" with a whole bunch of Indians, and they'd catch buffalo and have shooting contests, and by the time of the First World War, even Buffalo Bill had worn this thing out. But the American army, especially during the Spanish-American War, had adopted the visual stance of the cowboy. So in World War I the doughboys wore a hat called a "campaign hat" that was an abstraction on a cowboy hat. It had four dents in the top of it and was not an attractive hat. It was kind of goofy, but it was considered a cowboy hat.

After the First World War, the movie industry introduced a third- or fourth-generation abstraction on this cowboy thing. In other words, a copy of a copy of a copy. You look at Tom Mix, Tim McCoy, Gene Autry, and Roy Rogers and at some point you realize these are guys who are supposed to be herding cattle. Now, I herded cattle in the early '50s but I wore engineer boots and a straw hat, and I did exactly what the cowboys did in the 1890s. I had to catch cattle and then castrate them, run them into the stocks and take them to the butchers or the auction house, but I didn't have any of the effects. I didn't want to wear cowboy boots and look like a "cowboy."

So the thing became a moral issue for children. These rough-and-tumble cowboys who frequented whorehouses, had a short life expectancy, and lived catch-as-catch-can all of a sudden were virtuous people who lived on the prairie. The same things happened with the '50s. I saw the '50s and the '50s were either boring or terrible. But today there is this third- or fourth-generation abstraction about what life was like then, too.

Something interesting that I want to mention about hot rods was that you could have a really bitchin' hot rod in the '50s and '60s, you could put three or four thousand dollars in it, which was an enormous price back then, but you couldn't get a fraction of that out of it. The resale value on any modified car was zero. I remember when I first went to California I was reading ads for '32 Ford roadsters, real show cars, that were selling for twelve hundred dollars. There were no exceptions. There weren't wealthy hobbyists out there buying them and inflating the market. If you weren't having fun in the car, that was all it was, a losing deal. If you were involved in hot rodding you were some kind of dufus!

The hot rod started before the First World War by getting a touring car, taking the body off and making it into a race car. An old man once described to me how you made a speedster or an early hot rod. First, you got a Model T, you took the body off and threw it away, and then you went out and got a douche bag. You cut the line to the gas tank, because it was under the seat on a Model T, you moved the tank back, and you dropped the seat down, then you needed that eighteen inches of douche line to reconnect the tank. Think about that, the only thing you needed was 18 inches of douche bag line to make a hot rod. He said the biggest trouble with them, of course, was that all the weight was gone. These things got going so fast the magneto would blowout the light bulbs at night.

People used to say, "If a Model T isn't running right, let it sit a while and it will start running better." What would happen was that the ends of the magneto would develop a little rust and then it would make the connection better for a while, but people felt that the car would actually heal. They would add this humanist character to the cars. Well, I don't think there's any vehicle in the world, including a Volkswagen Bug with flower decals on it, more humanistic than a hot rod. They're humanistic almost to the point of being superstitious.

So they started making this exotic speed equipment for race cars that was immediately adapted in the late teens and early '20s for what we call speedsters. There were over a hundred manufacturers of speedster kits for Model Ts, and some of them were really beautiful. In '38 or '39 Bob Estes built this T roadster that had a single overhead cam in it with a '24 roadster body. He's driving through Hollywood and comes up on Clark Gable in a Duesenberg. So he races him and beats his ass, and Clark Gable wants to buy the car, and Estes says, "No way will I sell this car." But where were we? Ah yes . . .

Now the thing is, a long time ago in medieval history—the late-twelfth, early-thirteenth century—for jousting, knights developed a piece of head gear with a full face on it so you could no longer identify who was wearing the helmet. The knight would wear a surcoat with some simple emblem on it—a horse head, a shock of wheat, or something like that—and you identified him by the coat, and that evolved into heraldry. The twelfth century was a long, long time ago and it was primitive. They didn't have plate armor, just a helmet and chain mail, but they already had myths about King Arthur. There's no written history on King Arthur or the Knights of the Round Table. These knights created this romance about themselves, about chivalry and all this stuff that didn't exist—just like cowboys—they created a whole world that didn't exist.

They used to have a show before tournaments; there would be a big tent full of shelves with a hundred different helmets, each one with a crest on top of it. It was like a car show, showing off the crests with the coats of arms representing each knight. You'd go in there and be really impressed with the helmet and the crest and all that bullshit. The armor evolved into practical combat armor, but then all the noblemen wanted to be in parades, so they had to have special armor. So you had this really impractical armor with inlaid jewels and really ridiculous things. It got to a point of impracticality, especially when firearms were developed. It was just an archaic bunch of nonsense, like extreme show cars.

Likewise, hot rods started out simply, with this piece of douche line on a Model T, and with the introduction of the V-8 engine, they opened up to this whole variety of early-'30s cars. Plus, you could put the V-8 in the older cars. And, as I mentioned earlier, there was no financial reward in these things. Okay, then car shows came on the scene and hot rods started entering the realms of the abstracted cowboy and the suits of parade armor. You had a lot of "car show cars" that wouldn't function—you know, the thing that Ed Roth was "all show and no go." So this thing got to a point where you vicariously rode in Ed's cars; you stood there looking at his car and you vicariously saw yourself at the drive-in with some girl, but in reality this thing wouldn't run. So this goes on until the Vietnam War. The Vietnam War was a release for a curious energy in youth, where the repulsion of the war brought out a positive sentiment for intellectual education and kind of a rejection of the blue-collar ethos that hot rods always had. There resulted this big dip, a low period in the history of hot rods. They were making muscle cars then, which sold well, but it really put hot rods on a low ebb.

Okay, a decade and a half goes by and there's this resurgence of interest in this stuff. Even in the late '50s, early '60s, all the car bodies were pretty much exhausted, so all you've got from the early '80s up to now is what's been recycled and can still be found. And all of a sudden, all of that stuff became so valuable that only older, wealthy men could have it. It's reached this preposterous situation where enormous prices are being paid for exact reproductions of these bodies. The idea of taking an old passenger car and souping it up to where it would be a new car and making it obtrusive is abstract.

I observed it about fifteen years ago when I started seeing people becoming interested in the '50s cars and creating a world that was really never there. It's obviously only just starting; you've got wealthy gentlemen who would have previously only been interested in sports cars paying a quarter of a million dollars for a hot rod. It's like a traditional thing that's carved in stone now. Twenty years ago Ed Roth was at such a low point in his life, and now he's like the second coming of Christ. I only wish he could have lived another three or four years and seen Jesse James on television, seen these people reap this tremendous harvest that he suffered so much for. He died before that thing started climbing. Choppers were getting big but they hadn't hit television yet and now all these celebrities and sports stars are getting choppers. It's a must thing, you know.

I've always been a hot rodder, but I'd always been in fine arts and the two don't mesh. The people that make up the fine arts community are intellectuals and pseudo-intellectuals. They see dealing with machinery as menial and below their dignity. If you get around art people and start talking hot rods, they'll walk off. So I had to hide my affection for hot rods for three or four decades. It's bad karma and eventually I could no longer hide it. Now I'm known for being "the hot rod artist." I'm typecast like that. If I never drew another car for the rest of my life, I'd still be a "hot rod artist" because my work has that activated, modified, altered-ness about it. It gives off a hot rod feeling; there is a modification in the work. There's a sense of adventure and cavalierism. It's just in my work.

I've made a living selling oil paintings since 1970, and that's a curiosity. It's an odd thing that I can actually paint bewildering oil paintings and make a living at it. That's just a rare situation. I got a lot of money for those time-consuming paintings that Brucker bought, but to get a larger following I had to drop the price and spread out to a much larger buying audience. That's when the Zombie Mystery Paintings came in, and I found a peer group. For the kind of painting I was doing, there was not an official market, nor was it sanctioned or tolerated, so it was very, very difficult. I didn't have other artists I could go talk to. There were no other artists doing this stuff—it was not accepted. It was an age of abstract expressionism, doing surrealist oddball paintings was just not tolerated. I was partly working on Zap Comix, was one of the seven artists, and I had sold Brucker and a few other people oil paintings, so I launched myself. It was hard-going that first decade, the '70s. It was very difficult, but I never gave it up. I wanted to be a painter. It was sink or swim, and I had to do it.

I have converted more hot rodders to fine art just by getting them going to art shows. I said, "You don't like it only because you're not part of it. You have to go; if only snobs make it and you're not there to be part of the public, it's always going to be just for snobs." So hopefully my influence has lapped over to a number of other people. Trust me . . . getting Pete Eastwood to go to an art show is an unbelievable accomplishment!

"Are you Von Dutch the car striper?"

By Jack Baldwin

※

Car Craft, February 1956

"I'm Jack Baldwin of *Car Craft* magazine. Mind if I ask you a few questions for a story?"

"Not at all Mr. Ballman, go ahead shoot."

"Baldwin!"

"Oh yeah, Baldwin. Shoot."

"Have you got more of a handle than 'Von Dutch' or is that the whole name?"

"That's it . . . 'Von Dutch.'"

"How old are you Dutch?"

"Six Martian years, Mr. Ballwon!"

"Baldwin!"

"Oh, yeah."

"Does the fact that you wear a flat-top haircut have anything to do with your job?"

"Sure, with a flat-top I can comb it with a towel. Naw, seriously though. I take the cut hair and make brushes to do custom painting on golf balls."

"How do you manage to keep from getting paint all over you?"

"I don't. It's mass hypnosis. I'm not clean actually."

"Is this a special blend of paint you use?"

"Well, I'll tell you Mr. Bellman. The colored paint is Bulletin colors sign paint. The white is three brands thinned with a little 50 weight motor oil to give it the proper consistency. The white I use is WYLLES one stroke, Straight One Shot, and TW Single Stroke."

"What kind of brushes do you use?"

"They are imported from Bavaria. Made of Russian squirrel. I don't know what's the matter with American squirrels. Too squirrelly, I guess."

"You got any other trade secrets?"

"The biggest secret is to take your mistake and make it look like you did it on purpose. If I make a slip I go over to the other side and do the same thing."

"What do you do when you make a real boo-boo?"

"If I can't make it into something, off it comes. Sometimes I rub it off with a dry rag. But mostly I use my fingers. A rag is too fuzzy and leaves an uneven break in the line. It is cut off sharp when I use my fingers."

"How long have you been striping cars, Dutch?"

"I'll tell you Mr. Boleman . . . "

"Baldwin. B-A-L-D-W-I-N. Baldwin!"

"Sorry, Baldwin. I've been striping about the last 10 years profession-ally and about 20 years altogether for the kicks of it."

"Do you sign your jobs anywhere?"

"Sometimes, usually on the front or the back. I make tiny little letters that make it look like an imperfection. Then when people get up close to it they discover it's my name and they are real happy with themselves thinking they have discovered something."

"What do you charge for striping a car?"

"Flat six bucks an hour."

"Does that include drawing a picture or just striping?"

"A flat six bucks an hour! Drawing or painting, I don't care. A flat six bucks, I'll go 'til the guy tells me to stop."

"Did you ever eavesdrop on a crowd to listen to what they say about your striping?"

"Oh, man yes, that's a favorite pastime of mine. Usually I like what they've got to say. But some make me blow my top. They say, 'Look at that guy's eyes, he must be a wineo. He can't be normal. No normal man could paint straight lines.'"

"Well can they?"

"Sure, if they take their time. Like I told you. The secret in striping is loading the brush right, not the striper."

"What advice can you give to a rodder or a custom car owner who might contemplate doing his own work?"

"Go ahead, give it a try. Most people, or I guess anyone who wants to, could learn to be a car striper if they just learn to load the brush right."

"How did you happen to get started striping cars and cycles?"

"Well, personal pleasure at first."

"Have you ever had any art training?"

"Nope."

"This striping, will it take polishing and weather?"

"Sure, as long as you keep a buffer off of it. You touch it with a buffer and phhoost—it's gone. Any striping will stick if the surface is good and clean."

"You'd make a pretty good tattooer. Ever tried it?"

"Sure, the old fashioned method. You know, with India ink and a straight needle."

"Do you have any self-inflicted tattooes?"

"Nope, not one on me. Never liked anything so well that I wanted to carry it around with me for the rest of my life."

"Are your moods reflected in your work?"

"Definitely! The worse the condition, the better the job."

"Tell me, Von Dutch. Why stripe a car in the first place?"

"For the same reason a fellow puts on other goodies. For individualism. It helps cover up imperfections and distracts the eye from crude body joints. And it helps bring out good elements in design. Basically, it accents good features."

"Then you really think that striping a car adds something?"

"Sure! Modern automobiles need some human element on them. Without it they look as though they had been ground out by a mechanical monster—which they have!"

"Do you think we will go back to the days when they turned out factory striped jobs?"

"Naw, Mr. Balgan."

"Baldwin!"

"Oh yeah, Baldwin. Naw, I don't think so. You just can't go out and hire a guy and say, 'You're a car striper.' You can either stripe cars or you can't. Those that can are too unreliable. As for doing it with a machine it would be too static. There would be no human element like I said."

"I was thinking that maybe I could do some of this to my car. What do you think?"

"Sure if you load the brush right. That's the secret—loading the brush right. The more paint on the brush, the wider the line. The less paint, the thinner the line. That's why I go through all this business of slapping the brush on a piece of cardboard. When you have to stop in the middle of a straight line, the knack is to load your brush with just the right amount of paint so that you can pick up the lines again and have it the same width."

"What do you put down as profession or vocation when making out your income tax?"

"Professional bum. I just paint things."

"Do you paint anything besides customs or hot rods?"

"Oh sure! Radios, musical instruments and fancy boxes—anything! I even had a guy come in here one day with a Starfish he'd had in the family for years and paid me to stripe it. A Starfish!"

"Do you do much interior car painting?"

"Sure, about twenty-five percent of my work is done on dashboards and around radios."

"What kind of things do you paint?"

"Well, I'll tell you Mr. Balcom . . . "

"Baldwin!"

"Yeah, Baldwin! I'll tell you. It depends somewhat upon what mood I'm in. Sometimes it is the car owner himself who suggests the scene. I don't mean he tells me what to paint but he reminds me of something. Like maybe the guy looks like a spider. So I paint a spider. Or maybe he reminds me of a crazy landscape. So I make a surrealistic. Sometimes I slap on an inner-planetary scene. Or maybe music around radios. Anything that can't be obtained any other way."

"I've noticed this bloodshot eyeball with wings. It's sort of a Von Dutch trademark isn't it?"

"Yeah, I guess so. But what it means I can't remember. The first one I drew was way back in 1947 and I haven't any idea what prompted me to even draw it then."

"I notice that on some of your jobs you paint little sayings or quotations."

"You mean like 'Too much,' or 'Might As Well Commit Suicide,' or 'Humanity Is Tragic,' is that what you mean?"

"Yeah, any significance?"

"Sometimes, like 'His Taillight Is In The Way.' It was too! Some of the things I write on the cars are as confusing as my drawings."

"What's the average age of your customers would you say?"

"About six Martian years."

"When a guy comes for his custom after you have striped it, what kind of a reaction do you usually get?"

"Usually pretty good."

"What do you tell a guy who beefs about the way you painted his car?"

"_ _ _ _ _ _ _ _ _ _ _ _ !"

"Ever get tired of striping cars?"

"Heck yes. I'm good for about a year at a time at this then I go back to my regular job."

"Your regular job?"

"I'm a sign writer and a gunsmith by trade. I do action modifications and recaliber guns. I also make metal engravings on shot guns and that sort of thing."

"Well Dutch, I guess that about does it. Sure appreciate your help. Thanks for answering all my questions."

"Sure thing. What did you say your name was again?"

"Baldwin. You know like pianos, apples, and locomotives."

"Aw sure. Well bye now. It's sure been nice knowing you Mr. Jonathon."

2

How to Build
the Perfect Rod

Bud Crayne,
Boy Hot Rodder

By Henry Gregor Felsen

Hot Rod, 1950

Bud Crayne rounded a curve at fifty and faced into the setting sun. For the next ten miles the highway ran straight and level across open farm land. Ninety-nine out of a hundred drivers rounding that curve and coming on the flat immediately increased their speed. Bud held at fifty. He had his reasons for staying at fifty. Bud always had a reason for driving at a particular speed.

A new green Plymouth sedan came up fast behind Bud, honked imperiously and swept by. Bud glanced at the other driver as the Plymouth moved past and saw contempt in his eyes for the ancient-looking contraption Bud was driving. Bud watched the new car pull ahead and cut back in front of him, gaining speed and space. He estimated it was hitting seventy, and could tell it was working hard. He laughed to himself but he hated to be passed, even when he wasn't racing.

Fifty. The dual pipes were crooning throatily, the mill was turning like a charm. Bud looked in his rear-vision mirror, made sure the road ahead was clear, then swiftly checked his instrument panel. He noted and remembered the readings of a dozen quivering needles at a glance. Taking a pencil from behind his ear he jotted the readings on a pad strapped to his right leg. That was all for fifty. He stabbed the gas pedal with a gentle toe and his rod leaped to sixty. An easy, effortless sixty. A true sixty.

A short run and an instrument check at sixty. Then seventy. At seventy the dual pipes sang deeper, their rich powerful tones rolling back over the concrete road. At seventy the motor was happy, taking a full bite. Everything checked at seventy. A deeper stab sent the speedometer needle to eighty, and the RPM on the tachometer climbed.

The green Plymouth came into view. Whatever it's speedometer read, it wasn't grossing more than seventy or seventy-five. Bud's figures for eighty were on the pad. He wanted ninety, and the Plymouth was in his way. He moved slightly to the left and saw that the road was clear. He gave the Plymouth the horn, waited for the new car to wobble as the driver was startled, then moved to pass. Bud didn't look over to see the other driver's reaction. He didn't care about the other driver. He was interested in making his check at ninety and that was no speed to rubber-neck at.

As Bud started past the Plymouth the driver of the new car looked to his left to see who was passing him at this speed, expecting to see some more powerful new car. When he saw Bud's crude-looking home-made job matching wheels with him he almost ran off the road. Not willing to be passed by a car that looked as though it would fall apart at forty, the Plymouth driver tried to make a race out of it. Bud took him on.

For a minute the two cars raced down the highway side by side and only inches apart. As the Plymouth picked up speed Bud stayed with it, until he saw that it was running wide open. Then he opened up. Despite the speed at which he was traveling, he could feel his rear wheels dig the road as he gunned the motor. His car shot ahead and pulled away from the new car, gaining space with every second. The driver of the Plymouth saw it was useless to chase Bud and dropped back to a chagrined and disgusted sixty. He felt disgraced at having been out-run by Bud's stripped-down car, but he was judging from outward appearance alone.

It was a Jacob's coat of a car that Bud Crayne had built. The body had come off an old Ford coupe. Bud had sanded off the original black finish and repainted with a dull red prime coat. Some day he intended to put on a finish coat. Bud had also chopped three inches from the top of the body, streamlined the windshield, and added fenders from another Ford.

He had installed a dropped and filled front axle and cut the frame at the rear to lower the car another three inches closer to the road. As a result, his car looked as though every spring had been broken.

The dual chrome exhaust pipes gave the first hint as to what might be found under the dull red hood. The motor had been taken from a wrecked Mercury, rebored, equipped with a three-carburetor manifold, double springing ignition, re-ground 3/4-race camshaft, high compression head, and a score of other refinements and improvements devoted to speed and power.

In contrast to the usual greasy motors found under gleaming hoods, the nondescript body of Bud's car concealed a motor that shone like a warship's brightwork on inspection day. There was chrome wherever chrome could be used. The head, the acorn head nuts, hose connections, exhaust headers, pipes, filters, carbs and linkage system were all of chrome and spotless.

Inside the chopped stubby cab Bud sat behind a huge white steering wheel which, with the side-shifting assembly, had been taken from a Lincoln. The cab was upholstered in artificial red leather with a chrome dash and chrome instruments and knobs. The entire ensemble rode on an ancient Ford chassis with a newer Ford rear end. How all these odds and ends had been fitted together to make one car was the result of months of study, experimenting and hard work on the part of Bud Crayne. It had all been done in his spare time while working at the Avondale Garage and Service Station.

Ninety. Bud traveled the straight highway like a bullet, his pipes blatting against the hard road with the sound of a track racer. At ninety the road seemed to shrink to the width of his wheels, and when he went over small dips in the pavement his car seemed to be dancing lightly on its toes, ready to leap into the air.

Bud leaned forward, listening intently. He didn't like the way the motor was pulling at ninety. Now that his chrome mill was being pushed, it was working too hard for the power and speed it delivered. He pushed on the gas pedal, and altho he was rewarded with more speed the response was soggy. He pushed a little harder, almost all the way, and as he touched one hundred his motor faltered. Bud held at a hundred, listening. Better to figure out the trouble now and fix it, than find out later, when every ounce counted.

At a hundred his rod had a tendency to float, and he had to fight the wheel when he ran into sudden changes in the wind. A black dot coming out of the sun swelled up to a big tractor and trailer. There was no time to cut his speed as they passed. The noise of their passing was like a grenade exploding, and the backwash from the truck hit Bud like a solid blow. His car shuddered from the impact and pulled like a balky horse fighting the bit. Bud fought it through, but he was forced to the right of the road, and for a moment it felt as though his wheels were going to slide off the pavement and ditch him. He gave it everything and played for the middle of the road. He came out rocking and cut his speed, thankful there was plenty of room and no traffic.

Bud hadn't failed to note the details of engine performance in his burst of speed. He wrote them down on the pad strapped to his leg, then put the pad in the glove compartment. He looked at his watch and saw it was time to head for Avondale and work. He yawned. It had been a fairly dull run on the highway.

*Most drivers
quit easily at high
speeds. Not Bud.
He liked to win.*

Knowing how his car deceived by its looks, Bud liked to patrol that ten mile stretch of straight road. Whenever he could, he teased big cars into racing with him, and usually won. Sometimes he won because his car was faster, but when some unusually fast stock car could approach his speed, Bud counted on his superior driving ability and his nerve to beat down the opposing driver. Most drivers quit easily at high speeds. Not Bud. He liked to win.

On this late afternoon he had gone out primarily to check the performance of his rod, and the Plymouth hadn't given him much of a race. Now that he was headed back to the garage he was ready to tear into his motor and find out where it was weak. There was only one more thing he wanted to try.

Another mile down the road Bud turned north for the two-and-a-quarter mile run into Avondale. The moment he turned off the main highway he was on the stretch of road that all the local drivers regarded as a playground.

The road to Avondale ran straight for a mile. Then it broke to the left in a long, gentle, banked turn that was known as Ninety-Mile-Curve. When the road straightened again, it lay like an arrow for a little over a mile, pointing at the small town. At the end of the flat was an overhead railroad crossing, and the highway coiled into a tight S to go under the tracks. Once around the S and through the underpass, there was Avondale. The entire one unpaved business street of it.

As usual, the Avondale road was deserted. Bud shoved his rod up to ninety by slow stages, so that when he hit Ninety-Mile-Curve he was rolling steadily. Now for the test. He had installed an anti-sway bar and canted his rear springs. That, coupled with his low center of gravity ought to allow him at least another five. He tried the turn at ninety-five.

It was easy. There was a little pull, but nothing serious. His rod seemed to dig its nose in a furrow and come around without any serious danger of getting out of hand. His tires wailed a little from the side pull, but it was a pleasant sound. He came out of the turn holding a new record, determined to add another five when his mill was in perfect order.

Dropping back to ninety, Bud made a final test for stability. He pointed to the left side of the road, crossed the middle line, then turned back again. As soon as he was on his own side of the road he eased to the left again, and then back to the right. Rocketing, he rocked from right to left, rolling to the fine point where another touch would, pull his off wheels from the road. Back and forth across the road he rolled, mightily pleased with the way he could rock and roll without losing control or rolling over. He had the touch. He knew just how much, and how far. It was a wonderful feeling. It was important to know just how far he could push his set of wheels before he made his speed run to Trenton. He thought of mistakes in judgment that would roll him over as purely mechanical problems. It never occurred to him that he might be injured or killed, or that he should be afraid.

Bud cut the gun at the Avondale sign along the highway, went into the S-turn fast, and whipped around it with power on. He burned rubber in a joyful double turn, roared up a slight incline when the turn ended, and another hundred yards on he swung to the right across the gravel approach to the Avondale Garage and Service Station. He eased past the two gas pumps and the service station building and rolled into the open garage. The run was over. Reluctantly Bud turned off the ignition and climbed out of his car, stretching his arms.

Bud Crayne was a lanky, raw-boned boy of seventeen with a long face, bold, self-confident black eyes, and a thin mouth that almost always held a challenging, reckless smile. He wore an old fedora hat with the brim turned up in front and fastened to the crown with a giant safety pin, a tight-fitting black leather motorcycle jacket with zippers in the sides and sleeves and studded with metal buttons and faded blue denim trousers. On his feet he wore short leather boots ornamented at the ankle with small brass chains.

Bud's parents had died when he was in grade school, and since that time he had lived with a bachelor uncle who shared furnished quarters with his young nephew. At first the housekeeper where they lived had watched over Bud, made sure he wore clean clothes and ate his meals and left for school on time. Bud's uncle didn't know much about taking care of a boy, and let the housekeeper take over. As long as Bud was well and out of trouble, his uncle didn't worry.

During his early years Bud enjoyed an unusual amount of independence. The more he could look after himself, the more he was allowed to. He stayed out late, roamed when and where he wished, and learned a hard kind of self-reliance.

He had started hanging around Jake Clymer's garage almost at once. Jake let him stay, taught him about cars, and paid him for his work. Bud's real interest in cars led him to spend more and more time at Jake's, until, in his 'teens, he knew everything about cars that Jake could teach him, plus a good deal he'd learned himself out of books and magazines.

Bud had learned to drive while most boys were still struggling with bicycles, and once given this head start behind the wheel, he never relinquished it. He had always been able to out-drive the others, and his leadership behind the wheel was seldom questioned or (any more) challenged.

At seventeen Bud was his own boss, resented any attempts by anyone to guide or counsel (he called it interfering with) his ways, and he not only worked at Jake's, but practically lived at the garage.

Growing up in this way without a family, Bud always felt different from the other boys and girls in town, and was always a little apart from them. When they turned to the warmth and love in their homes, he, left alone, turned to the garage, and his car. The hours that others spent with mothers, fathers, sisters or brothers, Bud spent with his homemade hop-up. It was his family. He was in the habit—like cowboys who rode lonesome ranges for isolated days at a time and talked to their horses to break the silence—of talking to his car as though it were animate, and could understand, and sympathize.

His independence made him seem more mature than the other boys his age who yet had to ask parental permission to come and go. Bud regarded himself a man, and thought (he thought) like a man. He had a job, and as soon as he was graduated from high school, he was going to be Jake's partner in the garage. Content with this future which assured him an income and a chance to experiment with motors, he considered himself old enough to marry. When high school was over with, and he was working full time, he intended marrying LaVerne Shuler. Why not? He could support a wife, and, for the first time in his life, he would have a real home of his own.

Meanwhile, Bud worked for Jake in his free time. When he wasn't working he was on the road. He tinkered with his car for hours in order to have pleasant moments of speed on the highway. When he was behind the wheel, in control of his hopped-up motor, he was king of the road. When he was happy, his happiness reached its peak when he could express it in terms of speed and roaring power, the pull of his engine, the whistle of the wind in his ears, and the glorious sensation of free flight.

When he was unhappy, discontented, moody, the wheel again offered him his answer. At these times there was solace and forgetfulness behind the wheel. The motor snarled rather than sang, speed became a lance rather than a banner, and revenge against trouble was won through the conquest of other cars that accepted his challenge to race. And when he was alone on the road, his car and its speed seemed to remove him from the troubles that plagued him while his feet had contact with the earth. Once removed from bodily contact with the ground, once in motion, once in a world of his own making, he escaped his troubles and sorrows in speed, in the true touch of the wheel, in the trustworthy thunder of the motor, the rushing sensation of detachment from all that was rooted or planted in earth.

No matter what his mood or his feeling, his trouble or his joy, it made everything right and good to be guiding his car, the car he had built, that belonged to him, that owed everything it was to him. Not a day passed without Bud's taking time for a spin. It was more than a ride; it was more than speeding; more than killing time. In some ways these daily sessions on the road were his hours of meditation, of true self-expression, the balm for his soul and the boast of his spirit. In these flying hours he had sought himself out, molded himself into what he was, and found his creed.

Bud's car, variously called his baby, hop-up, strip-down, roadster, heap, hot rod, jalopy or set of wheels, was like Bud himself. In a way he had built a mechanical representation of his life, and its oddly-assorted parts could be likened to his patch-work past. Bud had started out in life as the son of two parents. Each part of his car had likewise begun life in a normal automotive way. Then had come death in his family. From a normal home

They were both a little different, a little apart, constructed partly by design and partly by accident, made of the materials at hand.

he had been thrust into an abnormal situation, and the product of parents was modified by the care of an uncle, and a strange housekeeper. From the wreckage of normal cars Bud had salvaged a part here and a part there, and assembled them, and modified them so they would fit.

Many people had helped design Bud's development. His parents, his uncle, the housekeeper, Jake, his friends, his teachers. He had been influenced by many sources as he grew, and not all the influences were compatible with one another. Yet each had had some effect on his character, and formed him into what he was, a composite person, belonging neither here nor there, and knowing no twin.

So was his car. From the wrecks and abandoned hulks Bud had taken a Ford piece here, a Lincoln piece there, a Cadillac piece somewhere else, reconciled their differences into one body, added something of his own, and created an automobile that was at once similar to and different from all other automobiles. It lived on the same food and obeyed the same laws, but, like Bud, it had no twin. They were both a little different, a little apart, constructed partly by design and partly by accident, made of the materials at hand, formed, as it were, by-guess-and-by-gosh.

No wonder then that Bud felt more than a pride of ownership in this fellow-hybrid that was his car. Made with the work of his hands and the thought of his brains, it was his totem, his companion, his dog, his drawer of shells, his treasured childhood blanket and fuzzy bear.

Together they were a team, Bud's car and himself. Together they had won local fame and leadership on the road and in the shop. And other boys who worshipped speed came to kneel before this stubby, squat, misshapen little god of speed, and to listen raptly to Bud, the cover-alled high priest of the cult. He held chrome engine parts before their eyes, sermonized on gear ratios, chanted of "gow" and "dig" and "drag," and blessed them with a benediction in the form of advice on how to run away from police cars.

Jake Clymer, Bud's boss, was stretched out under a muddy Chevrolet with a trouble light. When he heard Bud drive into the garage, Jake rolled out from under the Chevrolet and got to his feet, wiping his hands on some old rags. Jake was a lantern-jawed man of forty-five who wore rimless glasses and coveralls three sizes too big for his slight figure. "I see you're here," Jake said, looking at the clock on the wall.

"On time as usual," Bud answered.

"Have a nice run?"

"Fair," Bud said, lifting the hood of his car. "I chopped a new Plymouth without any trouble, but she didn't seem to fire right when I got toward four thousand RPM. I'll give my ignition system a look."

"Might be that new automatic pressure pump," Jake said. "But before you get lost with that, there's a little company business has to be done."

"Like what?" Bud asked in a bored voice.

"Like a grease job on that truck and a patch on that red tube in the corner."

"Okay," Bud said dispiritedly, hating to be torn from the interesting problem of his own mechanical troubles. He took down a large suit of stained coveralls from the wall and put them on over his clothes.

Jake grinned. He knew how Bud felt about doing jobs that didn't present a new mechanical problem, but they had to be done, and that's what Bud was getting paid for.

Bud got in the grease pit under the truck and knocked mud from a fitting so he could attach his gun. He worked with his hands, but his mind was busy with the probable causes of his own troubles. His fuel pressure hadn't shown any drop, so Jake couldn't be right about the pump. One of those carbs, maybe . . .

Jake walked over to the side of the pit. "How are you coming with your plans for that run to Trenton?" he asked casually.

"Okay. . . . What run to Trenton?" Bud's voice was suddenly guarded.

Jake chuckled. "It's no secret, Bud. Everybody knows you've test-run the distance a dozen times. Hear you and Walt Thomas have a ten dollar bet on it."

"We were just talking," Bud grunted; pumping grease. "I said I could make Trenton in thirty minutes, and he said I couldn't."

"It's forty miles," Jake said. "You'd have to average eighty."

"I can do better than that."

"And get killed trying," Jake said. "It ain't all on straight roads, Bud. You've got a full stop when you hit the highway, two big towns to go through and a couple of little ones. You'd have to be driving a hundred on the highway to make it, and we don't know what kind of traffic there'll be."

"I could still do it if I wanted to," Bud argued from under the truck. "I'd need a little more weight, because my baby tends to float after a hundred. But with a couple of sand bags and a passenger she'll hold. And I can touch a hundred and twenty if I have to, Jake."

"Passenger!" Jake laughed. "Who do you think would go on a ride like that?" He added soberly. "Don't let Walt Thomas get your goat, Bud. No ten dollar bet is worth killing yourself and maybe a couple of other people over. It's not right to drive like that on the highway."

"Did I say I was going to?" Bud demanded. "I just said I could if I wanted to. Somebody's been doing a lot of blabbing about me. I noticed Ted O'Day seemed to be hanging around this area a lot in the last week."

"That's the Highway Patrol's job," Jake said. "Ted's a good fellow."

"I don't care if he does hang around, Bud said defiantly. "I can run away from him any day in the week I want to. But just because I built a fast car, that's no reason for him to pick on me."

"You know what they say, Bud. Where there's smoke there's fire."

"Well, I'm not planning any speed run to Trenton," Bud said. "And you can tell that to Ted O'Day when you see him."

"You tell him," Jake said. "I'm going home to supper, and Ted's driving up now."

"I'll tell him," Bud said. "That uniform doesn't scare me."

Jake cleared his throat. "Say Bud, there's one more thing. . . . "

"On this truck?"

"No. What I want to say, Bud, is that I don't mind if your friends drop around to see you once in a while, but I'd rather they didn't make the station a regular hang-out."

"Okay, Jake," Bud said casually.

"You know how it is with a crowd of big noisy boys hanging around," Jake went on. "Ladies don't like to get out of their cars and it hurts business. You can see that."

"Yeah," Bud said. "I don't like a big crowd around all the time myself. But the drug store closes before we do, and since Pop Huggins started selling beer in the pool room you can't go in unless you're over twenty-one. Where else is there to go?"

"They might try home," Jake said. "Well, I don't mind a few boys around, but it's bad for business to have a crowd. Try to keep it down, eh, Bud?"

"Yeah, Jake," Bud answered. "I'll try."

" 'Night, Bud. That farmer says he'll be in for his truck a little after nine. Keep open for him, will you?"

"Yeah, sure," Bud said, gunning grease into another fitting. "I'll be here anyway. 'Night."

As Jake's legs moved out of Bud's field of vision, another pair moved in to take their place. Legs in brown boots and tan breeches. "Hello, Bud," came from above the legs.

"Hi," Bud answered shortly.

"How's your rod working?" Highway Patrolman Ted O'Day asked pleasantly.

"Fair."

Bud watched narrowly as the booted legs moved toward his car. He hated to have anyone touch it. "I saw you take that Plymouth," O'Day said. "He didn't have a chance."

"I guess not," Bud said noncommittally.

"You were moving pretty fast for the highway," O'Day said with mild reproof.

"There's no speed limit in this state," Bud came back. "Besides, I was testing my motor, that's all."

"What were you doing on the Avondale turn-off?" O'Day asked. "There is a law against reckless driving, and the way you were rocking back and forth across the road could be called that."

"It wasn't either," Bud said angrily. "I was testing something else. I looked. There weren't any other cars on the road. I didn't risk anybody's neck but my own, and that's my business."

"It's mine, too," O'Day snapped. "You know, Bud, there *is* a law against suicide."

"Oh . . . nuts!" Bud put away the grease gun and crawled out of the pit. He walked over to his car and leaned against it, wiping his hands on some old rags. "What are you following me around for?" Bud demanded. "I've never been in any wrecks, have I? Have I ever done anything I ought to get pulled in for? I obey lights and signs as well as the next guy. Maybe better."

Ted O'Day brushed off a place on the running board of the Chevrolet and sat down. He was a big six-footer with broad shoulders, a square jaw, light blue eyes and red hair. "You're all right, Bud," he said. "It's those other guys."

"Yeah," Bud agreed readily. "Those other. . . . What do you mean?"

"That's what they all say," Ted said grinning. "It's always the other guy. But forget it. I wanted to have a look at your motor."

"What for?" Bud asked suspiciously.

"Relax," O'Day laughed. "I saw how you rolled today. I'd like to see the power plant that did it."

"Okay," Bud said, feeling flattered. "I could have done better, but I'm having a little trouble somewhere. Maybe one of the carbs. . . . " He lifted the hood and proudly displayed the gleaming motor to O'Day.

The highway patrolman's eyes lighted appreciatively. He leaned across a fender and took in every detail. "Nice work, Bud. All by yourself, huh?"

"Oh, Jake had to show me a lot," Bud admitted blushing a little.

"Don't kid me," O'Day answered. "I know what Jake can do and what he can't do. Where'd you learn it all?"

"Out of books, mainly," Bud said. "All you have to do is follow instructions, and after a while you can try some ideas of your own."

"Got lots of them?"

"Yeah. Most of them don't seem to work, though."

O'Day pushed his cap back on his head and studied Bud's face. "You like messing with cars, huh?"

Bud nodded. "It's all I . . . It's . . . I don't know how to say it. But when I get working I forget everything. Sometimes I work all night and don't even know how long I've been until I see the sun come up."

"Plan to be a mechanic?"

"What else is there?" Bud asked. "Jake says he'll take me on full time after I'm out of high school in the spring. It's better than anything else I can get."

"Ever think of leaving Avondale?"

Bud shrugged. "What for? I'd just be a mechanic in some other shop, and maybe I wouldn't have the chance to do as much of my own work as I get here. I'll stick."

"What about college?"

"Not a chance. I don't have the money. Besides, the courses I'd want to take would be too tough for me to work my way through. I'm no Einstein, even if do like technical stuff. I'd need all my time for studying." A wistful look came over Bud's face. "I sure would like to be an automotive engineer. Boy I've got ideas about cars that if I had a real setup and money behind me. . . . Aaah, what's the use of talking?"

"Too bad," O'Day said half to himself. "You've got a lot of raw talent, Bud. You might do big things if you had the chance. Why don't you fight harder?"

"I'm satisfied the way I am," Bud said, dismissing his dreams. "I'll be out of high school soon, and I'll have a job. I'll be able to work on my own, and maybe invent something here. Anyway, I'll probably get married as soon as I'm set here."

"Married! At your age?"

"I'll be eighteen this summer," Bud said defensively. "It's just about settled."

"Who's the girl?"

"LaVerne Shuler."

O'Day nodded, his face expressionless. "I've seen her. Pretty."

"Yeah." Bud looked at his motor again, forgetting the rest of the grease job on the truck. "What do you think could be wrong? It seemed to be working fine until I got up around . . . around a hundred, and then it went mushy. I'd like to get rid of that bug."

"Don't blame you," O'Day said solemnly, holding back his laughter.

Both of them leaned over the motor while Bud examined the first of his three carburetors. "I want these jugs perfect," Bud muttered. "Can't take any chances conking out. . . . "

" . . . on the speed run to Trenton," O'Day finished.

Bud froze. The friendly atmosphere that had developed between the two was gone in a flash. "I don't know what you're talking about," Bud said in a flat voice.

"I do," O'Day said genially. "I heard all about it."

Bud faced the patrolman defiantly. "So what if I do want to make a trip to Trenton? Is that against the law?"

"If you try to make it in thirty minutes, it's bound to be," O'Day answered. "Don't be a fool, Bud. A run like that over the public highway and through towns is like opening fire with a pistol in a crowd."

"I know how to . . . " Bud began.

"Sure you know how," O'Day said. "I've seen you drive, and I'll tell you myself that I don't know anyone who can handle a car better than you can. But Bud, what about the people who might get in your way, and get rattled? Can you speak for the other drivers you'll meet in tight spots? You can handle the speed of a hundred, but can the people you meet?"

Bud looked at his motor thoughtfully. "I never thought about it that way," he confessed.

"That's the way it is, Bud." O'Day drove home his point. "You like cars, Bud, and you like speed. Okay. There's a place for experiments and for speed, but the public highway isn't that place. I don't want you killing others or yourself trying that Trenton run. You're too important, Bud. Here, in this little shop, you might find something that will make you famous. Do you want to risk losing that over a little speed? And what about LaVerne? Isn't she worth slowing down for?"

Bud nodded silently, reluctantly.

"I don't want to pick on you," O'Day said. "When you're out alone on the road, and the road is clear and you want to test something, you've a right to open up. But stay away from tricks like the Trenton run. It's like playing chicken, and rotation, and . . . "

"I don't do that crazy stuff," Bud interrupted.

"I know. But if you drive recklessly you're setting a bad example. The others can't match your speed, so they try to show off in other ways. In games. You're looked up to by the other fellows, Bud. They know you're tops behind the wheel, and they'll follow your example. Set a good one."

Bud rubbed his chin with his hand. "If you put it that way, I guess the run is off."

"Good boy," O'Day said. He prepared to leave. "Maybe some day when I'm off duty you'll take me out for a ride, eh?"

"Sure," Bud grinned. "Any time."

O'Day got in his patrol car and drove away. Bud went down in the grease pit again and continued his work on the truck. O'Day was okay, really. What he'd said made sense. No use getting knocked off just because a guy like Walt Thomas got under your skin. And he couldn't marry LaVerne if he cracked up trying to make Trenton in thirty minutes. No sir, LaVerne was worth more than showing up Walt Thomas. There wasn't going to be any Trenton run. He'd tell Walt, and tell him why—as much as you could tell Walt anything.

In his mind Bud could see how Walt would react to the news that the Trenton run was off. He'd blow to everybody that Bud had lost his nerve, and was chicken, and throw his big stupid weight around and make a lot of noise with his big stupid voice.

Bud jabbed viciously at the mud caked over an alemite fitting. It wasn't going to be easy taking any guff from Walt, because he knew he could make Trenton in thirty minutes. Once he did it, he could shut Walt up for good. Of course he'd half-promised O'Day not to make the run, but O'Day didn't understand. You couldn't let a guy like Walt crow over you for nothing.

Maybe there would be some other way out. He could take Walt out and scare the pants off him on the back roads. It wasn't really worth risking his car and his neck to win ten bucks from Walt. And O'Day was right about something else. LaVerne was worth slowing down for. A fellow who was thinking of getting married had to settle down. He couldn't spend all his money on auto equipment either, Bud thought. A lot of things would change after he was married. Anyway, that speed run to Trenton was off. He had bigger things to do. He'd tell Walt.

Then, in the distance, he heard Walt Thomas coming around Ninety-Mile-Curve as fast as he could travel.

Editorially Speaking

By Steve Alexander

❧

Hot Rod Magazine, September 1972

It was about 10 o'clock Monday night. The kid was asleep and me and the old lady were lying there, relaxed, watching the Democratic convention on TV. Willie Brown, leader of the California delegation, had just delivered an impassioned speech on behalf of seating the original California delegation. The entire convention had come to their feet and gone into a state of pandemonium following Brown's final plea of, "I did it for you in Georgia in '60. I did it for you in Selma in '64. Now do it for me in Miami Beach in '72."

The telephone rang. "Do it for me in South Gate. Now!" boomed the voice of Terry Cook, *Hot Rod*'s editor and my boss. Terry was calling from Alan Maas' shop in South Gate, California, where he, Maas and the *Hot Rod* staff had spent the previous 48 sleepless hours thrashing to assemble the '27 T street rod you have been reading about in these pages. Now it was my turn to help out.

The "South Gate Marathon," as it came to be known, had begun on Sunday afternoon when the freshly painted chassis had been delivered to Maas' shop. After a week of sanding their fingers to the bone, Don Kirby's crew had finally completed painting and detailing the chassis and fiberglass body. The chromed Jag rearend had been laid out in about 350 pieces on the floor and was ready to be assembled. The complete front end (springs, shocks, wheels, brakes, bearings, spindles, steering, etc.) also had been laid out on the floor. The radiator, transmission, steering column and wheel, power brake unit, radio, gauges, switches, lights, fuel tank, gas pumps and lines, brake lines, horn, relay switches, exhaust system, clutch and brake pedals, slave cylinders, motor mounts, etc., lay on the floor and on shelves, in boxes, in cars and out in the yard. The turbocharged Vega engine had just been hauled back from a long stint on Vic Edelbrock's dyno. After six months of parts chasing and preparations in Los Angeles and San Francisco, and on the very eve of the Street Rod Nationals, the incredible *Hot Rod* Magazine Project Street Rod was ready to go together.

Could it be done? Could Terry and the Pirates put it all together in time to drive it back to Detroit for the Nationals? The consensus around the office was that it couldn't be done, but that we'd give it a try anyway. And in answer to Terry's plea for help, the staff made their way, one by one, down to Maas' shop to help out.

On Sunday afternoon and into the night, Steve Kelly, John Dianna and John Fuchs joined Terry and Alan. Anyone else who happened to walk through the door was also put to work. This included Alan's mother, customers who came by to see how work was progressing on their own rods and even a South Gate policeman who cruised by to check out what was going on. The policeman wound up filling the transmission with oil before returning to patrol duty. (Unconfirmed rumor has it that Terry actually called Clyde Baker and Tom Senter in Detroit and Steve Green in Englishtown, but all three refused to fly back to flog on the rod.) The level of involvement became so intense in Maas' shop that nobody was ever quite sure whose beer can he was drinking out of or if the guy missing had gone home or just gone to sleep.

By the time I arrived late Monday night, only Terry, Alan and Steve Kelly remained to thrash on the rod. When I walked in, Alan had already crashed between the solvent can and the drill press, Terry stared blankly through bloodshot-red eyes, and Steve Kelly was wandering around polishing off the last of three half-empty cans of warm beer.

We thrashed for another 48 hours. The motor went in and out a few more times. John Fuchs disassembled and reassembled the front suspension so many times that he knows it like he knows the dimple on his secretary's kneecap. Steve Kelly finally fell out at about the 72-hour mark of the Marathon. Kelly was later to remark that if he'd listened to his old lady and gone to church on Sunday he would have missed Terry's phone call and his 72-hour ordeal as well.

Terry finally went to sleep in the truck at 3 a.m. Wednesday, waking at 7 o'clock that same morning. When he awoke, he turned to John Fuchs. "Where am I? What time is it?" John, always willing to have a little fun at Terry's expense, replied, "You're at Maas' shop. It's 7 o'clock Thursday morning. You've been sleeping for 28 hours!" Terry's eyes bulged in disbelief. He went back to sleep.

By Wednesday night the motor, trans, rearend and suspensions were in. Everything was wired. The body was ready to go on. The turbocharger was ready to be hooked up. The plan was to fire it up by midnight, take a hot lap around the block and then off to Detroit in a straight-through 48-hour kamikaze trip to the Nationals. But it wasn't fired up till 7 a.m.

Thursday. The hot lap around the block indicated that the rod needed some more suspension work and was overheating to the tune of 260 degrees, due to melting a thermostat when the motor was run without water a tad too long.

Terry and Alan looked at each other through screaming red eyes. They had it running. They could go the banzai route and make the Nationals by the weekend, but what would that prove? They would be risking their lives just to save face. Cooler heads prevailed. They booked airplane passage, and on Thursday afternoon, somewhat dejected and understandably exhausted, boarded the plane for Detroit. Incidentally, Terry, if you're still on the road when you read this, please look in your briefcase. You left town with three stories, including this month's "Editorially Speaking," and I need them to make the deadline.

Past Tenths

Bargain-Basement Performance
from Used Speed Equipment

By John Baechtel

※

Hot Rod Magazine, February 1990

Untold performance treasures are lurking in every attic and under every workbench, patiently waiting for enterprising hot rodders to liberate them from exile. Consigned to a vast underground graveyard of forgotten speed equipment, these discarded parts are the hidden treasures of hot rodding. Think of them as both past and future tenths, for whatever performance gains they offered in the past may still be there waiting to be applied on the cost-conscious hot rods of tomorrow. Judicious application of these components can reap substantial rewards and stretch your performance dollars for maximum effect. Unscarred by factory part numbers or casting numbers, old aftermarket speed equipment is relatively immune to the speculation that has driven the price of original factory hardware and O.E.M. restoration parts sky high. By comparison, uncommonly high value can be derived from discarded speed equipment because it is usually available for a fair and reasonable price.

Used equipment is not necessarily bad equipment. In most cases, the parts are still perfectly good, but the original owner no longer needs them because he has either changed vehicles or upgraded his machine with the latest high-tech pieces. For the cost-conscious hot rodder, this can mean a bonanza of high-performance equipment at a fraction of the cost of new hardware. The critical element is a broad awareness of all the basic pieces and a thorough understanding of which parts are worth buying and which parts you should pass up. This comes with experience, but there are some basic rules of thumb to follow.

Equipment that has no moving parts is generally a safe bet, as long as it hasn't been modified or damaged. Your primary concerns are cost, damage inspection, and whether it will fit your application. But you also have to select and combine used speed parts with the same care you would use in choosing new equipment. It's still the combination that counts, and since you aren't operating with the luxury of picking new pieces right off the shelf, you'll need to have a well-thought-out, long-range plan. This generally applies to engine and driveline combinations, where mismatched components can wreak havoc with your car's driveability and performance. It's important to determine the primary intent of your vehicle and stick to it. A great buy on a used tunnel ram from some guy's drag car is no bargain at all if the rest of your engine is geared toward smooth, economical street operation. So keep sight of your primary goal and limit your purchases to those good deals that will really work to your advantage.

Then again, if you're an experienced wheeler dealer, you may have the talent to buy and swap all different types of equipment with desirable results. For example, if you know someone who can really use that tunnel ram and you can get it cheap, maybe you can trade it for something else that you really need, or turn it over for a few extra dollars that can be applied to your own project.

Used speed equipment is all around you. All you have to do is keep your eyes and ears open, and take the time to follow up on the little leads you come across almost every day. Most local speed shops have a used-parts table full of goodies for sale on consignment, or a bulletin board full of 3x5 cards offering all sorts of high-performance equipment for sale or trade.

Speed shops also have cards from people looking for specific parts, so make certain you're not missing out on someone who is anxious to pay you money for some of the unused pieces lying around in your own personal stash. A lot of major cities also have "sale-and-swap" papers available at local grocery and convenience stores. If you're a dedicated speed-parts consumer, you can track down a lot of great buys by following the listings in these papers. Sometimes you'll discover almost new equipment for sale cheap, because the original buyer didn't install it properly or it didn't meet his expectations. Even if it didn't work for him, it probably wasn't the equipment's fault. A little knowledge and patience can often put that speed equipment back on the road in perfectly good working order.

Within your own circle of friends and acquaintances, you can establish a network dedicated to buying and trading parts while keeping an eye out for things that might be useful to anyone of you. Swap meets are still a great place to score good equipment and recycle pieces that you no longer need. There is usually a wide selection at swap meets, and you have the opportunity to trade parts on the spot without even using cash.

Engine shops, tire shops, and garages that have a few performance cars parked in their lots are also good places to look for parts. These shops remove a lot of speed equipment for people who need to make their cars legal for smog checks, or who just couldn't make it work right. Sometimes people leave the parts behind, and the shop will sell them cheaply to help cover expenses.

Whatever the source, good used speed equipment can help you build a terrific street machine for a lot less money. But it's also possible to buy a lot of junk if you're not careful. Some pieces are just too risky to pay anything for, while others are almost guaranteed to deliver on their performance promise. Intake manifolds are a good example. A '72 Edelbrock Torker intake manifold will run just as well today as it did when it was manufactured. As long as it is undamaged, there's no reason to expect any less performance. So if you can trade for it or pick it up for $30, you'll have a solid high-performance intake manifold that will give you miles of trouble-free performance, and we doubt that you'll ever notice any significant performance difference on a moderately modified street-driven machine. Manifold manufacturers have made changes and revisions on their products for decades, and while performance improvements can definitely be shown, the older manifolds will still perform almost as well if you apply them properly. The same rules of application apply. Single 4-barrel manifolds are preferred unless you're going more for show than go. There are even plenty of emissions manifolds around these days, so finding one that will retain your EGR valve shouldn't be that difficult. Generally, manifolds are a solid buy. They clean up easily and need very little repair. You may have to rethread a hole here and there but, in most cases, nothing too serious.

Other examples of speed equipment that are usually safe to buy include scattershields, air cleaners, valve covers, engine dress-up pieces, and most items that perform only one function that can't easily be compromised through abuse or misapplication. But the successful bargain hunter is wise in the ways of the jungle and tends to view most parts with apprehension—until shown otherwise. Camshafts are a good example. Even the most experienced shopper can't tell if a cam has a few lobes on the verge of going flat or if the timing dowel was misaligned. A used roller cam would be a safer bet than a flat-tappet or hydraulic cam, but unfortunately, most good street cams are not roller cams. A cam and lifters are relatively cheap compared to the cost of pulling a motor back down

to change the cam. And how do you know it's really the cam that the seller claims it is? Some cams are clearly marked, so you can determine the valve timing by looking it up, but you never want to take someone's word about a cam unless he's your best-trusted buddy. Even then, you only want the cam, not the lifters.

The same goes for headers. Unless you can find a part number stamped on the headers—and verify that they are in fact the correct headers for your car—they are almost guaranteed not to fit. Most used headers are in terrible shape anyway, so unless they are a set of original factory pipes essential to your 100-point restoration, buy new headers. One good application for used headers is a custom engine swap in which no headers are available. In this case, a used of headers could be modified to fit more easily than building headers from scratch. All it takes is patience and some basic welding skills.

Carburetors can be a great buy if you have some knowledge of them and are willing to sort them out. Most carburetor problems are caused by leakage, warped throttle bodies or metering blocks, worn bushings, and broken parts. A savvy carburetor person can fix most of these problems with a rebuild kit and pieces from other carburetors, thereby turning a $25 carburetor into a well-running piece of equipment. Just make certain that the carburetor you buy is the correct size for your application, and that it has the correct throttle arm and vacuum ports for total compatibility with your equipment.

Be careful when buying ignition parts if you can't arrange a trial run. Distributors aren't a bad buy as long as you can't wiggle the shaft inside the housing. They can be refurbished with new points, condenser, cap, and rotor for an inexpensive ignition upgrade, and at the same time you can re-curve them for greater performance. High-performance coils and electronic ignition boxes mayor may not be good. If you can try them out in advance, you'll know right away if they don't work. In most cases, the box or coil is all you get, and you'll have to comb the manufacturer's catalog for installation hardware.

Gauges can be a very good buy if you can find them, but it's difficult to determine if they're accurate without trying them. Mechanical pressure gauges are usually dependable, and electric gauges can often be made accurate with the addition of a new sending unit. Generally, pressure and temperature gauges are relatively safe buys, especially if they come installed in the manufacturer's own panel. Tachometers are another story. Some manufacturers such as Auto Meter will rebuild tachs to factory specifications, but after you factor in the shipping and repair costs, you might be better off buying a new tach. Most tachs are designed for multi-cylinder operation, but you should make certain that you're getting one that is compatible with your engine. In some cases, you only have to snip one wire, or reconnect a wire that has been snipped, depending on the application. A call to the manufacturer will usually clear up any questions you might have about making the right connections.

If you're starting to think that good used parts are too difficult to come by, please think again. We're simply suggesting some of the things you need to look for to make certain that you're buying a good or service-able piece. Almost any part can be defective or damaged through misuse, but that doesn't mean you can't find the good stuff. You'll need some experience and expertise if you're going to start buying things such as 4-speed manual transmissions, automatic transmissions, rearends, posi units, and clutch units, but these are all candidates for terrific bargains.

If a manual transmission will shift through all the gears and doesn't appear to have a lot of free play in the input shaft, it's probably service-able. Remove the side cover and examine the oil for metal. Traces will always be evident, but any serious damage will show up in the bottom of the trans. If none of the gears are chipped, the wear patterns look even, and the synchronizers aren't completely blunt, you can be fairly certain that the transmission is in decent shape. The same goes for an automatic transmission, but remember that there are a lot of hidden items you aren't going to be able to check out. In the case of transmissions, it's best to strike the lowest possible deal to keep yourself from getting hurt on repairs. A good automatic rebuild with a shift improver kit is still only a few hundred bucks, so try to get the trans as cheaply as possible.

If you're looking at a clutch, pressure plate, and flywheel assembly, or any of the individual pieces, make absolutely sure they are compatible with your existing hardware. In any used speed-equipment purchase, compatibility is king. Even if it's free, it's no bargain if it doesn't fit. Clutch discs should have plenty of lining left above the rivets and pressure plates should have all the levers in the same relative position. These can be difficult pieces to assess, but as long as there is no evidence of excessive heat buildup, you can probably use the pieces effectively. Numerous small spiderweb cracks in the flywheel surface are normal, so don't be alarmed.

Tires and wheels, on the other hand, are relatively easy to inspect. The most obvious thing to determine with a set of wheels is size, fit, and offset. If you keep a cardboard template of the bolt pattern in your car, you'll be able to check it against any wheels you come across. Backspacing and rim width are easily checked with a tape measure, and any damage to a set of wheels is usually easy to spot with a visual inspection. Steel rims are pretty straightforward, but you have to check custom aluminum rims carefully for cracks, chips, and other damage. As long as you're really familiar with your car and its requirements, you'll be able to tell whether the parts are going to work.

Sometimes it's even okay to buy speed equipment that's broken, damaged, or has parts missing. It all depends on your level of expertise and how difficult it will be for you to repair the item. It's also possible to adapt stock items off of wrecked cars to serve your purpose. As an example: With so many automatic transmissions and floor-shift cars around today, it's a snap to find a factory ratchet-type shifter that will do just about everything you need for 10 or 20 bucks at the scrapyard. The same goes for lots of other parts. Bolt-on parts are great, but hot rodding has more to do with fixing and modifying things to improve your car's performance.

You are your own best judge of what you need and how well you are equipped to deal with parts that need some work. Virtually everything you need to build a high-performance street machine is available on the used-parts market. From a simple set of traction bars to complete engines, it's all out there if you're patient enough to find it and savvy enough strike a bargain. With a carefully thought-out program, you could actually build a top-running street machine without buying one new piece of speed equipment. Even with all of today's high-tech improvements, cars aren't appreciably faster than they were 10 or 15 years ago, so all that old hardware must have worked pretty well. And once you become a religious trader and swap-meet devotee, you also may find yourself enjoying hot rodding more than ever, because it has become both afford-able and enjoyable.

"The '34 and I"

Dean Moon—speed shop owner, writer, photographer and constant drag strip competitor/spectator—has been associated with an ever-changing neat '34 Ford for as long as anyone cares to remember. In answer to the long-standing question of whence came the nifty little 5-window, Dean came up with this tale which we believe the readers of R & C will enjoy.

By Dean Moon

※

Rod & Custom, November 1955

It all started 'long about September of 1946. I had just returned to my home in California from an all expense paid tour of Japan—courtesy the U. S. Government—and was casting about in search of a reliable piece of transportation. While pondering the situation, a clean little '34 Ford passed the house—a bolt from the blue. I tracked the 5-window to its lair and found it to be the proud possession of an elderly couple who swore by the fuzz on the original floor mat that they were the coupe's second owners. And, yes, they were willing to sell.

After a quick once-over (two weeks) and a bit of thorough inspection (you had to be careful in those days), I decided that the coupe was ready for ownership by yours truly.

Now that I think back, I seem to recall that the exchange of names on the owner's certificate nearly didn't take place. However, finding that the original battery (now in its twelfth year) was still fit to argue with the 21-studder, I decided to take the plunge. Few coupes were in as nearly original shape as this one. 400 Yen didn't swing the deal, so I had to part company with a comparable quantity of U.S. currency. Any car was highly prized in those days—the war, you know.

The original 21-stud V8, which, I must admit, had seen far better days, was fired up and the new (to me, anyway) coupe and I started the homeward trek—home a garage filled with tools just waiting to be used and a stack of spare parts accumulated through the years which might just find a home in, or on, the Ford. The journey was most enjoyable. You know how it is, listening carefully as the tires bounced over the pavement, listening for any indication which would point the finger of misuse toward the former owners. To my utter amazement, however, nothing unusual or serious sounded amiss though the 12-year-old beneath the hood had barely enough oomph to propel the stocker along the streets. Apparently someone had appreciated the value of a really fine car and had treated it accordingly. It turned out that any ailment had been duly taken care of before it became too serious, the rigors of the 1,000-mile lube job had been adhered to. In short the coupe was a rare find, indeed.

Home at last. "Operation Rejuvenation" was about to get underway. Before one can commence a project such as I had in mind, though, one must decide just what step to take first. The upholstery? The "continental" kit? The pop-eyed headlights?

First to get the "deep six" was Henry's exposed spare. The continental kit would never make a comeback (remember, this was 1946). In quick order followed the 17-inch wheels and tires; said go-'rounds being replaced with a set of bright red 16-inchers—one for each of the coupe's four corners. Partnership between the '34 and I had continued for almost an hour by this time and I could tell that we were going to become inseparable buddies.

Late model sealed beam units replaced the frog-eyed lights, the tail-lights gave way to a pair of "teardrops" from a '39 Ford and the license plate was suitably framed and plunked down where the spare used to be.

A set of the popular (then, anyway) ribbed DeSoto bumpers—vintage 1937—were narrowed by 8 inches and the stock brackets reworked, and chromed, before installation.

Along about here, the '34 and I made up our minds to go all-out and make Operation Rejuvenation into a real spectacular production. Out came the dashboard. The stock instruments were replaced with Stewart Warner gauges—the dash being plated before replacement.

Time was passing swiftly—but the reliable old flathead hadn't completely given up the ghost as yet and it was still chugging along. Prior to changes beneath the hood, we decided that the hood itself should be altered—a filled, louvered or otherwise changed hood is nearly always an indication of alterations inside and this was about to take place. But, bodywork first. Going along with the fashion of the time, the louvered hood side panels were discarded in favor of a pair of solid panels sans the ornamental vents.

Really into the project by this time, Gil's Auto Body Works of L.A. was called upon to do something about the leaky insert panel in the center of '34's turret top. This problem was solved by fitting in a steel section and welding and hammering until the top looked as though Henry had intended it that way. Also to come under the torch at this time was the cowl vent. This had served no other purpose than to keep my feet wet in rainy weather—it wouldn't open anyway! The rear body seams that follow the contour of the deck lid went too, as did the exposed bolt heads on the front fenders.

Still not quite ready for engine replacement, we went ahead to improve the coupes stopability. This was accomplished through the courtesy of a wrecked-out '46 Ford which gave up its hydraulic stoppers and front spindles as well. The '46 was also relieved of its transmission (gears in same being replaced with a set of 26-tooth Zephyrs).

From various other cars came such equipment as the column shift and linkage, a new steering column (chrome plated), and a newer steering wheel.

The '34 continued to struggle along but with a little less effort now that the 59A engine had been installed. The year '51 was creeping up on us, though, and the great horsepower race had begun its rampant charge. Somebody victimized the mill with a portable grinder and a boring bar. Displacement jumped suddenly to 268 inches. Several other modifications at the same time resulted in our bringing home a mantel full of trophies. These were the direct result of a good many lakes meets and a run or two at the Bonneville Salt Flats.

Just as we were ready to cement our relationship a little more solidly, Uncle Sam again intervened so the coupe and I were off to see what we could do during the Korean conflict. As luck had it, though, duty this tour was strictly stateside. Salt Lake City was stop No. 1 where the coupe survived the winter far better than I.

Dozens of 800-mile shuttle trips between Salt Lake City and Los Angeles took its toll, but still the little '34 could get around. Then came a transfer to Georgia. The summer here made up for the cool winter we had just experienced but hot or cold, the '34 continued to tick.

Before being relieved of my job through an act of Congress, we took in a little spectating of races over the sand at Daytona and the same over the bricks at Indianapolis.

The trip home was made with no trouble other than the fact a trailer followed us all of the way—the latter being loaded down with a hefty 59L engine slated for installation when we had again settled down in L.A. As it turned out, though, the 59L made its home somewhere else for a

friend had taken me for a brief spin in a warmed over Studebaker V8. That ride was nice—in fact it was just too much. Those 5 main bearings and the overhead sprinkler system did it! 2 weeks and about 500 junkyards later, a nearly new '51 Stude V8 became mine for $200.00—hence began "Operation Re-rejuvenation."

With no information but with lots of effort, the V8 was soon functioning smoothly beneath the now-louvered hood of the 5-window. Along about here dropped axles, large rear skins and 15-inch wide-base wheels had taken over so the '34 was subjected to another transformation. 5.90s up front and 7.10s behind now stabilize my old friend who has averaged somewhat over 10,000 miles for each of the eight years I have owned it.

Henry's interior furnishing had really gotten me down by this time so John Bottenburg of L.A. was allowed to apply his talents with needle, thread and black and white Naugahyde. Driving home from the upholstery shop, a brand new '52 Mercury glided past and its Bittersweet shade left me gasping—with satisfaction, that is. So, Bittersweet it was—then the car shows began sending us home with more trophies to add to the stack.

Though the Studebaker engine was performing quite capably, it became apparent that a little altering was due here and there. The drag strip records were beginning to climb out of sight and we had to do something to stay with the competition. As it was, the V8 shoved us to 82 mph in the quarter mile, but a Howard M-5 cam, a Stu-V manifold with 2 97's, and a W & H igniter changed all that. Though the cubic inches were still as South Bend originally designed, the '34 and I made it through the end of the strip at an even 90 mph.

Along about here I started my Moon Automotive Equipment Co., so the '34 took up a role as guinea pig for new products. Consequently many variations have been made on the fuel system, transmission and engine linkages, etc. The coupe currently boasts, in addition to the stock gas tank, a 3 1/2 gallon fuel tank located in the trunk compartment.

Well, that pretty well brings us up to date. The '34 is still running with a lot of its original equipment left untouched since the day it rolled from the assembly line some 21 years ago. As for mileage, I piled over 100,000 on it since '46 before the speedometer conked out. I'll get around to fixing it someday, but it seems that a shop customer is using it as a loaner car every time I get a chance to work on it.

Oh well, I'll get around, to it soon for the Stude's ready for replacement. Who knows, maybe we'll see a fast-stepping Chevy V8 under the hood one of these days. If and when that day arrives, though, you can bet the '34 and I will still be the best of pals.

Now That's a Hot Rod

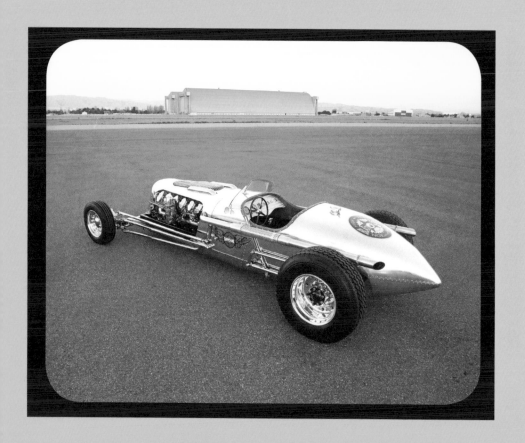

By Jay Leno

※

Popular Mechanics, May 2004

Jay Leno for *Popular Mechanics* (popularmechanics.com)

All of my car-owning buddies used to kid me because I never had a real hot rod. Well, a little over a year ago, a guy named Randy Grubb showed up to my garage. He was hauling a trailer with a car on it that he and a pal of his, Mike Leeds, had built. Unfortunately, the car had no rear brakes, headlights or turn signals and was far from road legal. However, it did have a 190-in. wheelbase and an engine from a M-47 Patton tank. Naturally, it got my attention.

So I handed over shopping bags full of $20 bills and the car was mine. And, it stopped all of that no-hot-rod nonsense I was hearing—in a hurry.

Enter Bernard Juchli, foreman of the "Jay Leno More-Money-Than-Brains Garage." Bernard has built numerous race-winning cars and worked on many projects over the years. He took one look at this project and said, "Just shoot me now."

As if getting this car road-worthy weren't already enough of a challenge, we soon had to replace the engine because somebody has opted to use radiator hose as an oil line. There I am, going down the freeway for the first time. I put my foot into it and *boom*! That 90 psi of oil pressure was too much for the radiator hose all 16 gal.—that's right, 64 quarts—of oil was gone in less than 10 seconds. That was the end of that.

This engine is an AV-1790-5B and it's 1792 cu. in. It has overhead cams and Hemi heads. Since it was designed to move a tank, it puts out 810 hp and makes 1560 ft.-lb of torque. But you can't just hit the local neighborhood NAPA store for replacement parts on one of these. Fortunately, a fellow by the name of Roy Smith ahs a surplus company in Augusta, Ga., and he has piles of them sitting there. He probably bought them for 5 cents on the dollar, but that's fine with me. There are guys who just save things, sort of like monks of the Middle Ages. They look at something and say, "Someone put too much work into this piece of machinery to just throw it away."

Remember, this motor was used in a tank that weighed 92,883 pounds—empty. Fully armed, the tank weighed 101,775 pounds. With 233 gal. of 90-octane fuel in its tank, the Patton would travel about 80 miles. That's about one-third of a mile per gallon. The engine was origi-nally built under license by Chrysler, and cost the government $110,000 in 1953. Today, a complete rebuild would cost $4500. How's that for reusing the nation's tax dollars?

With the engine handled, we turned our attention to getting all of that power down to the ground. So we replaced the transmission. The one in the car came out of a Greyhound bus. It had about 200,000 miles on it, and it was slipping continuously. So I called my friend David Killackey at Performance Allison Transmissions in Azuza, Calif., who pronounced, "There's only one transmission that could do that job: the Allison HD4060 6-speed." We got one from GM Powertrain. I wanted the transmission geared so that when the engine was running at 800 to 900 rpm, the car would be moving about 80 mph. This is an American car, powered by an American tank engine, and the power is being put to the ground by an American transmission, by Allison.

I called the folks at Allison and told them my needs. They, of course, asked, "What vehicle is this for?" When I said it was for a car with an engine from a Patton tank, I was put on hold. I really thought that would be the end of it. But, no, they came back and they were very excited. These people are engineers and they love projects—especially hot-rod projects. We took the car over to General Motors' Proving Ground in Arizona to get it specially calibrated. Steve Spurlin, from Allison, knew just what to do. "When we're through with it," in told me in serious truck-engineerspeak, "it will easily handle your duty cycle."

We added, among other things, rear brakes with vacuum boosters front and back, a new starter motor, an entire new electrical system, rear springs and an electric pre-oiler pump. We even added a Ki-Gas system—like many superchanged cars use—to inject raw fuel and prime the motor before starting. And we have mufflers, so we're socially responsible.

This isn't a car that when you take it apart and drop something you hear *bink*. You hear, *Clunk*! *Bang*! The engine alone weighs 2100 pounds. The car weighs 9500—nearly 5 tons, but one one-twentieth of what the tank weighed. This thing is *faaasssttt*. Best of call, it's hilarious to drive. The size is what's the funniest. The engine alone is 6 ft. long. The car looks like a roadster on steroids. When Arnold was on *The Tonight Show*, I brought it in to show him. I said, "It's the Terminator car." He loved it.

Since the engine is air-cooled with huge fins and cam-driven fans, it's like driving with your face in a hair dryer. On the coldest day of the year, I'm driving around with short sleeves. People think, "Wow, what a macho guy." But really, macho or not, I have a 100° breeze in my face even if it's 30 below.

This is the only car I've ever had with an engine that can actually overcome the brakes. You put your foot on the brakes as hard as you can and hit the gas, and it still pulls. It's ridiculous how much torque there is. We had to reinforce the frame because it was twisting like a coat hanger. We installed a Rockwell 3.78:1 airlocker rear end, like you'd use on a huge dumptruck. It costs $4200 and it's made of "unbreakabillium." With it, we can really light up the tires, which travel 11 ft. per rotation.

I have aircraft-engine cars, of course, like my Phantom II Rolls with a Merlin V12 from a Spitfire fighter plane, but this if my first tank-engine car. We're branching out. Truth is, this is not that different from an airplane engine. Except that they didn't make a whole of gasoline engines for military tanks. The first time someone hit one with a grenade, the Army brass went, "Oh." So tanks went diesel. The Army doesn't use Patton tanks anymore, but I'm using up those old engines. And now the Army has heard about my car. They want me to race it against their tank at Fort Irwin, Calif. My strategy is simple: Just stay out of the way of that gun turret and I'll be fine.

Building Your Own Hot Rod

By Robert E. Petersen and
the Editors of *Hot Rod* Magazine

❧

The Complete Book of Hot Rodding, 1959

Telling a fellow how to build a hot rod is just about as ridiculous as telling him what he should eat for breakfast. No two hot rodders have the same likes and dislikes and this is the reason there are as different hot rods as there are hot rodders. The only thing that all hot rods have in common is an engine that has been reworked to make the car perform better, or a larger displacement engine of a different make that was installed with normal engine swap methods.

A fellow can want a hot rod for several different uses and for each use there are many different ways in which he can accomplish his goal. If hot rods were divided into groups according to the reason for which they were built, the largest group would include those for normal driving, the second would include cars for drag racing, in the third group would probably be cars for track racing, and cars for straightaway competition such as on a dry lake or at Bonneville would comprise the smallest group. It's practically impossible to reduce hot rods to any smaller denomination than this because a hot rod of nearly any body type can fit into any of the groups. Exceptions to this would be dragsters, Bonneville streamliners, and track roadsters.

Since the time of the Model T there have been several cars that hot rodders have accepted over other types and makes as basis for modifications. It wouldn't be unreasonable to consider some of these cars, which are all of Ford origin, as hot rod "classics." That all the classics are Fords is more than just a coincidence because the name Ford has been synonymous with hot rods for longer than the present generation can remember. The reasons for this are the result of the way Fords are built and merchandised. Fords have always been small cars, and it is one of the first considerations for a hot rod that it be small. By being small, Fords have also been of comparatively light weight. This also fits into hot rod requirements. Fords have always been among the industry's lowest priced full-size automobiles and, for this reason, Ford has built and sold more passenger cars than any other manufacturer. This has made used and wrecked Fords plentiful and cheap, and price has always been something a hot rodder has had to consider. Through some quirk of fate, Fords have always had engines that are easy to work on and that are highly adaptable to hot rodding techniques. The engines respond readily to improvements and they stay together remarkably well when subjected to normal hot rod abuse. Added together, these things make a combination that until recently no other car could come near equalling. But now, Chevrolet, with its comparatively new and exceptionally adaptable V8 engine, may possibly take over Ford's position at the top of the hot rod ladder.

Chevrolet has paralleled Ford in car size, weight, production, price, and appearance for many years but until 1955 they were handicapped by engines and transmissions that only a Ford-hater could like. When a Ford owner told a Chevy lover that he had better paint his stove-bolt green so he could hide it in the grass alongside the road and watch the Fords go by, he meant what he said. Six-hole Chevys couldn't stay close to a Ford, and even when they were reworked, a reworked Ford would go around them. But when Chevy engineers got the go-ahead from the big-wheels that determine policy to modernize their powerplants for 1955, the result was a terrific blow to Ford superiority. To this date Ford hasn't been able to completely recover their former performance edge.

Starting with the Model T, the first of the Ford classic hot rods was the '27 T roadster. The only part of this car that actually qualifies as being a classic is its body. At one time roadster bodies of this vintage were very much in demand for both street rods and competition cars. Next was the Model A roadster. It was used in its entirety, first with reworked Model A engines and then with reworked Model B and flathead V8's. It was a favorite for street and competition. After the Model A came the '32 roadster and three-window coupe. The roadster was much more popular than the coupe for both street and competition but enough of the coupes were used to qualify it as a classic. Next were '34 three-window coupes, then '36 three-window coupes, and then '40 coupes and sedans. At one time coupes of all these years were very popular and it was common practice to chop their tops. They made good cars for street or competition.

The last of the classics were '49 and '50 Ford coupes and sedans. These were the cars that were instrumental in starting the tremendous move to engine swapping. Later model Fords and other makes of cars were used for countless engine swaps after 1950 but there's something lacking about these later models that keeps them out of the classic category.

All the classics mentioned have been used in various forms for competition of all types. Model A and '32 roadsters were used when hot rod track racing was first started but it wasn't long before they were replaced by cars that had Model T roadster bodies and special frames. And later builders of the faster cars gradually changed from stock bodies to special bodies they made themselves. The first of these special bodies were narrowed stock bodies. A slice was taken lengthwise out of a roadster body and then the two sides were welded together, leaving just enough room for the driver. Next were the airplane belly tanks. Special frames were made for the tanks, which were in halves, and one half was used for the bottom of the body and the other half was used for the top. Holes were cut in the tank for the axles, exhaust pipes, the driver's head, and anything else that wouldn't fit within its confines. These were the early "streamliners."

The last and most professional appearing of the special bodies are the enclosed wheel streamliners built for Bonneville. These streamliners consistently run over 200 miles per hour and the fastest one to date has turned 272 mph. Some of them have aluminum body panels and others are constructed of fiberglass.

Many hot rods for competition purposes are built from the ground up. All of them use standard passenger car running-gear components but the components may be extensively modified to conform to the car's specifications. Frames for cars of this type are often from '32 or Model A Fords, narrowed, shortened, and otherwise modified. Frames built after '32 consist of members that are too heavy for competition hot rod use. A shortage of early frames and a desire for something better has led many fellows to build frames from lengths of steel tubing. Members for frames of this type are cut from the steel tubing and welded together to form a unit of adequate strength and stiffness for the application.

Most competition hot rods have roadster or coupe bodies, in standard or modified form, with special noses and hoods to give them some degree of streamlining. Many of them are fitted with full belly pans. Others have special bodies ranging from a cockpit between or even behind the rear wheels, as is customary in modern dragster design, to covered wheel streamliner bodies.

Suspension can consist of leaf, torsion bar, or coil springs, but torsion bar and coil springs are definitely in the minority. The front spring is usually some model of Ford transverse, or "cross" spring, or a special spring of similar design. The number of leaves in the spring vary according to the weight of the car and the stiffness desired and the spring is mounted either ahead of, above, or behind the front axle. On track cars the shackle at the left end of the spring is anchored so it can't move to prevent the frame from moving sideways in relation to the axle when the cars are in turns. The mount on the frame for the spring is usually of the "suicide" type that consists of a bracket welded to the forward side of the frame's front crossmember. Some of these brackets, especially on track cars, are adjustable so the frame can be raised or lowered in relation to the spring and axle. This is done to enable the car's handling characteristics to be changed.

Dragsters usually don't have any rear suspension. The frame is bolted tight to brackets welded to the rear axle housings. This same construction is also used for some straightaway cars and streamliners. Drag and straightaway cars that have rear springs usually have a spring of the cross type similar to the one on the front. Rear cross springs are longer and stiffer than those used on the front of the car and they can be mounted ahead of, above, or behind the axle assembly. Rear spring brackets on the frames of track and some straightaway and drag cars are adjustable to permit the frame to be raised or lowered in relation to the axle so the car will handle better for track racing and so the rear tires can get the best possible bite for drag racing and straightaway running.

A Bad Day
at Black Rock

By Brian Brennan

※

Street Rodder, March 2001

All of us grow up knowing there are some rules that we had best adhere to. For instance, never drive cross-country without first giving your street rod a once-over in the maintenance department. Never leave home without your driver's license, insurance card, and a backup plan should something go astray. And of course, always, always insure your car.

I have always been a believer in lots of insurance for my cars, street rods or otherwise. And, guess what, on more than one occasion I have had to use it. The first time occurred back in 1969 when my very cool looking and hard chargin' dunebuggy was stolen. After some debate with the insurance company, I finally got my money and off I went.

The second time occurred in 1980 when a woman ran a stoplight (while munching on a hamburger) and broadsided my '29 on Deuce rails. The ol' Magoo-built highboy took quite a beating, to the tune of $10,000-plus in 1980 dollars! Oh yes, she was insured and that worked out well, but not until a great deal of gnashing of teeth on my behalf.

You know, it isn't the collecting of the money, the paperwork, or the hoops the insurance company makes you jump through that's the terrible part. It's dealing with the clean-up and the energy it takes to start anew that makes for a tuff time. Oh, well, onto the present.

One of our sister publications is *Classic Trucks* magazine. Former *Street Rodder* staffer Jim Rizzo heads it up. Riz has been having so much fun at *Classic Trucks* that he made me envious. So, I talked Jim into letting me put together a '67–72 Chevy pickup. Well, that turned into a '72 Suburban that was spending its life as a surf wagon near my home in SoCal. The intent was to rebuild the truck and turn it into a staff wagon to tow magazine projects as well as drive to a number of events. Sounded good. It was working oh so well until one Saturday morning.

Did you know that while traveling 70 miles per hour on a freeway you can catch on fire? You can, and I can prove it. Turns out the timing chain gave up the ghost and the resulting backfire through the carburetor started the fire of fires. Until that Saturday morning I hadn't actually experienced first-hand the incredibly helpless feeling that accompanies such a mishap. I know what it's like to have a car stolen, or have a car demolished, but never a fire. Unless you walk around with a fire extinguisher or pull over (while on fire) next to a fire station, all you can do is stand there, make sure you get everything out of the truck, and pray no one is injured.

You can call 911 and have the fire department come but inevitably they get there in time to wet down a black and burnt framework that was once a pretty neat classic truck. It's a bummer. Well, I knew my co-workers and peer group at the magazine would take both pity and sympathy on me and shower me with emotionally charged outpourings intended to make me feel better. I thought you might like to read some of them. What I received back was swift, but not exactly what I had envisioned:

The Top 10 Reasons Why Brennan Burned His Suburban to the Ground

Freelancer supreme Ron Ceridono was quick to keystroke a few bits of e-mail wisdom:

"Couldn't afford a real Manuel Reyes flame job."

"Was following the smoke in hopes a free barbecue was nearby."

"Was hoping to get his photo in *Rod & Custom*'s Roddin' at Random." (That's downright cruel.)

"Silly attempt to ride in fire truck and run the siren."

"No one would give him a free Halon system."

But alas, I knew fellow Editorial Director Randy Fish would be somewhat more sympathetic. Well, what do you think?

"Brennan was ashamed of the 'Cruizin' fender emblem and didn't have access to the cage nuts that held them on; hence, he tried to melt them off. (That's cold!)

Then my good buddy, Scott Parkhurst, from the *Popular Hot Rodding* staff, chimed in with "PPG's new 'Cajun Blackened Beige' finish is sure to be a hit." (And I thought he was my friend!)

Surely, Damon Lee, fellow staffer on *Classic Trucks*, would provide some solace.

"I always liked the nickname 'Sparky.'"

"We told Brennan that he couldn't re-heat Krispy Kremes with a cigarette lighter, but he wouldn't listen!" (That's brutal.)

"And they said he wouldn't be able to get the heater working."

"Let's see, 'righty tighty, lefty loosey.' Man, replacing fuel lines is hard!"

"See, I told you that rewiring this thing would be a piece of cake."

"Maybe now they'll let me on the staff of *Hot Rod*." (That one is particularly spiteful.)

Even *SRM*'s very own editorial assistant Corinne Hamilton, who heretofore was a very sweet and harmless individual, chimed in with her two cents' worth.

"Rather than cancel his corporate AmEx, he figured it'd be easier to melt it down."

But the most painful swift blow of the mighty pen came from my one and only neighborhood friends, Paul and Joyce Cain. (Actually, they're a new couple to the neighborhood and had the misfortune to be cornered by my husband as he proceeded to tell them how great he is because he can work on his own cars. Guess he won't be having that conversation any time soon. —*Fireball Brennan's wife, Kim Brennan.*)

The two of them sent a condolence card that I thought smacked with a bit of sarcasm. Actually, I was impressed with just how much effort he put into the custom-made car. I wonder if his boss knows how much time he spent on it.

Well, you get the drift. Insure your street rod and everything else you have, 'cause you never know.

No Miracles!

By Barney Navarro

❦

Hop Up, February 1952

There is no easy path to high horsepower. No gadget or item of speed equipment will convert your sluggish family bus into a "supersonic rocket." If such things did exist, Detroit would use them and save millions of dollars. The power output of an engine is governed by sound engineering principles dependent on physics and chemistry, not witchcraft.

The hopping up of an engine consists of improving the two basic factors which govern the horsepower rating, namely, torque (twisting ability) and RPM (revolutions per minute, engine speed). Any change that improves one or both of these factors, without sacrificing too much of the other, will raise the horsepower rating of an engine. If torque is doubled and RPM remains constant, horsepower will be doubled. The same holds true for RPM. If it doubled with the same amount of torque, horsepower is again doubled. Such conditions rarely if ever exist in actual practice but are only used as an illustration. Actually, torque drops off considerably at the point where maximum horsepower is developed but the percentage of drop is less than the percentage of RPM increase.

In the majority of cases, when the hop up treatment is applied to the family bus, torque increases are desired. Such increases aid acceleration and hill climbing ability in top gear. On the other hand, the performance of the family car will meet with great disfavor if the hopping up process leaves it with less hill climbing ability and acceleration in top gear. This condition can be, and is quite often, brought about by making changes that increase RPM but reduce torque. Why, you may ask, do we lay so much stress on torque? Simply this, horsepower is totally dependent on two factors, torque and RPM. The only way that horsepower can be developed thru an RPM increase without a torque increase, is by changing to a lower rear end gear ratio. Of course, the majority of enthusiasts will object to this type of change because they like to limit their alterations to the engine only.

If you wish to add a single item of speed equipment to help you pull a trailer coach, don't choose a race-grind camshaft as that item. This may sound silly but it is being done occasionally. There is no race cam grind on the market that can improve the pulling ability of a stock engine. Some modified cams do less to destroy the original pulling ability . . . but none of them improve it (stock passenger car camshafts are designed to produce maximum torque without too great a maximum HP sacrifice). Of course, if you wish to change your rear end gear ratio from 4 to 1 to 5 to 1 in order to take advantage of the higher peak RPM, this will help you pull the house trailer, by developing more horsepower at the same road speed.

Race-type cams are equipped with valve timing that enables an engine to get a heavier charge of fuel at high RPM. This is accomplished by holding the valves open longer. The intake stroke of an engine has a duration of 180° when considering the piston travel only, but the intake valves are kept open much longer. There are many reasons for this longer duration, but one of the main ones is due to the fact that the fuel mixture has inertia. In other words, it is difficult to get the flow started into the cylinder as the piston starts down on the induction stroke and, at the other end of the stroke, the fuel has enough momentum at high speed to continue flowing even after the piston starts traveling upwards. This momentum increases with RPM so the intake valve can be left open longer with a high RPM engine. Of course, the long valve duration will cause some of the fuel to be pumped back into the induction system at low engine speed. This will cause the engine to develop less horsepower at low speed with race timing than stock timing. Everyone wants a cam that will produce maximum acceleration and maximum horsepower but you can't "have your cake and eat it too."

The simplest change causing the most effective torque improvement can be attained by installing high compression heads. This makes a very noticeable improvement because pulling ability is increased the most in the driving range between 30 and 50 mph. But again we cannot accomplish miracles by this change alone. Many fantastic claims have been made for compression increases but the small increase in ratio that is possible with a passenger car will rarely, if ever, raise the horsepower more than 10%. The low octane rating of pump gas limits the compression ratio of L-head (side-valve) passenger car engines to 8 or 8 1/2 to 1. These ratios are only made possible by the use of aluminum alloys in the manufacture of high compression heads. Aluminum has a faster rate of heat conductivity, consequently, the surface of the combustion chamber is kept cooler during the early part of the combustion cycle, the period where detonation takes place. By keeping the chamber cooler, the tendency toward detonation and pre-ignition is reduced. Even with the use of aluminum, higher ratios than those outlined above will cause detonation and pre-ignition.

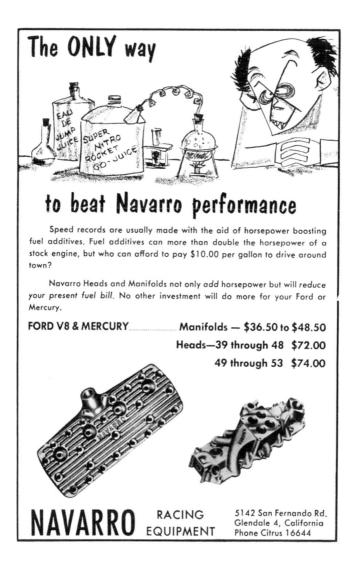
Another item of speed equipment about which many misconceptions center, is the dual intake manifold. The misinformation surrounding this item is almost as bad as the impossible expectations of a cam. "Doesn't a dual manifold use more gas," most people will ask? This question cannot be answered with a simple yes or no but the answer is nevertheless a simple one. An engine requires just so much fuel to deliver a given amount of horsepower, so the addition of another carburetor won't make

it consume more unless you place a greater power demand on the engine. Under increased power you will use more fuel because, after all, you are not going to get something for nothing. The basic reasons for installing a dual manifold are to get a more even fuel distribution and to improve the breathing ability of an engine . . . the latter being the principal reason. Unlike the high compression head, a dual manifold does not improve the torque or horsepower output of the average engine unless it is turning more than 2000 RPM . . . converted to miles per hour, this would be between 40 and 45 in top gear. The useful speed of the manifold is, of course, much lower in 1st and 2nd gear, which is self evident when accelerating thru the gears. At speeds over 15 mph in first gear the average Ford will have its acceleration improved by a dual manifold. However, maximum advantage is not derived from this unit until the engine is close to the RPM where maximum horsepower is developed. This horsepower increase will range between 7 and 8% with a Ford V-8 engine.

Big men are more powerful than little men, and it is the same with engines. A large engine has a better chance of producing high torque than a small one. Being that torque is still the factor in which we are most interested, increasing the size of an engine is the best way to effect an improvement. There is no single item of speed equipment that will make as much difference in torque as is gained by boring a Ford V-8 to 3 3/8 inches and stroking it 3/8 of an inch. This procedure will add 57 cubic inches to the displacement of the engine and will allow your car to climb hills in high gear that it used to struggle on in second. Now that the ideal has been illustrated, you are probably wondering about the disadvantages. As is always the case when you reach for the best, cost rears its ugly head. Fifty-seven cubic inches will cost you $234.00 for parts and services even if you do all of the work of disassembling and assembling.

Magicians may pull rabbits out of hats, but horses are a much bigger problem.

3

History of the
Hop-Up Movement

The Golden Age of Customs

By John DeWitt

✠

Cool Cars, High Art:
The Rise of Kustom Kulture, 2001

At the end of 1953, the year the Hirohata Merc caused such a sensation in the car world, the list of the top-ten best-selling records for the year contained not a single song that can be easily connected to any emerging youth culture. The number-one song, the theme from the Hollywood costume drama based on the life of Toulouse-Lautrec, was "Song from *Moulin Rouge*" by Percy Faith and his orchestra. A catchy pop instrumental, "April in Portugal" by Lee Baxter, was number three. The only singing group, hardly doo-wop, who made it to the list was the Ames Brothers with "You, You, You." . . .

By the end of the decade a revolution had taken place. Every single one of the top hits of 1959 was either a genuine rock 'n' roll song or performed by a newly created teen idol. . . . What is significant about [this is] the almost total dominance of the music market by teens. By 1959 teenagers no longer existed on the fringes of the culture, forming what today is called a niche market. By 1959 teens were the market. . . . By the end of the decade, teens had developed a full-blown culture. They looked different, they talked different, and they acted different from even what today are called "twenty-somethings." . . . No longer proto-adults or innocent youth, they created a unique position for themselves in opposition to both the values of maturity and the limitations of childhood. The generation that created this culture would come to influence not only the record charts but every aspect of American life for the rest of the century as well. Their experience was rapidly becoming the American experience.

Rodding and customizing, an important part of this emerging culture, also moved from the fringe to a place a little closer to center stage. Rods were no longer shown in just teen exploitation films, they had become domesticated, a part of the American television family. In an attempt to lure teen viewers to the *Life of Riley*, Chester Riley's son Junior was given a neat chopped and channeled Barris-built '34 Ford coupe to exasperate his father with. Bud Anderson did a little rodding in his driveway on *Father Knows Best*. Not only did Rick Nelson sing rock 'n' roll at the end of episodes of *Ozzie and Harriet*, but he had a beautiful green Deuce roadster for at least one episode. In 1958 television even had a hot rod star; Norm Grabowski's beautiful T-Bucket was driven by Ed "Kookie" Burns on *77 Sunset Strip*. The car drew as many young viewers as the plots. As a result of the exposure, it became the most famous rod in the country, inspiring dozens of imitators while creating a whole new class of rod.

In the real world, drag racing was well on its way to becoming a major professional sport and not just the pursuit of devoted amateurs although the strip was still a place where almost anyone could drive up to see what his car could do in a quarter mile. Strips had been opening throughout the decade from Maine to California. In 1957 *Life* magazine reported that there were 130 strips in operation in forty states. *Life* estimated that they drew more than two and a half million spectators and over 100,000 racers. The article counted 15,000 car clubs which were adding about 1,500 new members a month. Some of the more famous drivers traveled as many as 60,000 miles a year getting to races. Strip owners had begun paying appearance money in order to ensure that the best drivers and the fastest cars would race at their strip. Prize money became more than a token amount to accompany a trophy. Even a top prize of one thousand dollars for winning top eliminator was a significant amount of money in 1959 that allowed builders to continue to improve their cars and their elapsed times.

The rapidly growing auto parts industry began to see advantages in backing the most successful drag racers. In exchange for token amounts of money by today's standards, decals from cam makers, tire manufacturers and oil companies began to appear on dragsters.

Drivers were becoming stars. And California no longer had a monopoly on cars or drivers. Don Garlits and his series of "Swamp Rat" dragsters from Florida successfully challenged west coast cars. His speed of 183.66 mph at the end of the quarter mile in 1959 was the fastest ever run to that point. Nicknamed "Big Daddy" in the early sixties, he would soon become the most famous and successful of all drag racers, the Babe Ruth of drag racing, who introduced many innovations to the sport. The Ohioan Arfons brothers and their wild airplane-engine–powered dragsters also drew a lot of attention. Other important drivers arrived on the scene from Michigan, North Carolina, and Texas.

The National Hot Rod Association no longer completely dominated the sport. NASCAR briefly flirted with drags. In 1956 the American

Hot Rod Association (AHRA) was formed to compete with the NHRA as a sanctioning body. The AHRA, in contrast to the NHRA, allowed the use of the more powerful, and more dangerous, nitromethane fuel which allowed the AHRA to leap ahead of the older body in top-end speeds and elapsed times. *Hot Rod*, closely tied to the NHRA and its emphasis on safety and regulation, largely ignored AHRA events, and the competition became intense and bitter. Because of the excitement created in AHRA events with runs approaching two hundred miles an hour in the quarter mile, the NHRA retreated and approved fuel cars in the early sixties.

Drag racing nevertheless still had difficulties with its image. Even as late as 1957 there was significant opposition to the very idea of drag racing even away from the streets as a sport on sanctioned strips. Despite the fact that organized drag racing is a relatively safe form of auto racing, the National Safety Council (NSC) issued a bizarre recommendation aimed specifically at drag racing—stock cars, sports cars, and Indy racing, all with many more fatalities than drag racing, were not included: "The National Safety Council opposes speed contests. Since speed violations are so often involved in traffic accidents, the National Safety Council cannot condone speeding even in the name of competition" (Maremont 1957, 15). The Council urged rodders to pursue economy runs and offer driver clinics instead of drag racing. Needless to say, the NSC didn't win many hearts or minds among hot rodders.

The overall growth of the economy at the end of the decade played a crucial role in the development of a car-based youth culture. In 1957 *U.S. News & World Report* surveyed the economic accomplishments of the preceding ten years. The results inspired the editors to trumpet "10 Amazing Years":

> The last year of an amazing decade is about to end. . . .
>
> In one brief 10-year period, America's face was remade. Vast suburban areas sprang up to receive millions of Americans pressing out from cities. Ribbons of superhighways were laid across the country. A huge expansion of air facilities tie the nation into a compact unity.

Whole regions changed their complexion. Deserts were turned into boom areas. Power was harnessed on a stupendous scale to ease the burden of work.

Nearly 30 million added people were provided for, and on a steadily rising standard of living. A car was put in every garage, two in many. TV sets came into almost every home. There was a chicken, packaged and frozen, for every pot, with more to spare. Never had so many people, anywhere, been so well off. (in Satin 1960, 16)

Fueled by the growth of an economy that put more money in their hands (about $10 billion in 1959), teens were able to spend more time and more money with other teens and create their own culture as an alternative to one based on safety and security. As a result teen life became more and more separate from the adult world. There were movies aimed at them, as well as magazines, books, drive-in restaurants, clothing stores, and radio stations that catered almost exclusively to teen taste.

One of the most visible signs of teen opposition to the dominant values of success and security was found in the cars they chose to drive. More and more they were choosing rods and customs. By the end of the decade driving a car was a necessity if a teenager was going to have a social life. And teens were no longer limited to buying old jalopies: "It is taken for granted that every teen-ager will learn to drive and that, if he does not have a car of his own, individually or as a member of a group, he will certainly have access to one" (Bernard 1961, 2–5).

During the second half of the fifties interest in customizing grew at an explosive rate. Significant new cars were being built all across the country by new builders who ranged from driveway customizers to the emergence of a new group of creative professional designer/builders. Northern California builders like Joe Bailon, Joe Wilhelm, and Gene Winfield began to compete with George Barris for the title of "King of Kustoms." Among the twenty-eight candidates for "Custom of the Year" in 1958, *Motor Life* selected four Bailon and four Winfield customs and six by Barris. Painters like Von Dutch, Dean Jeffries, and Larry Watson fundamentally changed customizing by making paint treatments equal in importance to bodywork in reworking stock designs. These builders and painters defined the Golden Age of Customs—with each producing a number of distinctive masterpieces.

Although customizing was spreading quickly across the country, California remained its artistic center. It is interesting to note that of the twenty-eight candidates for *Motor Life*'s 1958 award only five were not California cars. But there was a growing number of builders outside of California who were not slavish imitators of the California style. The Alexander brothers in Detroit and Darryl Starbird in Kansas began to build cars of national significance. Bill Cushenberry left Kansas in 1958 where he had been building customs and dragsters to open a shop in Monterey where he soon became the preeminent builder in central California. Bodymen Bill Hines and "Korky" Korkes and painter/photographer Andy Southard all built interesting cars before they found the lure of Kustom Kulture irresistible and headed west.

In addition to major shows like the Oakland Roadster Show on the West Coast, there were now major shows in Hartford and Detroit, as well as in Nebraska and Kansas where new cars could inspire backyard builders. By 1959 there were more than ten magazines devoted in whole or part to customizing. . . .

The impact of Detroit's exploitation of the Kustom Kulture also helped shaped the growth of customizing. By the mid-fifties Detroit had become more attuned to the growing market for flashier and higher-performance cars, influenced, at least in part, by customizers. The year 1955 marked the first appearance of what would become the consummate fifties cars: much chrome, wild colors, gigantic proportions and, of course, the fin. The 1958 Lincoln Continental Mark III was 229 inches long (more than 19 feet!). True fins, not the little bumps on the backs of early fifties Caddys, dominated Detroit automotive styling and seemed to grow every year. By 1957 almost every manufacturer had a model with some sort of fin. Every configuration was employed. There were vertical, horizontal, angled, and bigger fins. And chrome was everywhere—side trim multiplied, hood ornaments became engorged, and taillights were encrusted with the silver metal.

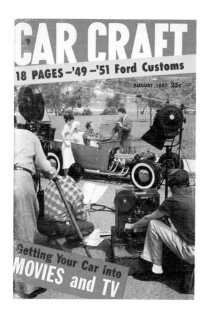

The year 1955 also marked the appearance of Chevy's first V-8 after decades of offering the same basic six. Soon there were a number of performance packages available direct from the factory which offered combinations of hot rod favorites—fuel injection or multiple carburetors, dual exhausts, and stiffer suspension. In 1957 you could buy a 283ci Chevy that produced 283 horsepower—matching the hot rodder's old ideal of one horsepower per cubic inch. Plymouth offered its Fury in 1956 with a 240 horsepower "Hy-Fire" V-8 as a special hardtop model with gold trim. Chrysler began offering its high performance 300 series in 1955 with a 300 horse Hemi engine. Although the luxury 300 series was not directly aimed at a hot rod audience, Chrysler's Hemi engines would soon become the standard engine in top dragsters. In 1955 the Corvette, introduced in late 1953, also finally got a V-8 and the first Ford Thunderbird appeared, giving Americans an option of two Detroit two-seaters.

It was not technical innovation, however, but styling that dominated Detroit's productions in the fifties. Although there is disagreement over this point (Ganahl 2000, 68), many ideas from Kustom Kulture, whether through direct influence or coincidence, were incorporated into the new models: both two- and four-door hardtops with rakish roof lines became a standard body style for all makers; the '55 Chevy came with hooded headlights; and scoops, mostly nonfunctional, were added to hoods, roof lines, and side panels of a number of models. Grille shells began to be integrated with the bumpers on a number of models; the exhaust of the '55 T-Bird exited through ports above the bumper like many customs; dual headlights, first used on the "Wild Kat" pickup by Barris in 1956, became commonplace on production cars by 1958. Dealers offered continental kits as an option. The traditional Detroit range of colors—black, white, red, beige, blue, and green—was enlivened with a whole range of new tints that evoked warmer climates like southern California: pinks, aquas, and salmons, often applied in two tones with the chrome strips used as color dividers the way Barris had done on the Hirohata Merc. Hudson and Packard even tried three tones in an ill-fated move to stay ahead of the competition. At the end of the decade metallic paints were widely available.

Changes in styles accelerated. Model changes had been occurring in three- or four-year cycles, the '49 to '51 Ford and the '49 to '52 Chevy, for example, where one body style received minor trim changes for each new model year until a major change. By the mid-1950s Detroit offered major, sometimes radical, changes from year to year. The '55 to '56 Chevys were fairly close in style, the '57 was a fairly big departure, the '58 constituted another major new direction. There was almost nothing the '59 Chevy had in common with the '58.

Despite the stylistic innovation on Detroit's latest creations, customizers were not deterred from their desire to modify stock models. They still found lots to do. As far as they were concerned Detroit still hadn't gotten it right. Detroit lacked restraint with chrome. There was still much too much trim and too many ornaments that often obscured lines on the new models. And they didn't sit right. Cars always needed lowering. The stock paint in stock colors just didn't measure up to custom colors and didn't even come close to the new paint treatments like paneling and scallops.

With a greater sense of daring customizers turned their attention to a wider variety of vehicles. The line between hot rods and customs became blurred. Barris customized a Model A pickup truck, "Ala Kart," with a completely customized front end including quad headlights which won the "America's Most Beautiful Roadster Award" in both 1958 and 1959, and he created a custom front end on "The Emperor," a Deuce roadster that won the award in 1960. A little later Bud Pearce built a pickup custom/rod, with an upholstered top and unusual Jaguar engine, out of a 1930 Ford.

Early fat-fendered Fords also received the full custom treatment. Bill Cushenberry's "Matador," a 1940 Ford coupe, is a particularly fine example. Its body was totally reworked: chopped two inches, sectioned four and a half inches, with deep sculpted fender insets and hand-formed front grille.

Contemporary pickup trucks, largely ignored by early customizers, became more and more popular as candidates for the full customizing treatment. Barris's "Kopper Kart," a 1956 Chevy with a radically reworked body, had matching front and rear grilles that were both copper plated. . . .

With the increased number of models and trim levels provided by Detroit, customizers were blessed with an abundance of parts to use on the older models they still favored: the '49 to '51 Mercs, '49 to '52 Chevys, and Shoebox '49 to '51 Fords. Packard Clipper taillights, Plymouth grilles, and Pontiac side trim, as well as a host of other parts, could be used to give a new look to older cars. . . .

No longer did the customizer have to rely primarily on collaging existing parts or cutting away from the stock body as the means of transforming a stock car. A new aesthetic, a kind of expressionism, began to emerge which left no part of the car as it was and which allowed much more freedom to the customizer to create his own fantasy of a particular car. These new directions were closer to the art of true sculpture than assemblage. By the end of the decade many customizers moved away from using stock cars as the starting point and began creating one-of-a-kind cars from scratch.

Ardun White Paper Part I

Tracing the Development and Manufacture of the Ardun Engine Kits

By Tom Senter

Rod & Custom, May 1971

Beginning a three part series on the overhead conversion which ultimately revolutionized modern internal combustion engines and more importantly, transformed Ford's lowly flathead (valve in block) into one of hot rodding's greatest record go-getters. Ardun! Its history, tragic in some respects—colorful always, is perhaps the thing which attracts its following. There are, perhaps yourself included, those who ignoring opinion, love and advocate the underdog. Powerplant underdogs . . . there have been many. Obsolescence their only real fault, the warmed over vintage mill brings to its builder both heartbreak and ecstasy. This, without question, is the Ardun. R&C is proud to bring you author Senter's "Ardun White Paper"; the most comprehensive work on the subject ever compiled. From start to finish, development, history, finally, assembling the beast, you won't be able to put the next three issues down. —Ed.

I would like to acknowledge the following for their valuable assistance in preparing this document: Clem Tebow, Jerry Darien, Cotton Werksman, Chuck James, Tom Ruddy, Roy Richter, Bob Estes, Ray Brock, Hot Rod Magazine, Racing Cars *by Richard Hough, Iskendarian Cams, and Bud Bryan.*

My thriving curiosity for mechanical things and my love of tradition, memorabilia, and historical documentation kindled a long smoldering desire to learn the story behind the famous Ardun. I first discovered there was such a thing seventeen years ago through the pages of *Hot Rod* magazine. To me, *Hot Rod* was a looking glass, through which at age eleven, I could fly down the salt at incredible speeds or dazzle my pre-teen associates with a cut down Ford Roadster, a robust flathead engine arrogantly daring the competition to accept the challenge.

The fellows on my block—the big kids—had neat cars. One was a '50 Ford Coupe with a brand new Olds in it. I slapped out fires on the staggered-four with a rag while he tried to get the angry thing to light. One guy had a beautiful lavender and white Caddy powered ski boat AND a dragster. He used to make furious passes down our street in the digger while we blocked traffic at the cross street. The '49–'50 Olds craze was on and I made a couple of bucks pinstriping dashboards. The die was cast: I was a car nut. It was to be a few years before I got my first one (a decrepit '34 Buick Coupe) and in the interim, I substituted car magazines for school books. My grades suffered, my parents never accepted the idea, but I memorized many of those articles . . . and Ardun was King.

Dave Marquez' Deuce B/Hot Roadster was really the first Ardun powered car to grace a *Hot Rod* cover, even though by that time (July '56) it was pretty clear that the small block Chevy would fall heir to the throne occupied by the flathead for twenty years.

In that same issue, Ray Brock (now a Petersen VP) authored what proved to be the first and last comprehensive article written on the Ardun overhead conversion kits.

Through the years, Ardun powered cars set records in hundreds of classes. The engine became a legend in its own, time. Ardun builders were different, innovative, individuals, usually bucking the odds against stronger, modem OHV motors. I vowed someday to build an Ardun powered Roadster.

Time passed, I built Chevies instead, and went to the drags. I was thrilled by flag-started contests between Garlits and Karamesines at Riverside, Mooneyham and Reath at Bakersfield, and Stone-Woods and Cook and Mazmanian at the Beach. Chuck James' Safeway Sandblasting '40 Willys was the only Ardun still running at the drags of any notoriety, and this awesome Coupe proved to many a C/Gas Supercharged competitor that the King still lived . . . the beat went on.

Through the years, I had been a devoted fan of the wonderful heads, but never an owner. Then in 1966 I found a set. A mechanic, who had accepted a pair of the heads and a few pieces as partial payment of a customer's bill a few years back, agreed to let me pull the dusty stuff off his top shelves if I would get it out of there. He didn't have to ask twice. I didn't even have anything to put it in except a tired '57 Chevy. But when I got the glorious equipment home and cleaned it up, I realized that it was the inspiration for my Roadster.

I hunted down fellows who might have precious parts or some first hand information, and I learned that one reason why more builders don't become involved in projects like this is the difficulty and frustration of trying to breathe life into an era which is past. But more important, I also discovered that there are many enthusiasts who love the old Ardun engines, especially those that ran them during the fifties. Many racers, who built dozens of different engines, fondly recall the Ardun as their favorite, relating the place, day, and hour when they broke such and such a record using the hemi heads. Considering the small number of sets produced, the list is long and formidable. But to really tell the story of the mighty Ardun, I should start at the beginning.

Throughout the twenties and thirties, Chevy fours and sixes, Ford Ts and As logged thousands of raucous competition miles, performing like champions for battalions of builders and racers. They were fitted with every conceivable modification. Beautiful accessory heads dressed the two hundred inchers: Riley, Rajo, Fronty (designed by the Chevrolet Brothers), Hal, Cragar (originally called the Miller-Schofield, designed by Miller), Cook, Super Winfield . . . from high compression flatty to exotic twin cam overhead conversions. They ran at Indy, the boards and dirt tracks, and later, the drags and Sepulveda Boulevard.

But the Ford Motor Company was busy after the Great Crash, and in 1932, Henry Ford lifted the wraps off the infamous flathead V8. Intended as the means for capturing the sales lead away from Chevy, the engine delivered cheap, rugged power in a package that was easy to maintain, and '34 and again in '38, the flathead, with ridiculously low cost and high torque for its day, proved itself at intersections all through the States those post depression years, by leaving the most expensive Buicks, Auburns, and Packards in a cloud of dust. John Dillinger was so pleased with the performance of his '35 while eluding the police, that he wrote Henry Ford a letter, thanking him!

As the war approached, the scrappy V8s locked horns with the durable fours, and became the new champions in the race for speed and power. The redoubtable A-bone was displaced as throneholder, just as the flathead itself would be twenty years later. Designers and engineers—trained and backyard—experimented, modified, and tweaked: 180 degree cranks, pointy cams, more carbs . . . try it, see if it works; swap the intake and exhaust ports. The ideas were endless; the engine produced nearly triple its rated horsepower.

Overhead valves were not a new idea. Some of the more expensive American designs featured them. Even the Chevy Brothers tried the idea on a V8 in 1917. European designs were considerably more sophisticated than our own. The 1914 Mercedes 4 1/2 litre Gran Prix machine used single overhead camshafts and four valves per cylinder; the '23 model sported 7 litres (420 inches), and was supercharged. Indeed, the French 3 litre Peugeot, built in 1913, used the first TWIN overhead cams, and won the Indianapolis race of 1913. The Peugeot was thrashed to victory by Jules Goux, reportedly assisted by no less than four bottles of the finest French Champagne, consumed in long pulls during tire changes. In fact the Peugeot twin cams were the inspiration for the fabulous Miller engines, which metamorphosed through the years to become the incredible Offie.

No, the flathead, with its siamesed center exhaust ports running through the bowels of the block, cooking the coolant was about as trick as an anvil. But the lower end, by the standards of the day, was pretty good. The crank was counter-weighted and pressurized. The trio of mains were stout enough for much heavier loads than experienced in stock form. For many hot rodders, the magnetic attraction, the love affair with the cast iron thing, began because it was there. They were available by the hundreds, and they were cheap. It could have had seven cylinders and NO camshaft; they'd have figured out a way to make it wail.

When the Japanese launched their attack on the Pearl, builders laid down their tools and trundled off to foreign soil. Some took advantage of the opportunity to study what was developing on the other side of the automotive globe. Perhaps some studied European head designs and had time to think about them. Others have been involved in engine design in the aircraft industry. Whatever, a number of advanced rocker arm overhead valve designs materialized in the years following the war. Their application: the flat-head Ford V8. Detroit had not yet made the breakthrough . . . the incentive was there.

A number of talented designers tooled up their favorite ideas for helping the 24 studder to breathe. Lee Chapel's cast iron Tornado heads were a record breaking success, pushing his C/Streamliner 224 MPH at Bonneville in 1952. Then Rudy Moller and Kenny Adams built a pair for

One conversion kit was destined for tremendous racing success and lasting popularity, unmatched by anything produced in the Golden Years after the war: the famous Ardun.

C and T Automotive that rocked the racing world by smashing the International Class C Streamliner record in 1952, a record held by Germany's Auto Union since 1939. Riley built a few sets for V8s. Stephens and Alexander tried new designs. Art Cummings and Joe Davies each cast sets bearing their names. Most of the efforts were individual, with only a few sets of any one design ever produced. Occasionally, a head or two, and a few rockers, maybe with valve covers, will turn up at a swap meet, years having passed since the assembly ran. Most of these side-show freaks representing someone's still-born Indy effort, or prowess with a lathe and patterns, remain conversation pieces, gathering dust on shelves and work benches.

Except one. One conversion kit was destined for tremendous racing success and lasting popularity, unmatched by anything produced in the Golden Years after the war: the famous Ardun. The reason for their longevity, aside from notorious performance increases, is that they were manufactured in some numbers. Spare parts were available, and as a matter of fact, parts were made for thousands of kits. The actual number of heads cast is nearer 200. Searching out the history of the Ardun brings some interesting facts to light.

Zora Arkus-Duntov is the father of the high performance Corvette, and the whole super-car phenomenon. He joined the engineering staff of General Motors in 1955 and changed the original six cylinder, powerglide, plastic runabout to the most versatile and ferocious Grand Touring car made in the United States. Few Chevrolet engine builders are unfamiliar with the legendary Duntov camshaft, which for $27.95 over the parts counter, would outperform nearly any other camshaft for the small-block Chevy.

But fewer still modern day enthusiasts realize that Mr. Duntov made a very significant contribution to the racing world (without being fully aware of it at the time), nearly three decades ago. Born in Belgium sixty years ago, and raised in Russia as a boy, he developed his superior mechanical skills in the highly advanced engineering schools of Germany. A handsome leading man type, speaking with a thick accent, he suggested to his brother Yura, that they venture to America and establish an engineering research and development company.

His precise and logical mind and terrific capacity for problem solving, and Yura's business and administrative skills, quickly established the Duntov Brothers in New York as a formidable enterprise. Their first endeavor of note was a development as an outside contractor for the Ford Motor Company. Large trucks had developed the unpleasant habit of consuming engines, due to excessive overloading and heat, and a sorrowful lack of torque for these loads. The 24 stud flathead (the same used in passenger cars), devoured rods and pistons and persisted in cracking themselves in the valve seat area, at an expensive rate.

During a stretch with the Talbot Automobile Company, Zora became intimately familiar with the most advanced European valve gear and combustion chamber design. He put his experience to work to design a pair of sophisticated cylinder heads, made of heat treated aluminum, featuring hemispherical combustion chambers, radially inclined overhead valves, and replaceable bronze valve seats and guides. All this in the interest of higher outputs at lower temperatures. Tooling was completed and the Brothers lent their name (**ARkusDUN**tov) to the marvelous hemi head kits, and the Ardun Engine Company was launched.

Early tests revealed that some changes in the water jacketing around the intake valves and the length of the lifter would be necessary, but further research and development was limited. By the time two hundred sets of the heads and parts for a few thousand more had been manufactured,

Ford was installing the larger, more reliable Lincoln V8 engine in the 1949 trucks. The Ardun kits were not practical for passenger cars without extensive modifications to the engine compartment sheet metal (as you might guess if you've ever seen one of these dudes), and for the moment it looked like the Ardun Company might not even recoup pattern and material costs, let alone the research.

But the actual casting of many of the heads and parts had been done across the Atlantic in England (in the interest of lower costs). The enterprise caught the attention of Sidney Allard, a manufacturer of custom built sports/racing cars, equipped, curiously enough, with early Ford running gear and flathead engines. Through negotiation, a project originally destined for yeoman duty in a lowly 3/4 or one ton truck made its way into the racing world through the back door. The Ardun went airport racing in Allard sportscars. But it was no racing engine. In all fairness it wasn't meant to be. The deep shrouding of the spark plugs made battery ignitions impotent. For racing, cartridge plugs and magnetos allowing 45 degrees lead were a must. The simple, single carburetor manifolds, head gasket problems, rocker arm failure, and numerous other maladies occurred precisely at the time one clever and well fixed builder dropped a brand new OHV Kettering Cadillac engine in his Allard and began to run off with the goodies. If you know anything about racing, you are aware of how long it took the crowd to ape the winner. There wasn't time to fiddle around with this fugitive from a garbage truck. "Get me one of those bloomin' Caddies! Anyhow, if God had wanted rocker arms on a flathead he would have put them there." So much for Jolly Old.

But a representative from the Stevens Motor Company of New York had observed the Ardun-Allards in action in England and found himself with a good opportunity to represent the Ardun Engine Company in the U.S. for sales and distribution in the face of the invasion by the Yankee overheads . . . which he did. Stevens Motor Company New York became sole U.S. distributor for the kits, and for all practical purposes, Zora washed his hands of the whole thing.

Sometime in late 1948, two active lakes racers, named Don Clark and Clem Tebow, were operating a small machine shop in a garage in

Hollywood. Both were interested in engine design, especially the hemi-chamber, and were continually trying any new idea, experimenting with fuels and untried concepts. In an automotive trade magazine (like *MOTOR*), Don spotted a cutaway drawing from a brochure of the Ford flathead block fitted with the Ardun kit as it might be used for passenger car or marine application.

Excited, the fellows examined the drawing carefully and concluded that possibly here was the answer to extracting large additional quantities of horsepower from the most popular hot rod engine in the world; at least it was worth investigation. Whether Duntov appreciated the popularity of the flathead as a hot rod engine is uncertain; it didn't make any differ-ence. With the C & T boys on the trail, the Ardun was sure to figure heavily in the racing scene.

In the July 1949 issue of Bob Petersen's spanking new *Hot Rod* magazine, an article titled "Overhead Design" made brief mention (and I mean one small paragraph) of the new Ardun Conversion Kit which had been unveiled the year before.

Bob Garrett, founder of Speed-O-Motive, had four sets shipped to California, from New York. When they arrived, he found himself a little short—the sets sold for $500 per copy complete. As a result, Howard Johanson, of Howard Cams, took a set off his hands; Bob Estes, a Lincoln-Mercury dealer and active racer, bought a set, and Clem and Don ended up with a set.

The C-T boys went to work on the package, which was, of course, an unknown quantity. The SAE paper showed that the Ardun factory had performed brief dyno tests using a 239 CID stock block Ford flathead engine, 7:1 compression, equipped with "water pumps, exhaust mufflers... a standard dual (throat) Ford carburetor . . . but without generator."

Dated February 1947, this test engine netted 175 HP at 5200 RPM, a 75% increase, and 225 ft/lbs of torque at 2500 RPM. The Stevens brochure suggested multiple carburetion manifolds and " . . . pistons for various strokes, bores, and compression ratios, from 8:1 to 14:1 . . . " could be supplied upon request. The above figures were allegedly obtained by bolting the kit to a stock flathead in three hours on a Saturday afternoon, just following the instructions. Insert pushrod B into valve hole B!

However, no one else had been able to get anywhere near those figures. As far as the factory version of the Ardun was concerned, as a racing engine, it made a great boat anchor. But the potential . . .

Don's highboy seemed a likely place to start looking for the right combination. The Deuce had seen more than a few trips to the lakes, and also doubled as a street machine, as many an early lakes runner did. The fellows began working on the great thing, communicating with the Duntov Brothers, Yura answering most of the mail. But for the most part, they were on their own.

After tinkering and modifying of all sorts, Clem and Don married the push rod contraption to the fenderless Roadster to put it to the test. They rolled the black highboy out one morning at the 1950 SCTA meet and ended up with a few wide-eyed believers. As might be expected, a few problems manifested themselves in the valve spring area, and the head seal would require some new ideas, but next year they made the trek to Bonneville. While earning a reputation as the noisiest car on the salt, Don captured the SCTA Class C/Street Roadster record in 1951, with a velocity of 162.162 MPH, a two way average. Scritchfield take note. Thus, Don's Roadster became the first successful Ardun in competition. A dyno test at Wilcap in November 1951 provided the first real successful results of their racing development: 303 HP at 5250 RPM using Champion R2s, a Vertex, A Herbert Roller, and 25%. Fuel was an unknown quantity then. Clem said later: " . . . they told us not to go farther than 25%. Hell, we should have thrown in the can, label and all."

In the meantime, *Hot Rod* magazine, April 1950 ran a small ad in the new parts column: *"The Ardun Overhead Valve V8 engine conversion now being manufactured in England is available for distribution throughout the U.S. by Bell Auto Parts of Bell, California. They have recently received a shipment which is obtainable for V8 and Mercury engines, and have one unit in operation on their pickup truck."*

Wild. An Ardun on their pickup truck. This is the same one that had the Kinmont disc brakes on it. But as a matter of fact, Bell Auto Parts only stocked four sets and never really had much success with sales. Nevertheless, the Ardun was on the map and the race was on. Yet, the engine would continue to remain within the use of a closed circle of enthusiast, a small number of fellows who are always the ones fiddling around with new ideas and different ways of doing things. Also, the heads were expensive (still are), and to many a racer an additional expense of $400 or $500 could not be justified. Many a builder did not have that much in his whole car. Today, while tracking down the facts on the Ardun, one is immediately confronted with the fact that everybody has heard of it, but very few people know anything about it. Even the fellows who actually built and raced them are hard pressed to remember many details. From the rumblings that I pick up lately it is quite possible that the Ardun is about to enjoy a renewed popularity that is more widespread than when the engine was in its heyday.

Next month we'll take a look at some of the most famous Ardun racers and their accomplishments. You might just recall Ruddy and Weinstein's modified low-boy (1955), or Chuck James' Elephant Ardun Safeway Sandblasting C/Supercharged Willys Gasser (1963).

Ardun White Paper
Part II

*True Bolt-on Horsepower . . . the Ardun. Undisputed King of the
Overheads—for a While at Least. Exciting Moments in Hot Rodding Which
Set the Pace for a Glorious Racing History that May Never Be Topped!*

By Tom Senter

※

Rod & Custom, June 1971

Last month we recorded the odyssey of the Ardun Engine from Germany, to New York, to England, back to New York, and finally El Mirage. This month we're going to journey through the pits of the past and have a look at some of the equipment. Ardun powered cars had a habit of setting records and in many cases, pushing the mark out of reach for years. I'll get to one interesting example later.

In the long run, Clem Tebow and Don Clark ended up with more Ardun parts than anyone else; all the parts available in fact. As owners of C and T Automotive, they were two of the most active racers on the West Coast. One of their most notable achievements was in 1952, when they hauled home the International Class C Streamliner record, held by the Nazi Germany effort since 1939, with the Hill-Davis "City of Burbank" beauty. The record breaking motor was a 264 CID Merc with hemi heads patterned after a Rudy Moller, Kenny Adams design. (Clem owned this engine until late last year when he sold it to someone in Texas who faithfully promised him that it was to be put into a street machine. We'll see.) Two 291 CID Arduns sat impatiently in the push truck in case the small motor fell short, but they weren't used. As Clem tells it: "We set the record with the Moller-Adams. We'd have gone faster with the Ardun, but there were no tires in the country that could cope with their speed potential." The C Streamliner project put C and T on the map.

Don and Clem, who had their wrench turning fingers in a whole lot of pies besides running the booming business, learned that Howard Johanson was burning up the sprint car tracks with his Ardun Sprinter cranking out around 270 HP, so they decided to see if the new OHV combination would produce results for them on the dirt. Their 284 CID (3 5/16 x 4 1/8) carbureted Number 22 ran so well that Al Bish the driver won every event that he finished. One day late in 1952, a fellow in Texas called Clem and said: "Hey! Me an' ma daddy would sure like to have one of them Ardun kits." So the fellows sent some heads to Texas and A.J. ran off with everything in sight.

Don Clark ran his Ardun at Bonneville but he also drove the Deuce on the street. One night in the early fifties, Don and Clem motored up Sepulveda to the old Saugus strip for the night drags. These were the days when spectators would line the strip with their cars and turn on the headlights when two cars made a pass. They pulled the mufflers off, and ran 110 MPH on used Indy tires (18 inchers) using high gear only, with 3.52s in the quickie. Don says he boiled the hides right through the eyes. The record at the time was only 116. He liked the hemi Ford well enough to slip a set of the heads under the hood of his '50 Ford Coupe and he drove that around for a while.

In 1953, the C-T fellows coupled up with the people behind the Glaspar fiberglass sports car project. They lifted the Ardun directly out of the sprinter and dropped it in the '39 Ford chassis used for the Glaspar Sporty. Off came the alky carbs and on went the gassers. (Limeys frowned on alky, and they weren't crazy about '39 Ford running gear either.) Their driver didn't have a big time license so he had to run in the amateur race on Saturday. When the flag dropped, forget it, he was out of sight at the first turn. Sunday he's promoted to full race driver like the big guys. After blowing off Balchowski, Phil Hill's Ferraris, and everyone else, a needle valve stuck in one of the 97s (that's odd), and the funny thing burnt down. Nobody was sorry. Later this same combination blew off Briggs Cunningham's Chryslers at the March Field Road Races.

Clem suggested once to the Ford top brass that valuable publicity could be gained by exploiting the success of the Ardun in racing. They answered by saying that because it didn't look like any stock passenger car engine, nobody would be impressed. Quite a contrast to factory attitudes of recent years. How many Falcons have you seen lately running around with Indy Cammer engines in them?

Clem and Don built many engines through the years, and were benefactors to hundreds of racers. They ran the lakes, Bonneville, the drags, sprints, and sports cars. But the engines they remember most fondly were the ones bearing those fabulous Ardun heads. Don sold his half of C and T to Clem in 1962 and Clem sold the whole works in '66, and there are no more Ardun parts at C and T Automotive.

When the word got around, there was a scramble for the equipment and the records toppled. Paul Sylva trailered his B Modified Roadster to Bonneville in 1952, and ran 157 MPH with a 258 incher, featuring one of Stuart Hilborn's new fuel injectors. He took home top speed honors at the 1953 Russetta meet at El Mirage with a 154 blast. Charles Scott, better known as the owner of Scotty's Muffler Shop, sent them home mumbling to themselves with a record breaking 201 MPH pass in his B Lakester at the 1953 Bonney Nats. Later he chased the belly tank down the Santa Ana Drag Strip at 140. Bill Burke pushed a C-T Ardun to 167 at Bonneville in '53, and Art and Lloyd Christman, running a much modified rear engine Coupe went 160 with Harry Duncan's 258 incher the same year. Remember, these are all three-main, cast iron Henry Motors.

In 1955, LeRoy Neumayer solved his pushrod problems with chrome-moly tubes and rushed his tank to a 205 MPH clocking on 50% nitro to break into the rare air of the 200 Mile Per Hour Club, which had only a dozen exclusive members at the time. Tipping the can to 75% produced 215 one way, and a long walk back to the pits for LeRoy. Belmont SanChez campaigned a '34 Ford Coupe, a Bantam Roadster, and a new Studebaker Coupe (one of the slick new Raymond Loewy designs) at Bonneville in the early fifties. He teamed up with Clark Cagle, a very active and inventive Ardun pioneer, and they tweaked the Cagle-Lemmon-SanChez C Studebaker to 167 MPH in 1955. Alex Xydias, Keith Baldwin, and Buddy Fox (of blown flathead fame) wrote their Ardun powered So-Cal Speed Shop chopped '34 into the history books with 175 MPH blasts down the salt in 1954 and 130 MPH trips at Santa Ana, using every bit of their 258 inches.

Bob Estes, a Lincoln-Mercury dealer and sponsor of the Hill-Davis "City of Burbank" record breaking Streamliner, was a devoted racing enthusiast for many years. His beautifully prepared racing cars competed at Indianapolis, the dirt tracks, sprints, and Pikes Peak.

He entered a 59A flathead powered car in the 1948 Indy 500 and returned in 1950 with the Ardun powered number 82. Called the Poor Man's Novi by trackside buffs the car set a qualifying mark of 124 which stood as a record for semi-stock block engines for a dozen years.

Estes, a personal friend of Duntov's, still has his Lincoln-Mercury dealership, a Volkswagen agency, and he is a Lamborghini distributor as well. His collection of exotic racing machinery includes a Type 35B Bugatti racing car (now in the Briggs Cunningham Automotive Museum), Fronty DOC T engines, Cragar DOC As, a DOC conversion for the old Y-block Ford V8 which he designed, and was a forerunner to the famous Indy 4 cam Ford V8, and the famous one-off Davies DOC heads built for the flathead.

Bell Auto Parts, C and T, and Speed-O-Motive continued as suppliers until 1955 when this ad appeared in *Hot Rod* magazine for C and T Automotive:

"This company has obtained the entire Ardun stock left in America including six sets for V8-60. Price $375, down from $500."

The Moorpark address was given. Six sets for V8-60 . . . where are they now? Bet you didn't know they made an Ardun for the V8-60. I can see it now: A Bo Jones type modified bucket with an Ardun equipped V8-60 in it. Blown maybe. Right on! Rumor has it that they are floating around the San Francisco area, and one man is reported to have all of them.

Tom Ruddy attended the drags at Long Beach in '52 and '53 with Clark Cagle and Joe Mallard, who were running a new swing-axle dragster. He was a member of the Dusters, a Russetta Timing Association Drag Club, and was also a sailor at the time. A friend, Marty Weinstein, was running a flathead Roadster and Tom commuted from his San Diego Navy Base to drive for Marty on weekends. Weinstein's partner had gone to high school with Belmont SanChez and pretty soon the talk centered around putting a pair of Ardun heads on the Roadster. Joe Mallard found a set up north at Romeo Palimides' place. Palimides owned a small wheel company that cast wheels out of real Magnesium. It was later to be widely known as American Racing Equipment. The heads were reported to have been new, but when Tom got them home he found that they had suffered the indignities of a terrible porting job. Some of the ports cleverly routed gasses right into the water jackets. Tom worked on them two weeks with heli arc and die grinder and put the save on them.

The crew went to work building the Platypus-nosed Bonneville car in 1954. The first trip to the salt in '55 resulted in a 180 MPH speed running Class C Modified. The engine was a 5/16 plus .030 by 4 1/8 290 incher, and it packed a 430 HP wallop on 85%. That's with the stock 21A rods, $1.00 apiece, rebuilt exchange. Clem bought them by the gross and would send out three sets to get eight good ones. That same year (1955) Buddy Fox's blown flathead went 188 but couldn't back it up. Don Waite held the B Modified record at 187 with a De Soto Hemi (what ever happened to those little gems?) and the C record at 186 MPH with a carbureted flathead. At that time, Class A was the smallest, B the next larger, and so on up.

Tom worked in the balancing shop at C and T after discharge from Uncle Sam's Peacetime Yacht Club, experimenting with balancing techniques. He claimed having no main bearing trouble using Wilcap steel center and front main caps. The traditional 3/8-inch overbore was shunned by Ardun builders because most of them ran heavy nitro loads. They also preferred late blocks because few of them had been relieved. Tom got two good sets of Victor sandwich-type head gaskets and used only one set for years.

In 1956 at Bonneville, the Summers Class C Modified Roadster laid down a 192 pass to snatch the record from Don Waite. Tom and Marty waltzed in two days late and ran a 192 right off the trailer with the Ardun. The next day, they topped 200 and killed two birds with one stone: They stole the record from Summers who held it only one day, and they became the slowest member of the 200 Mile Per Hour Club with a two-way average of 200.009. To this day Ruddy and Weinstein hold this distinction.

The boys returned to the salt in 1957 with a spanking new motor in the now famous Modified. Waite still held the Class B record, and Ruddy and Weinstein saw nothing wrong with owning both the B and C records, so a 268 incher was put to work. On a warm-up run an intake rocker let go, and Tom poked through the five mile eyes at 192 at 4500 RPM on seven good cylinders. He got out and told Marty: "This thing runs like a pig!"

Pulling the rocker covers exposed the gremlin. The next day the '56 Chevy station wagon was summoned to push the Modified for what seemed like miles. Tom finally clutched off at 90 MPH and high-geared it right up to 199 (this time on eight). They backed it up with a 197 and snatched the B record, now the possessors of a matched pair. That mark stood for 12 years, the oldest in the books, when in 1969 Bill Taylor of San Diego thumped down the course with an average of 201 MPH in his Modified T Roadster. And just to keep things in the family he captured the record with a 258 inch Ardun!

The boys ran the Modified at the drags in '55 and '56 running 138–140 MPH, but it was too heavy. So the same team built the famous Bantam Roadster. (These fellows obviously got along well together.) The 1400 pound metal flyweight was a familiar sight at Bakersfield and Long Beach from '57 to '59, earning Top Eliminator honors at Bakersfield in 1958. The 291 incher ran a Vertex, 55–60 degrees lead, Hilborn squirts, and 80 to 90%.

They fought some terrific battles with Jazzy Nelson's incredible flathead Fiat Coupe, with times around 150 MPH and ETs in the nines. All this, mind you with the same set of heads.

Tom put them to work for the last time in 1961 in Dale Warner's Guasti ski boat. This time he chose a 284 incher (5/16 x 1/8) to push the 16 1/2 footer through the Chrondeks at 92. This number ET'd like a bandit; it fact, it was never beaten. Tom ran Middle Eliminator many times and points with pride to a defeat of the 110 MPH blown fuel Chrysler "Woodpecker."

In the late fifties, Motor Monarchs club member Dave Marquez campaigned one of the most beautiful Deuce Highboy Drag Roadsters. Inspired by Frank Iacono's fabulous Jimmy Coupe, Dave built an orange and white B Hot Roadster that stood as a flawless example of workmanship and inspired many another racing Highboy.

The *HRM* July 1956 cover car snatched Best Appearing accolades wherever it performed. The sleeved and stroked 235 inch Ardun ran Hilborns, an Isky no. 2 cam, Smith pushrods, Edelbrock pistons, and a Vertex, and grabbed Top Speed Honors at the Great Bend Nationals in 1955.

Speeds of 120 on 50%, a quick class change with a removable body upping this to 130, made the Marquez Ardun Roadster a car long remembered by racing enthusiasts and *Hot Rod* fans.

Our tour through the halls of Ardun history would not be complete without some notes on the last really serious competition effort with the Ardun engine. And these wars were fought in the heat of the toughest West Coast drag strips, against the fastest big-buck gladiators.

Not long ago I stopped by Safeway Sandblasting, Culver City, to have some parts cleaned and had a cup of coffee with the owner Chuck James. I'd like to relate what one man's romance with the marvelous heads finally accomplished. Chuck, a very pleasant and helpful fellow, told me he bought his first set from Farrel Backer back in the mid-fifties. Backer drove for Tim Woods (later of Stone-Woods and Cook).

Back then, Chuck says the stuff was easy to come by but nearly impossible to keep together, at least for him anyway. But he had good reason for saying this. Chuck worked for years with the engine solving two knotty problems; making it live, and increasing. I said *increasing* the horse-pressure. The first dilemma was solved with the help of the world's largest center main cap. . . . The second with a 6.71 GMC blower pumping 24 pounds boost through those heads into that pre-war lower end. Incredible!

Nobody was even running blowers then. Cal Rice, Garlits, all the shoes were still using unblown carbureted Chryslers. A special one-off manifold was fabricated to marry the huffer to the motor. Nobody ever manufactured any racing manifolds for the Ardun . . . the Crower log was a kit.

Eventually, Chuck's stump puller motor ended in the famous "Safeway Sandblaster", the orange '41 Willys Coupe; 2800 pounds, 1000 of it lead in the trunk. If you ever saw it run, you know what a handful it was. There began the most successful string of wins and the most awesome sounds any Ardun engine ever made.

I can't write down words that express what that wheezer sounded like, but if you ever run into me, just ask and I'll do my best to give you an imitation.

I remember sitting in the bleachers at Bakersfield 1965. The Coupe pulled to the line and the fellow next to me asked: "What's in the Willys?"

"Blown Ardun," I said.

"That's a truck motor," my neighbor said. "They don't buzz."

Just then Bones cleared it out once with one quick blast of throttle: BREET! He slipped the Hydro in gear and the whole car reared back on its haunches. In a second the tach read 8000, Bones made the one to two shift, and I helped my associate return his jaw to its normal position. I can't write down words that express what that wheezer sounded like, but if you ever run into me, just ask and I'll do my best to give you an imitation.

The 292 incher ran 9:1 compression, assorted cams, Pontiac and Buick rods from Crankshaft Company, the aforementioned 6.71, a two-door Hilborn, a La Salle gearbox, and later a Hydro. This animal cranked

8800 RPM and put out . . . are you sitting down? 527 HORSEPOWER on gas on Isky's dyno in 1962. This was enough to fling that 2800 pound Willys down the quarter in 10.80 at 125 MPH, running C Gas Supercharged. Lou Sales made the Hydro adaptors and Chuck says this was the working set-up. Later he switched to a Torque-Flite but it didn't swing the heavy Coupe out of the gate like the Hydro. Want to hook a Torque-Flite up to your flathead? The adaptors, which represent about $500 in machine work, are still floating around.

The blown head gasket problems were solved with O rings and paper gaskets cut out of old Drag News. The Coupe used to spit out rods and gaskets while Bones rapped it in the PITS before Chuck engineered the bugs out. He says he had $2500 soaked into that motor. Anyone who ever heard it or saw Bones Balough make a pass in that '41 Willys will never forget it. Maybe that's a low price to pay for a sort of immortality.

The last time I saw the Coupe was at Bakersfield '66. Bones leaped out of the gate, made the one-to-two shift, broke an axle, and DROVE on two wheels for 300 feet, clear over to the chain link, to keep from going over on his head. That thing was an animal! The last of the prehistoric meat-eaters.

The engine found its way into a digger, finally putting an 8.98-164 MPH run on the big-end clocks. Chuck believes this is the only time a flathead block ever made it into the eights. Some of Chuck's parts are spinning around in my motor and I'm proud to have them.

You know, one of the things that made Hot Rodding and engine building the great fun that it was in those days was the endless scrounging. And what you couldn't find, you made. A group of racers watching Tommy Thickston show off his latest two-barrel high rise manifold personify those simple, misty days.

Unorthodox, weird designs appeared by the hundreds because one or two professional builders didn't mass produce the hot machinery that raised hell after the war. They were constructed by hundreds of different guys wearing tanker jackets and jeans, and hundreds of different ideas were the result. This trend continued until sometime in the mid-fifties, when the tide turned. Little by little, the fabricated was replaced by the ready made. Less work was done at home and more in the flourishing shops across the country. In all fairness, these shops and the Speed

Equipment manufacturers did provide valuable service and parts to many fellows who would not have been able to build a car otherwise, myself included.

But somewhere along the line the whole idea of Rodding got lost in the shuffle; it became a contest of Top-My-Trick-Stuff and many talented enthusiasts hung it up because it wasn't fun any more. All through the sixties, the manufacturers made more and more goodies available in blister packs. Detroit joined the fray and a charming old lady collecting Social Security could blow the doors off the hottest late-forties machinery.

"Write your name on the line, Son and carry the wheels across the intersection."

How many youthful car buffs in the computer sixties are going to spend two, three, or four *years* building a car? Spend that long paying for one, OK, but build one?

Drag strips replaced the lakes as the Hot Rodders test bed and competition grew to the point where money was so essential for even a chance of winning that the fun left drag racing too.

So what happened? Not long ago, some guys realized that Early Ford bodies were hard to find, the pieces were badly rusted, prices climbed out of sight. Fiberglass replicas were all over the place. Flathead stuff was getting scarce let alone someone who could really build one any more, or wanted to. Flathead stuff! Everybody had four banger and flathead parts lying around. Guys that had never built a flathead had gaskets, two-jug manifolds, and a few 97s hanging in the garage like props just so the place would look like you played with cars.

Somewhere along the line, so much stuff got thrown away or junked that it's getting a little hard to find now. You've got to ask around some. People laugh sometimes when you trundle into the speed shop for a gasket set for a '46 Merc. "You're livin' in the dark ages, Pal." Thanks.

Rusted, bent body panels have to be saved and patched. Junk Deuce frames, maimed by less able assemblers, need hours and hours of work to make them live again. You have to scrounge for usable parts—good heads and cranks, a serviceable quickie. Because he couldn't care less what happens to the stuff, beware of the newly arrived enthusiast who walks up to you and says: "I'm looking for all the Cragar OHV heads I can get my hands on."

Detroit went horsepower nuts in the sixties, it's old hat now. You can go down and buy 625 HP in a crate, if you have the scratch. The funny thing is, everything under the sun was tried for thirty years to extract more power from Detroit's passenger car engines. Then some Hot Rod types (like Duntov) get jobs in Detroit and Dearborn and a few years later, even the hero cam grinders realized that factory Super Stock cams were the only ones that really put any horseponies in the more sophisticated muscle motors. But the government and Insurance Companies will put the screws to that pretty soon. So, a chapter in the automotive saga comes to an end.

All this brings us to what Traditional Rodding is all about. The time has come. The old stuff is trick again, and it's fun, and it affords the opportunity to be different and inventive.

I hope you've enjoyed reliving these very few nostalgic moments. Maybe you were there at one of these meets. There are many more fellows whose names belong in the Ardun Hall of Fame: Jack Ewell, Kent Babler, Jerry Darien, The Sandoval Brothers, Cotton Werksman, Don Apenfels . . . many I have doubtless failed to mention. My apologies. Maybe we'll hear from you.

In the first "Hot Rod Magazine Street Rod Quarterly" we'll bring you PART III. We'll follow the construction of my blown street Ardun and relate valuable hints and suggestions to those who may be undertaking the reincarnation of one of these exciting motors. The text will represent all the information currently available on the state of the art. One thing will become very apparent: having a pair of Ardun heads is a long way from driving it into the swap meet parking lot.

* Note: *Rod & Custom* was merged with *Hot Rod* after the June 1971 issue, so Part III of the series of articles didn't go quite as planned.

Street Rodding

State of the Art

Street rods have been around forever,
but until recently they've hardly been anywhere.

By LeRoi "Tex" Smith

Street Rodder, May 1972

Suddenly it's 1948. A strange and wonderful metamorphosis has come over hot rodding in this past decade, a change quiet and subtle but ever so decisive. Street rodding has surprised all but those who know by emerging as a major factor in the hot rod sport, ranking second to none as foundation for automotive enthusiasm these next many years.

Street rodding has always been around, but it has taken back seat to the more glamorous aspects of hot rodding simply become they were more spectacular. At first it was the local half-mile fairgrounds dirt track, where grandpa could whistle his stripped Model T through the oval with other Frontys and various homegrown overheads. The street machines came on fairly strong during the 1930s, when emphasis shifted to Southern California and the dry lakes. The strip-downs were still very much a part of things, but in the warm Southwest car enthusiasts could gather at dry lake beds and test their efforts for top speed. These first events were far from organized, but they were fun. All you needed was a set of wheels, in any condition, and you were legal.

The speed equipment industry was born at these early meets, initially as a personal thing and then to supply the demand from rodder friends. In fact, the industry really didn't boom until the late 1950s, when so much emphasis was directed at making Detroit street iron run better. Back then, you would drive your only form of transportation around town all week, make special adjustments on Saturday, and run on Sunday. Later, when roadster racing on oval tracks became popular (just before and after War Two) it was common practice to zip over to the track, pull off the windshield and headlights, race a few laps, put everything back in place and drive home. Now, those were *really* dual purpose cars.

Toward the end of the 1940s, the street rod had begun the slow evolution toward better suspension, better and more flexible power, workmanship that was detailed, and advanced design. Shows like the Oakland Roadster Show and highway events like the famous Rose Bowl tour sponsored by the Pasadena Roadster Club helped prove that a good street rod was more than a strip-down. But along came drag racing and the hot rod sport was soon divided.

In the beginning, everyone tried to run a dual purpose street rod/drag machine, but that proved entirely unfeasible. Just as the street roadster could no longer compete successfully on the circle tracks, the press of serious drag racing radically altered the concept of a dual purpose rod. More and more emphasis was on making street rods competitive. Engine setback, driver relocation, body gutting; everything was done to make the hot rod win races. And the street rod almost disappeared from the street.

Ready availability of new Detroit cars and a growing economy meant we could then have a neat car to drive, as well as a hot rod to play with on the quarter-mile. The drag strip became more and more crowded, and definitely more competitive, until anything remotely resembling a street machine was hopelessly outclassed. Besides, who wanted a chopped '32 coupe anyway. The stockers and dragsters were more exciting.

It was into this low point in street rodding that some Los Angeles enthusiasts introduced the L.A. Roadster Club. The group was active and received publicity in leading hot rod magazines. The idea spread slowly at first, until other roadster clubs were formed. Then came coupe and sedan clubs, and finally, clubs for old cars in general. Which brings us to the state of street rodding today.

Frankly, street rodding is more exciting now than at any time in the past, because anything can be an acceptable hot rod now, not just a 1932 Ford. Those of us intimate with hot rodding the past many years began to comment on the move toward diversified street machines during the early 1960s. The current rage for restoration of old cars was just beginning then, and we felt that surely this interest in making a car look original would overflow into rodding. Where before the emphasis had been on stripping fenders, the new breed of rodder went out of his way to find original accessories. The first changes showed with the Ford crowd, but by 1965 there were a number of unusual marques showing on rod runs. Chevy had come back strong, and there were several Buick and Dodge tourings in the ranks. Vehicles that would make poor restorations because of a parts shortage were being turned into premium street machines.

These same cars had been built sporadically during the past two decades, but never in sufficient numbers to attract attention from serious rodders. By the mid-Sixties there were enough older rodders, fellows who had been away from rodding for several years, to support the new building styles. At the same time, there were a number of builders anxious to construct something from the gaggle of interesting automotive parts introduced in recent years. From this curiosity came the Jaguar XKE and Corvette suspensions, the disc brake swaps, the torsion bar and coil-shock springs, and such radical departures as the VolksRod. Sophistication of a very advanced degree has overtaken street rodding.

Mechanically, street rodding today is about five thousand percent superior to what it was twenty years ago. Back then, we built with what we had, which meant almost exclusively Ford parts. And we didn't do a red hot job because most of the enthusiasts were relatively young and had a rather limited experience in things automotive. Now, two decades later, we are fortunate to have a tremendous international automotive experience to draw from, a fantastic array of spare parts at reasonable prices, and a less limited imagination.

No matter how much the old pre-1948 Ford suspension contributed to hot rodding, it was really a most rudimentary form of suspension. On the other hand, when coupled to the type of frames common then, and the body styles, that particular suspension is still adaptable. Beam and tubing front axles are going to be with hot rodding for years to come, and the transverse rear spring is super simple enough to adapt to any modern dead axle. Even the Corvette with its independent rear end found the transverse spring acceptable. The point is, improvements in modern street machinery have been made where they are most important: Brakes, steering, spring rates, roll centers, transmissions, engines, cooling, etc.

Of course, there is hardly a corner of the country where a rodder can't get parts or quality work. And even if he finds the local radiator shop or welding specialist can't help, relief is as close as the ads in a hot rod magazine. I remember not too long ago it was very difficult to get Heim rod ends or Dzus fasteners anywhere outside Los Angeles. Now both are prominently advertised in car books.

The modern street rod builder is faced with a far more exacting task than in years past. Let's look at some examples. A few years back one of the L.A. Roadster members came by my house with a ragged '29 roadster. He had just found it stored in a garage, where it had been since the early Fifties. He was going to replace the flathead with an Olds engine, but after getting into the project, he found the only thing retained from that original rod was the '32 frame (which had to be boxed and modified significantly), the body, and the front suspension. In making changes, he found the original work had been something less than painstaking. Back when, we just sort of hacked things off with a torch and let it go at that. There were a few precision builders, but not many. Doane Spencer was such a builder. Doane's

Mechanically, street rodding today is about five thousand percent superior to what it was twenty years ago.

old '32 roadster is now in the hands of Neal East, who is restoring it to original including a flathead engine. Restoration of old hot rods has come on strong recently, spurred by Bud Bryan's construction of a new "old" '29 and Jim Jacobs' rebuild of the Niekamp '29. Neal tells me that a full report on his machine is being readied for *Street Rodder*, and I hear Duane Kofed plans a similar report on his revamped Dick Flint roadster. But in the case of Kofed, the powerplant will be modern, along with an updated undercarriage. The point to be made is that even the old time hot rods are being given different treatments. Some are being restored (tried to find speed equipment for a Ford flathead recently?) while others are original in outward appearance only. There is no longer a restraint on what is, and what isn't, a true hot rod.

A lot of the liberal attitude toward modern street rodding can be attributed directly to the rod run. Following the much publicized early runs of roadster clubs on the west coast, similar highway tours have cropped up across the nation. In the midwest and east, where weather isn't always sunshine and smog, the closed cars have long been more popular than roadsters. Rod runs bring out these cars by the gross, and the more unusual machine is likely to get the greatest approval. Early Pontiacs, Rocknes, Studebakers; it doesn't matter as long as it is more rare than the Ford and Chevy. And even in the popular Ford ranks, the once ignored body styles are getting attention. It wasn't long ago that a Model T sedan was considered only one step removed from insanity, and you were really off the deep end if you built up something like a 1937 or '38 Ford. Nothing could be that ugly, we surmised. Now these styles are much sought after. Which goes to show what we knew.

At the same time, the car does not need to be something from the late 1920s to be rod material. A 1939 Buick sedan with twin sidemount spares is extremely popular as a contemporary street rod, and it may have either a late model Buick V8 for an engine, or a modified early straight eight. While emphasis has been on the pre 1949 series car as a true rod, this definition is too restrictive to be honest. A 1963 Chevy II can be a pure street rod; it is a matter of tasteful design and good construction. It won't be as rare as a 1931 Chevrolet cabriolet, but just wait a few more years. Often I reflect on the relative value of time and cars. Just after War Two, a Model A was only fifteen years old. Which is the age of a 1955–'56 Chevy today, so if the street rod enthusiast is honest with his evaluation of suitable street iron he will not rule out the late models.

If workmanship becomes the criteria for judging good and bad street rods, the sport takes on an entirely new meaning. At the first Street Rod Nationals in Peoria, I happened to be standing in the parking lot at the headquarters motel when a new arrival parked his '39 Chevy sedan. A little rough around the edges, it was obviously the driver's first attempt at a street rod, and chances were he came from a small town where there were no other rods. Everything went ok until he spotted a similar '39 at the other end of the lot. Casually enough he sidled up to the flawless red two door and took it in very carefully. A work of art, this Chevrolet could have run away with class honors at any show. Disappointment welled in the newcomer's eyes, but the frustration didn't come until he returned and looked his own car over again. In an explosion of silent fury he started kicking the door panel and fender, distraught that his pride wasn't as good as he thought. Wife and child were bundled back into the car and away he went, not bothering to stay for the meet. I saw him again this year, with the same '39. But what a change in the car. It wasn't loaded with expensive chrome, but detailed workmanship was everywhere. Like so many other rodders who finally get to see what the best hot rods look like, he had gone home determined to make his car just as good as the next. And he had succeeded.

Street rodding has flowed into every corner of this vast continent, touching the lives of car enthusiasts in every city and village. The only valid prediction to make is that rods built primarily for highway use will double and triple in number the next few years, and that quality will continue to rise. Already craftsmanship of the better machines surpasses all but the most elite racing cars, machines that often cost up to fifty times as much to build.

Street rodding is a very personal thing. Thank gosh we all get a chance to share in it.

The Hot-Rod Culture

By Gene Balsley

※

American Quarterly, Winter 1950

I

The following statement by Thomas W. Ryan, director of the
New York Division of Safety, presents the typical image of the hot rodder
in the mediums of mass communication. He is shown as a deliberate and
premeditated lawbreaker: "Possession of the 'hot rod' car is presump-
tive evidence of an intent to speed. Speed is Public Enemy No. 1 of the
highways. It is obvious that a driver of a 'hot rod' car has an irresistible temptation to 'step on it' and accordingly operate the vehicle in a
reckless manner endangering human life. It also shows a deliberate and
premeditated idea to violate the law. These vehicles are largely impro-
vised by home mechanics and are capable of high speed and dangerous
maneuverability. They have therefore become a serious menace to the
safe movement of traffic. The operators of these cars are confused into
believing that drinking is a competitive sport. They have a feeling of
superiority in recklessly darting in and out of traffic in their attempt to
outspeed other cars on the road . . . "[1]

This point of view is lavishly dramatized in the comic-strip character
Hot Rod Happy, a lawless, spoiled, delinquent, disrespectful cad, who is
the antithesis of good, clean-living American youth. Recently Hot Rod
was near death as the result of an automobile accident for which he was
apparently solely responsible. Presumably he has returned as a cautionary
exemplar of the evils of the hot-rod culture.

The hot rodder's picture of himself is somewhat different, though
obliquely cognizant of the mediums' image. Thus, in a letter to the creator
of Hot Rod Happy protesting the cartoonist's picture of the hot rodder,
a hot-rod organization wrote as follows: "A hot rod accident or incident
is newsworthy, while an accident involving ordinary cars is so common
that it is usually not newsworthy. We wonder whether you appreciate
the very real contribution that the hot rod industry, for it is an industry,
has made to automotive transportation. The automotive industry has
the equivalent of a million dollar experimental laboratory in the hot rod
industry from which they can get valuable technical information free of
any expense or risk of reputation . . . "[2]

The publication of the hot rodder, *Hot Rod* magazine, which claims
a circulation of 200,000, devotes many of its editorials to presenting

a true picture of the hot-rod car and driver. One of them said, "A real hot rod is a car that is lending itself to experimental development for the betterment of safety, operation, and performance, not merely a stripped-down or highly decorated car of any make, type or description, or one driven by a teen-ager. As to the menace or nuisance element, very few hot rod enthusiasts want to risk their specialized equipment for use as battering rams. The fact their cars are built so that they attract attention becomes an automatic psychological brake which governs their driving activities . . . "[3]

II

Most Americans are sure that American cars are the best and cheapest in the world. They will argue that we are the leaders and innovators in motor-car design. Judging from the Detroit car one sees on the street, it looks as if Americans believe that "chromium makes the car" and that only a big, heavy car will hold the road. The predispositions of American automobile designers shine through the enamel and chromium strips. This standard of taste appears to be as unshakable as the erroneous American belief that the cars and drivers at the Indianapolis Memorial Day Race are representative of the best in the professional racing world. In contrast to this complacency, the hot-rod culture is committed to the everlasting modification of what it casually calls "Detroit iron"—the American production car.

The hot rodder and his circle are highly articulate in their objections to the Detroit product as an automobile, and the reason is that they have little respect for the Detroit solution of a problem in transportation, engineering, and esthetics. The hot rodder says that this production car is uneconomical, unsafe at modern road speeds, and uglier than it has any right to be. What is more, it is too costly, too heavy, and too complicated by class and status symbolism to be a good car. Designed in ignorance of the hot rodder's credo that driving should not be so effortless that one forgets one is driving until after the crash, this car appears to the hot rodder to be a sort of high-speed parlor sofa. In general, the hot rodder protests against the automobile production and merchandising which fail to give the public a sufficiently wide range of models to permit judgments of value. The huge scale of the hot rodder's protest is immediately suggested by the sales of its parts industry—a cool eight million per year gross income.

III

When the hot rodder rebuilds a Detroit car to his own design, he is aiming to create a car which is a magical and vibrant thing. Yet, back of his dream design we can see the workings of the practical engineering standards that dominate the hot-rod culture. There are sound reasons for the hot-rod builder's selection and rejection of the various components of the Detroit car.

Any given car, when rebuilt by the hot rodder, can be loosely assigned to one of four classes of design. Let us talk in terms of ascending ranks of merit or prestige, distinguishing two illegitimate and two legitimate categories of hot rods. Implicit in this description is the assumption that the hot rodder has the knowledge to be critical, that, in fact, he possesses a kind of critical responsibility.

Cars rebuilt by means of the simplest changes can be classed in the lowest, the fourth rank. The owner in this category changes only the exterior of the body. He is, unfortunately, aided by the countless manufacturers of doll-up accessories, who provide such mechanically useless items as cutout mufflers, "supercharger pipes," and the ubiquitous Buick-like ventilator ports that do not ventilate. The owner of this kind of car spends most of his time driving around, playing proactive tunes on his four-note horn while flying three foxtails from his car aerial.

Transformations in cars of the next higher rank are dictated by considerations of function, although ornamentation may still be used. While in cars of the lowest category the engine remains substantially unaltered, the engines of third-rank cars are changed in order to increase horsepower and acceleration. A number of manufacturers make accessories which can be attached to their cars by fans with a minimum of mechanical skill. The old part, in most cases, is removed, and the hot-rod accessory is merely bolted on. The higher horsepower obtained is often dangerous if other compensations are not also made.

Now who are the mediums talking about when they speak of the irresponsible hot rodders? They are talking about cars in the two lowest ranks. Actually such cars are hot rods only in the loosest sense of the word. This was recognized by an official of the California Highway Patrol, who said in a letter to the editors of *Hot Rod* magazine, "Along with the true hot rodder will come the chaps with the shot rods."[4]

When we move up to the second rank we cross the line into the true mysteries. The hot rodder in the second rank strips his car of all chromium and ornaments. He lowers the body of the car, often as much as ten inches, to increase roadability and safety. He stresses clean lines, lightness, simplicity, and gasoline economy in his design. He may not change the chassis but he will surely add disc or hydraulic brakes if needed. He has failed in his avowed objective if the car is poorly constructed, or if it is not safer, better looking, and more efficient than ordinary cars. His car is a pleasure car, and all the changes he makes are practical for everyday road use. If he happens to be interested in competition he is likely to drive against time at the dry lakes outside Los Angeles, or at the various national meets. Generally, however, a great deal of his time is spent talking about performance figures with his cronies at the garage or at his hot-rod club; dry-lake racing tends to force him toward ownership of a top rank car.

What are the cars of the top rank? They are superstreamlined, often made of surplus aircraft wing-tanks, and will run only at top speed. They can be started only if they are pushed, one of the many reasons why they cannot be run on the highway. They are of interest in the hot-rod complex mainly because their owners are the designers and innovators in the hot-rod field. Many automotive manufacturers, knowing the excellence of the timing apparatus at the lakes, time their own test models there.

Between August 21 and 27 of this year at Bonneville Salt Flats, Utah, there were hundreds of sleepy hot rodders fuming around trying to gap spark plugs and adjust carburetors in the early morning dark; these were the dry-lake drivers of the fourth category. They made dust and noise, and broke AAA records as soon as it was light enough to run. The stark, white salt desert, the blue of the far-off mountains, the brilliantly colored cars, and the tight roar of those engines drew hot rodders from all over

America. To those who savor the smell of gas fumes and hot oil as others savor mountain air, a week at the salt flats is a kind of oil-drunken ecstasy. Driving against time, not against each other, mixes competition with teamwork in an unforgettable blend.

IV

While the hot-rod culture can be seen largely as an engineering protest against Detroit, some students of American culture have looked for other sociological and psychological meanings in the activities of the hot rodder. The hot-rod culture has been called an attack on the existing channels of expression—channels which grant success and acclaim only to those who fulfill certain occupational roles. It is said that the hot rod is especially suited to this search for spheres in which it is possible to obtain nonoccupational status because its prestige points are exhibited freely and personally in the very act of driving it. David Riesman and Reuel Denney have emphasized that the hot rod is more than an isolated phenomenon, that it is rather a single example of a process that may go on in the consumption of all mass-audience products. "As the hot rodder visibly breaks down the car as Detroit made it, and builds it up again with his own tools and energies, so the allegedly passive recipient of movies or radio, less visibly but just as surely, builds up his own amalgam of what he reads, sees, and hears; and in this, far from being manipulated, he is often the manipulator."[5] Thus, apparently, the consumer can attain a measure of autonomy despite the attempts of mass-producers to channel consumption in "respectable" directions. The hot rod has offered a real challenge to the automotive producers in the past—a challenge that threatens to grow. It is even thought that since the hot rodder is a good critic of the automobile, he might also be a good critic of many other industrial products; indeed, he may, in some instances, generalize his critical flair to include such subjects as politics and modern art.

Such hypotheses suggest that we need to learn more about the formation of a critical attitude among consumers of our mass-produced commodities. They also suggest that we might use small samples such as the hot-rod culture in order to obtain insight into the psychological processes, methods, and standards employed by the critical consumer.

And, of course, it we assume that the hot rod is a key variant in the mass-consumption complex, the logical next step is to know more about the hot-rod culture itself. Perhaps the researcher will find this easier than many other comparable investigations, since the hot rodder is highly articulate about what he is doing and his car is as concrete a piece of data as one could wish.

Notes

1 *New York Times*, June 19, 1949.

2 *Hot Rod* magazine, September 1949, p. 4.

3 Ibid., December 1949, p. 6.

4 *Hot Rod* magazine, May 1950, p. 7.

5 "A Research Program in American Leisure," mimeographed study, University of Chicago, page 4.

Remembering Pete

Hot Rod's Founder Was
One in a Million

By Ken Gross

Hot Rod Magazine, August 2007

The world of hot rodding owes an inestimable debt to Robert Einar "Pete" Petersen.

Petersen who passed away on March 23 from complications of neuroendocrine cancer, was a true American success story. Born in east Los Angeles in 1926 and modestly self-described as "just a kid from Barstow," he founded one of America's most successful magazine publishing companies.

Nearly 60 years ago, at barely 21 years old, Petersen set out to create a national publication to cover the fledgling hot rod community. *Hot Rod* magazine, and many other successes that followed—*Motor Trend, Rod & Custom, Car Craft, Guns & Ammo, Teen, Savvy,* and *Skin Diver,* to name just a few—grew beyond his wildest expectations. Bob Petersen was a self-made, tough, street-smart guy who never forgot his humble origins, and he was quietly modest about his remarkable achievements.

Actor James Garner, his close associate for over 35 years, says, "Pete didn't classify his friends by their social status. He was either your friend or he wasn't." John Dianna, a longtime Petersen honcho and now CEO of Buckaroo Communications, adds, "If he liked and trusted you, you were his guy for life. Pete was a man's man, a rugged individual with a certain magnetism that definitely contributed to his success."

Looking back, it took guts to establish *Hot Rod* magazine in January 1948. "Hot rod" was a pejorative term. Pete had the vision to see that hot rodding was more than a bunch of kids racing at the dry lakes and on the street. It was becoming a major sport. Alex Xydias, founder of the So-Cal Speed Shop, recalls, "We didn't really like the term 'hot rod.' That's what the *Los Angeles Times* and the Hearst newspapers used when they wrote about 'speed-crazed kids racing on the streets.' We called our cars 'roadsters.' For a long time, the SCTA (Southern California Timing Association) didn't even let coupes and sedans race at the dry lakes."

Dean Batchelor, in his book *The American Hot Rod*, tells this story. "The last SCTA dry lake meet in 1947, on October 19, sticks in my mind for several reasons. Alex Xydias and I had driven up to El Mirage in my roadster, and it would be the first run with my new flathead engine. We drove up Saturday to make it easier to get ready for Sunday's time trials. While walking around the pit area, a young guy neither of us knew collared Alex to show him the layout for a new magazine he was going to publish. He didn't say, 'I'm thinking of publishing it.' He said, 'I'm going to publish it.' He discussed the magazine's proposed coverage with Alex, how it would be circulated, and other things related to the publication's format, and then he asked Alex if he would advertise his speed shop in it. Alex put him off by suggesting he call or come by the shop during the week. After he left, Alex turned to me and asked, 'What do you think? Will it work?' My reply was, 'I think it'll sell great in Southern California, but I can't see much success in other parts of the country.'

"Right. I've eaten those words many times since 1947. The young man was Robert E. Petersen, who with Bob Lindsay started *Hot Rod* magazine, the circulation of which has since topped 1 million copies per month."

Hot Rod magazine made its debut at the First Annual *Hot Rod* Exposition at the LA National Guard Armory. Years ago when I asked Pete about using the name *Hot Rod*, he said matter-of-factly, "That's what they were called. Anything else wouldn't have been believable."

Right from the beginning, when he and Bob Lindsay put the money together to publish the magazine's first issue, Pete understood the business potential in selling advertisements to budding speed equipment manufacturers. His original assignment had been to gather ads for the hot rod show program, but (typical of this hard-driving businessman) Pete went far beyond that simple brief. Despite his youth, he somehow knew that if he could help focus this growing passion and contribute to making hot rodding legitimate and safe, the sport would grow—and it would last.

It's the stuff of legend that Petersen hawked the first issues of *HRM* for 25 cents each on the steps of the Armory. Pete was told he couldn't sell his magazines inside. His show partners were annoyed that not only had he sold plenty of ads for the program, he'd also sold them to run in his new magazine's first issue.

Optimistically, and again typical of the man, readers of Volume 1, Number 1 were invited to place a subscription order. The price was $3 "throughout the world." Pete later said, "That's how we got enough money to eat some nights. We'd be at a drive-in or a race, and we'd say, 'Let's go sell some subs.' We'd sell 'em, then we'd have enough money for supper."

Alex Xydias didn't buy an ad for his fledgling So-Cal Speed Shop in that first issue of *Hot Rod*. He finally got in on the third issue. "I couldn't see that a magazine that just went to a few dry lakes racers would ever be successful," he confesses. "Our customers might have come from as far away as the San Diego Roadster Club, but we didn't have many guys from Fresno in the SCTA. Of course, when I did place an ad, and started getting orders from guys all across the country, I realized Pete was right. If it weren't for *Hot Rod*, how else would a guy in Ohio who wanted a Winfield cam know where to buy it?"

"Soon I bought even bigger ads," Alex recalls. "I wanted my little shop in Burbank to look as big as Roy Richter's Bell Auto Parts. With his magazines, Pete gave us all that chance. I've heard people say the speed equipment manufacturers made Petersen rich, but it's just the other way around. Thanks to his magazines, he made many people successful and wealthy."

HRM was tiny at first. Pete's partner Bob Lindsay, initially managed the office side of the business. Pete sold subscriptions, wrote and sold advertising, took many of the photos, planned editorial, and even wrote copy. Sometimes he really had to work to get an advertiser. He liked to tell a story about Vic Edelbrock, Sr., a winning dry lakes racer who developed and sold speed equipment out of his gas station on Highland Avenue in Hollywood. At first, Edelbrock didn't want to buy ads. After Pete convinced Vic to spend some money on quarter-page ads (by writing the copy and photographing the equipment himself), Edelbrock complained that his phone was ringing off the hook "and we [didn't] have time to pump gas." To cut down on phone calls, Pete convinced Edelbrock to offer a catalog for 25 cents. Vic soon said they were making a fair amount of money selling catalogs to people all over the country, but the work involved in responding to the mail meant they still didn't have time to sell gas. Petersen recalled that he gently suggested to Edelbrock that perhaps he wasn't in the gas station business anymore and that now he was a "speed merchant."

In his book *Hot Rod Pioneers*, Ed Almquist quotes Petersen as saying, "We sold most ads to small businesses who didn't know any more about guaranteed circulation than we did. We'd show them the magazine ad, collect for it, and then rush back to pay the printer."

Wally Parks, 14 years Pete's senior and president of the SCTA at the time of *Hot Rod*'s germination, was highly respected in the hot rod community. Pete clearly understood that Wally could be of inestimable help in many ways. Early on, he retained Parks to be the editor of *Hot Rod*, because he knew his experience as a dry lakes racer and as the SCTA's leader provided the credibility his fledgling magazine sorely needed.

Almost as soon as *Hot Rod* could stand on its own two feet, Petersen was back in January 1949 with *Motor Trend*, "The Magazine for a Motoring World." It was a more broadly focused monthly that covered the new-car industry, road-tested new models, and attracted an even wider variety of advertisers than *HRM*. Alex Xydias says, "Only 23 at the time, Pete realized there was a need for a national magazine that covered both domestic and imported cars. Besides," Alex laughs, "he knew selling an ad schedule to Ford Motor Company was worth a lot more than selling a handful of small ads to speed shops."

Asked the secret to the success of his publications, Pete responded, "We hired talented guys who really knew about the subject matter: cars, guns, surfing, skin diving, whatever. We could always teach people how to write," he'd say, "but it was more important that they knew what they were talking about." And he could pick 'em: Wally Parks, Barney Navarro, Eric Rickman, Bob D'Olivo, Don Francisco, Roger Huntington, Ray Brock, Racer Brown, Tex Smith, Tom Medley, Alex Xydias, Don Prieto—the list goes on and on. That style of knowledgeable, in-depth reporting gave *Hot Rod* and later, *Motor Trend*, authentic, first-person validity. From the beginning, *HRM* was written by experienced, respected authorities.

"Pete was a wonderful judge of people," says Checkered Flag 200 chairman, car collector, and former Petersen Museum board member Bruce Meyer. "He could read them astutely, and he could recognize opportunities. He especially valued loyalty and trust. No one I knew had so many 30- to 40-year-old friendships. He gave so many people great opportunities.

Carroll Shelby, Pete's close friend for over 50 years, says, "Bob Petersen started more institutions than anybody I ever knew, and he didn't always get credit for what he did." Characteristically, Petersen was modest about his role in establishing the NHRA (National Hot Rod Association) and SEMA (originally the Speed Equipment Manufacturers Association, now the Specialty Equipment Market Association). From the beginning, he understood that legitimizing this so-called outlaw hot rod sport required a bona fide trade organization and a national club so guys all over the country could feel they were a part of something more important than fixing up old cars, dry lakes competitions, and even street racing. Bob Petersen helped underwrite both organizations and played a key role in their expansion. Besides being the right thing to do, it was good for business, and despite his lack of formal education Pete was instinctively an astute businessman.

After starting as a messenger boy at MGM Studios, then working with Hollywood Publicity Associates, then founding and expanding Petersen Publishing Company into a world-renowned firm, Pete later developed Petersen Aviation, a jet aircraft charter company; an ammunition manufacturing firm; a Paso Robles, California, winery; and a juice-bar business. He possessed extensive real estate holdings. He invested in ideas he valued, such as a new engine design with Carroll Shelby. A silent partner in many ventures, Pete had an instinct for a great idea and loved making a good deal.

Truth be told, Bob Petersen really liked hunting and fishing more than he liked automobiles. His stellar arms collection, especially the personal guns of Samuel Colt, astutely purchased over a long time, remains priceless. "He was a voracious reader on subjects he liked," recalls John Dianna. "And he was extremely knowledgeable about collectible firearms."

Pete always had an instinct for a bargain. About eight years ago when he bought a 135 M Figoni et Falaschi Delahaye, we were at a Ford Motor Company dinner, and the Bonhams & Brooks auctioneers in Carmel had called Pete so he could bid by phone. As the bidding soared to over a million dollars, he wasn't at all perturbed.

"What do you think?" he asked. I replied that it was a lot of money and the car probably needed a re-restoration. He responded, "Where would we get another one? They only made 11 of these, right?" He'd done his homework. As the price went up in $50,000 increments, Pete commented dryly, "I sure hope this ends soon; I'm really getting hungry." He won it with a $1.35 million bid; we returned to dinner, and other than telling his wife Margie about it, he didn't say anything. He was quietly pleased, like the cat that had swallowed the canary. And as was true so often, Pete was right; today, that Delahaye is worth more than three times what he paid for it.

You'd never want to play poker against Bob Petersen. He could be very, very tough. He subtly intimidated Natural History Museum President Jim Powell back in the days when the LA Museum of Natural History operated the Petersen Museum. Despite holding two Ph.D.s, and through no lack of trying, Powell

Truth be told, Bob Petersen really liked hunting and fishing more than he liked automobiles.

could never figure out Pete's intentions. Normally erudite and cool, Powell would stammer and hesitate in a conversation with Petersen. When Powell authorized a trial press release indicating that the Natural History Museum would have to close the Petersen Museum because funds were not available to continue running it, Pete countered by quietly threatening to sue him and the entire Natural History Museum Board. Jim Powell retreated and the release never went out. "They'll have to come to me, eventually," Pete'd say with a grin, referring to Los Angeles County's disposition of the Museum. And eventually, they did.

Pete and Margie generously established a foundation to purchase the museum from the County of Los Angeles. To no one's surprise, the property on Fairfax and Wilshire in Los Angeles has appreciated well beyond the price they paid for it. And all the cars are worth more, too.

The best part of my job as Petersen Museum director was having long lunches with Pete, where he'd talk about hot rod and racing personalities, noted movie stars (he knew a lot of Hollywood and film industry people), celebrities, and politicians. He was modest about his friendships, he appreciated loyalty, and he withheld criticism of people for the most part, especially if a person was deceased. Pete was a very classy guy, in ways that transcended his obvious wealth. And he had an intense competitive streak.

One day he brought a bound volume of the first year of *Hot Rod* magazine to lunch. We leafed through a few issues, commenting on people and the feature cars he remembered. He reflected on an April '48 cover that showed Stuart Hilborn and his record-setting lakester, the first fuel-injected hot rod and the first streamliner to top 150 mph. "I took that picture in front of Stuart's mother's garage," Pete said. "Any idea where that car is now?" I told him that the Hilborn car had disappeared after a brief appearance at a dragstrip in Kansas many years ago, and that Bruce Meyer had placed some ads in *Rod & Custom* looking for it. He said, "Well, you'd better find it before he does." And he meant it.

Pete was the only guy I knew who could use the words Montrachet and shithead in the same sentence. He could be both crude and sophisticated, often at the same time. But that was part of his charm. Confident without being overbearing, with a well-developed sense of humor. Pete had an uncanny ability to read an ongoing situation almost as though he were outside watching events transpire, and then say the right thing at the right moment. John Dianna remembers that Pete would sit through day-long business meetings, often without a comment. "But at the end of the day," Dianna recalls, "he'd say a just few insightful things, and they'd encapsulate and focus everything that had been said." Like the skilled hunter and fisherman he was, he had incredible patience. He didn't have to make the first move; he instinctively knew how and when to make the one that would count. Bob Petersen would have been one hell of a gunfighter in the Old West.

While he was a bachelor, Pete dated some of the most beautiful women in Los Angeles, but that all changed when he met Margie McNally, a lovely New York model and former Miss Rheingold. Carroll Shelby remembers meeting her on Pete and Margie's first date. "I started to say something about women we knew, and then I said I had to get my date home before her husband got there. Pete kicked me under the table. 'Why'd you do that?' I said to him. 'I really like this girl,' Pete replied." He proposed to Margie on that first date. Adds Shelby, "After Pete met Margie, he was never interested in another woman."

Pete was very devoted to Margie. Their lives suffered a great tragedy when their sons Bobby and Ritchie were lost in an airplane crash when they were just boys. It would have destroyed many marriages, but it brought Pete and Margie closer together. In later life, they were very generous to organizations like the Boys & Girls Clubs and the Thalians, supporting the Mental Health Center at Cedars-Sinai Medical Center. The Petersens helped countless Los Angeles kids, even though they'd lost their own.

Carroll Shelby recalls: "We were friends for over 50 years. I owe Pete a lot. When I introduced the Cobra, he helped promote it with articles about the car in *Hot Rod* and *Sports Car Graphic*. Every CEO in Detroit respected him. He'd tell everybody, "You should see this new car Shelby's built. It's a winner."

So was Robert E. Petersen.

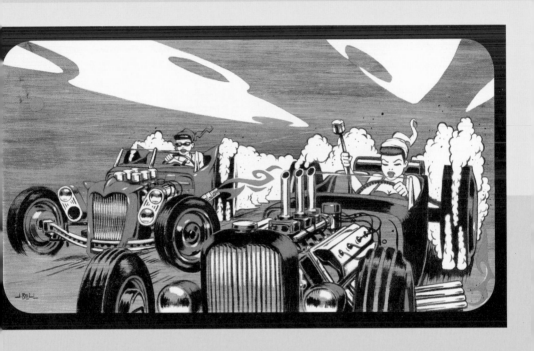

4

Dragging and Driving

What is Bonneville?

By Mark Dees

※

How to Go Racing at Bonneville, 1980

This is supposed to tell you how to get your car together and go fast for a slight amount of fame and glory on the saline wastes. Speaking for myself, I have received damn little fame and glory for all the time, blood and money I have spent on innumerable Bonneville projects, even those which performed as planned.

Why then do I continue to do it, and why should anyone else do it? In the event Thawley has omitted the fact in the following pages, one good reason is that I can use obsolete equipment, as the Bonneville racer does not have to concern himself very much with the tire, chassis, or camshaft of the month. That makes things cheaper, or so I keep telling my wife. Note that I said obsolete, *not* worn out. Some weathered Salt Rats may use seven-year-old valve springs and eight Stromberg 97s instead of a fuel injector, but I don't recommend it. Some go to Bonneville to tour the cathouses which lay (good word) at all western approaches to the area, and if that's your reason to go, it doesn't matter how worn-out your valve springs are so long as your personal equipment is in good shape.

As most people who race on the Salt or visit the Nationals every September will tell you, the principal reasons for their activity are subjective, that is, personal and often undefinable. Maybe if I just dredge up a few images from memories of over 25 excursions to the wilds of Utah, you'll get the idea.

Bonneville is the getting there—thrashing on the car to the last minute and driving for hours through some of the most desolate land in the country, usually at night. It is boring to some, but relaxing to me—except for the constant fear at the threshold of consciousness that the trailer will break, blow a tire or dump the whole rig into a canyon.

How can I ever forget the time I was clipping along at some 80 MPH in those dear dead gas-abundant days of yore when I saw one dim headlight coming up behind at a fearsome rate of speed. As it passed me, I saw it was attached to a '40 Ford sedan delivery, hoodless, with a 6-71 blown Olds roaring away, driving Ford, trailer, and lakester at 125 MPH up the southern reaches of Montgomery Pass. The apparition faded in the distance, its departing aspect lit only by a kerosene railroad lantern swinging from the trailer. Thus Tom Beatty was wont to make his passage through the night.

Bonneville is open space in which the city-dweller's soul expands. We never travel there without stopping at night and shutting off lights, engine and the music from a hundred western radio stations, just to stare at the sky and drink in the starry firmament and its implications. If the sky is cloudy, we watch for the lightning flashing over the distant ranges, like artillery fire in another country.

Bonneville is sociability—rolling into Jim's Place or the Western, to meet old friends and talk cars, "Have you seen the Markley's new roadster?" "Did you see Bob so and so?" "Yeah, he was just putting the rods and pistons in when I left Santa Barbara," "What class are you running this year . . . not C Fuel I hope 'cuz that's what we're doing . . . " "Did you check out the Green Lantern when you came through Ely?" "Do you have an extra room lined up for my friends here . . . ?"

Bonneville is the last stand for iron Chrysler, De Soto and Dodge hemis. Have you ever stood at the timing stand when the Allen-Parker belly tank comes through? It's that little speck moving at the head of that great roostertail of salt . . . usually only the cars that are making horse-power do that. Listen to the howl of that 25-year-old engine bounce off the mountains and reverberate around the bowl of heaven as it drives an equally old car with exiguous suspension and dubious streamlining at close to 300 MPH, snarling defiance of wind resistance and age.

Bonneville is a wild ride. Over 200 MPH in a lot of Bonneville cars, particularly the first ride or two after a layoff, is like going over Niagara in a barrel. Just aim 'er down that line, push the pedal and hang on. Everything vibrates, you can't read the instruments, the damn thing slips on the salt and if it's got any punch at all, tries to come around on you so that you have to backpedal a bit and launch it again after it steadies itself. After a run or two you are in the groove, can take time to read instruments, fiddle with the wheel a bit, and steer for the best parts of the course. By the end of the week it's second nature and all you worry about consciously is the damn tach, and knowing you need to break the record in your class.

Bonneville is weird machinery and people that flourish nowhere else. Flathead Camaros, 235 MPH Studebakers, 210-inch-wheelbase Model B Ford lakesters, twin-turbo Panteras, full-streamlined fuel motor-scooters, the nastiest open-frame Harleys you ever saw, a biker stripping out of boots, brain basin, and leathers to reveal a young dolly in a minimal bikini, and most beloved of all-old Ford roadsters and coupes, some immaculate (with not a single Ford part of any kind, just modern running gear and fiberglass replica body), others with as much salt-streaking, dents and corrosion as a Malaysian tramp streamer . . . with no speed differential to speak of between the two types. I've seen naked women changing spark plugs. I've seen steam-powered contrivances that just teakettled in the pits, and Mickey Thompson leaving the line in his LSR car sounding like he had enough horsepower to launch himself into orbit.

All the above is that much worse if the salt is rough and you don't have rear suspension in your car. In the return road, which is never graded for some reason, the beating your car takes as it is pushed as much as eight miles back to the starting line tears at your heart . . . so much so that many guys load the thing back on its trailer for the trip.

Bonneville is quiet triumph, as when you've just made a run on a record attempt on Saturday afternoon, having hung three or four strong competitors out to dry with a final pass that gives you the record at a speed that they will have trouble reaching for years to come. You roll into the impound area grinning, someone hands you a beer and you pull off helmet and firesuit as the congratulations are passed around. You usually have some champagne and maybe another couple of beers, and you pull down your trusty motor in a happy fog of self-esteem and satisfaction.

Bonneville is bitter disappointment, as some other guy goes through the victory routine in the impound area as you load your salt-spattered racer together with a couple of trashed shortblocks. The drive home is really a drag, as you think of all the bills at home, all the people who will ask "HowjadoatBonneville?" to which you have to say "Took a big shit, I did," and all the salt that has to be flushed off the damn thing lest it turn into a mound of rust. Little by little the pain goes away, and in a few weeks you are saying to yourself—"I'm going up there next year and blow those characters into the weeds"—and by the end of the next summer the pattern is repeating itself, thrashing, bashing, kiting checks, all to get your rig together, loaded, and on its way.

Bonneville is all this and more, for better or worse. I'd like to tell you about it. Wait for me in the Stateline bar about midnight or so on the first or second day of the next Nationals. I'll stagger in, dirty and sleepless with a half-finished car out in the entryway. Buy me a Daniels on the rocks and before I turn in, I'll have a thing or two to say . . .

Warming Up

By Robert C. Post

%%

*High Performance: The Culture and Technology
of Drag Racing 1950–1990, 1994*

I had no idea it would get as big as it did, but I didn't see any reason for it not to always be a good moneymaker.

—C. J. Hart, 1961

On a crisp Sunday morning in 1949 a group of hot rodders converged on a stretch of two-lane road north of Santa Barbara. The road ran westerly towards the ocean from California's Coast Highway, Highway 101. Ordinarily, it provided access to a landing field at Goleta, but on this April weekend a half-mile had been closed off with portable fencing. Although the site was well known among local street racers, this was a special occasion—a match race between two out-of-town celebrities, both of them dry lakes veterans, Tom Cobbs and Fran Hernandez. Cobbs had been winning races all around Los Angeles in his Ford roadster, a 1929 Model-A body channeled over a '34 frame. The engine was a '34 V-8 with a Roots blower from a GMC diesel truck or bus fitted on top as a supercharger. Cobbs had challenged Hernandez, who raced a fenderless but otherwise stock-bodied '32 Ford three-window coupe with a new Mercury V-8 that had been over-bored and stroked to 3 3/8 X 4 1/8, 296 cubic inches compared to Cobbs's 249. But there was no blower on top, just three Stromberg carburetors on a special manifold.

There were marked contrasts between the two racers themselves as well as their hot rods. Cobbs was called "a clever engineering sort who could afford, as heir to tobacco fortunes, to experiment and to test on Stu Hilborn's dynamometer." Hernandez, who managed Vic Edelbrock's place on West Jefferson Boulevard in Los Angeles, was "a scrappy master of machine shops." Cobbs hung out in the beach town of Santa Monica with Hilborn, who manufactured fuel injectors for dirt-track racers, and Jack Engle, who was one of the first southern Californians to go into business regrinding Detroit camshafts, changing lobe profiles to alter valve timing. Hernandez's buddies were Bobby Meeks, who worked for Edelbrock, too, Ed Iskenderian, a onetime apricot pitter from Fresno who had a cam grinding shop just down the street from the Edelbrock Equipment Company, and Lou Baney, who rebuilt engines in a shop on South Normandie.[1] Nominally, Cobbs's roadster was in "legal" trim and could be driven on the streets, but Hernandez's coupe lacked such niceties as headlights and mufflers, so he had towed it in with a pickup.

Other hot rodders—nearly all of them young men around twenty, with just a few girlfriends in evidence—showed up to participate, to drag it out with one another, but the Hernandez-Cobbs match was the feature. Everyone crowded up close for a good view, either at the starting line or near the finish, where there was a hump and the roadway narrowed to cross a culvert. The course that had been marked off allowed racers three-tenths of a mile to accelerate and sufficient room to stop before coming to a sharp turn beyond the culvert. Hernandez's coupe was balky about starting, so it had to be hand-pushed and fired on compression. When it finally kicked over, the exhaust fumes immediately betrayed the presence of something other than gasoline. Cobbs may have been surprised, but Hernandez already had a reputation as one of the select few who were expert in setting up Stromberg carbs for nitro.

Side by side, a few feet apart, Cobbs and Hernandez edged towards a white line across the blacktop, where the starter stood holding a flag on a wooden stick pointed towards the ground. Then, just as all four front tires touched the line, the starter yanked his flag skyward. Open headers roared and Hernandez jumped out in front while the roadster spun its tires, filling the air with clouds of white smoke. Although Cobbs finally regained traction and was closing the gap toward the end, Hernandez's deuce crossed the culvert a length ahead. He quickly gathered his things, while his friends bolted a tow bar to the frame of his coupe and hitched it to the pickup. Then he was gone.

Word of the outcome quickly got around, and hot rodders rehashed it long afterwards, a diversion known as bench racing. Cobbs had changed to lower rear end gears, thinking (mistakenly) that this would give him an advantage out of the chute—could he have won with "lakers gears" like Hernandez had? Did that "Jimmie" blower really produce 10 pounds of boost, as some people said? What kind of load was Hernandez running, anyway? The collective memory later coalesced as a tale titled "The Day Drag Racing Began," which was reprinted time and again.[2] While eyewitnesses could attest to its essential accuracy, it had all the makings of a classic legend. The details need not be taken literally.

Clandestine drag racing had been going on for some time, of course, but what was unique about this particular event is that officials of the

Santa Barbara Acceleration Association had sought, successfully, to have the California Highway Patrol confer approval: The races at Goleta were not against the law. That nicety aside, one might denominate "the day" as almost any day (or, more likely, any night) in the late 1940s and the place as being Arrow Highway in the San Gabriel Valley, Riverside Drive in the San Fernando Valley, Culver Boulevard in West Los Angeles, Baker Street between Harbor and Bristol in Orange County, or anyone of many other spots—in Texas or Florida, even in Michigan, Illinois, or Ohio, as well as in California—where hot rodders raced unlawfully. Drag races that were not only legal but also in keeping with commercial conventions were not established until a year after "the day" at Goleta, at an air strip in Santa Ana, California.

Soon enough similar events were being held in Caddo Mills, Texas, Zephyrhills, Florida, and elsewhere, but Santa Ana (which for some reason the racers always pronounced Santee Ana) is the place where drag racing had its inception as a commercial enterprise—or, to be more precise, where the *staging* of races had its commercial inception, since the making and selling of hot rod parts was already established in the hands of people like Vic Edelbrock and Ed Iskenderian.

Although the reader will find me yielding to temptation in the narrative that follows, seeking to denominate "firsts" is not a terribly profitable exercise. What is important to establish here is that some time close to the midpoint of the twentieth century an activity was invented—or, again for precision, an activity invented previously was endowed with formal sanction. Given that activity's thoroughgoing transformation in the ensuing forty years, it is worthwhile to take a look at the Santa Ana Drags. The instigator was one Cloyce Roller Hart—"C. J." Hart, also known as "Pappy." Hart was thirty-nine in 1950, having left Findlay, Ohio, for California with his wife, Peggy, and their two young children after some colorful innings as a moonshiner and roustabout, among other things. Hart always cautioned that he "didn't invent drag racing." He had done a lot of it himself around Findlay, even as a teenager, and reckoned that dragging on public thoroughfares must have been going on "ever since there was cars!"[3]

But street racing took off by orders of magnitude in the postwar years. There were thousands of unmarried males, many of them ex-GIs, with plenty of spare dollars, enhanced mechanical skills, an assertive bent, and a love of speed. As the sociologist Bert Moorhouse writes, after the war "the 'hot rod' became significant in the lives of a large number of (mainly young) Americans."[4] Many of these young men also had a dubious sense of social responsibility, and the press relentlessly flaunted an image of the hot rodder as "a deliberate and premeditated lawbreaker."[5] No doubt the "hot rod menace" was overdrawn in the newspapers and in a genre of fiction purveyed by Henry Gregor Felsen and his followers. Nevertheless, street racing had clearly become a problem of major proportions by 1950, particularly in California. People were getting killed in hot rods, and by hot rods.

"Throw 'em all in jail" was one response. But among the ranks of citizens who tried to address the problem constructively the idea of "giving the kids a place to race safely" began to seem like better tactics. Indeed, this became the primary rationale for the establishment of drag strips nationwide in the 1950s, although it was probably not what was foremost in C. J. Hart's mind. Hart had been an inveterate street racer himself, and a good deal of what was really exciting about it was that it *was* illegal.[6] What nobody enjoyed however, were the busts, an ever greater likelihood as the police infiltrated drive-ins and other hot rodders' hangouts to gain advance information and as "engaging in a speed contest" became the costliest of all citations. Besides, Hart thought, there could be money made in staging legal drag races.

Aircraft landing strips and taxiways, smooth and uncrowned, had always seemed like ideal places for drags, and in Santa Ana, where Hart operated a used car lot on Bolsa Avenue, there was a sleepy little airport behind Newport Bay. In concert with two partners, one of whom promoted motorcycle races and was in a position to provide insurance, Hart approached the airport manager and struck a deal to rent an unused runway every Sunday "for 10 percent off the top." All told the initial investment was less than a thousand dollars. Hart recalled that "about the only thing [he and his partners] had to put in there was an ambulance, and . . . some kind of concession for the food, and insurance, and trophies."[7] The first day for the Santa Ana Drags was Sunday, June 19, 1950.

Five days later the North Koreans came across the 38th parallel, and what ensued in the Far East was bound to put a crimp in any recreational activity attractive to draft-age males. Still, within a few months enthusiasts who usually spent their Sundays at El Mirage were showing up regularly at Santa Ana. There they could race one another as well as get timed. To supplant stopwatches Hart had designed a timing system with a pair of photoelectric cells that activated a clocking device set up in an old hearse parked at the finish line. Although it would gradually become clear that quick start-to-finish elapsed times were what won drag races, C. J.'s device recorded only top speed at the quarter-mile mark, or perhaps a little beyond—1,320 feet had not yet been established as conventional. The fastest run in 1950 was 120 miles per hour, clocked by a gutted '34 Ford with hand-formed bodywork in front, four rear tires, and a big question mark painted on the side. The "?" was campaigned by Harold and Don Nicholson, brothers from Pasadena in their early twenties. The boys from "Nick's Speed Shop" were already legendary around local drive-ins like Larry and Carl's for their street-racing exploits.

Or, rather, 120 was the fastest run by an *auto*, for Al Keys had topped 121 aboard two different fuel-burning Harley-Davidson motorcycles, Joe LeBlanc's "Beauty" and "The Beast" owned by Chet Herbert, who ground cams for automobile engines which utilized roller tappets, like Harleys. Weight did not matter a great deal at the dry lakes, where there was more than a mile to get up to speed, but already it was becoming obvious that weight was a key constraint on a drag strip. A hopped-up Harley 74 on fuel could put out a lot of power, while the overall weight was far less than any automobile, no matter how ruthlessly it was gutted, no matter how many nonessential parts and pieces were removed. Not that hot rodders had not begun trying, almost at once in fact. A lakes veteran named Dick Kraft had stripped a roadster all the way down to bare frame rails, calling it "The Bug," and a lot of other people would be thinking along the same lines, that less was more.[8]

Certainly, creating a "rail job" to gain an edge was much cheaper than investing in a full-house engine with such expensive refinements as a stroked crankshaft (i.e., reground with a longer stroke). At that time it seems unlikely that anyone had ever spent as much as a thousand dollars on a vehicle intended solely for the drag strip. The ease with which one could jump right into the thick of things contributed to an initial surge of participation. Several other California strips had opened by 1951, including one near Monterey Bay, at the Municipal Airport in Salinas, and another at New Jerusalem, near Tracy. On Armistice Day, 1951, a strip opened north of Stockton which was known as Kingdon and was managed by Bob Cress, a Stockton policeman. Yet another of the first strips was located in Saugus, just beyond the northern rim of the San Fernando Valley. It was run by Lou Baney (née Aloysius James Benedetto), a thirty-year-old confrère of the Edelbrock-Iskenderian circle.

Baney was an operator, a man whose organizational skills and entrepreneurial flair would make him a major presence in drag racing for many years. He had headed the Russetta Timing Association, a rival to SCTA. He had raced track roadsters on local ovals such as Carrell Speedway against men like Jack McGrath and Manuel Ayulo, who went on to the big-time on the "champ car" circuit that included the Indy 500. He had even tried to make a deal with the manager of the Santa Ana airport for staging drag races there but lost out when his partner got cold feet. After Hart's venture caught on Baney talked with Lou Senter, in whose shop he did engine work, about launching a rival strip. With five hundred dollars borrowed from Senter's brother and another five hundred dollars from Baney's dad, the two of them incorporated as Sports Events, Inc., and scheduled Sunday races at a place called Six-S Ranch Air Park. "The strip was short and a little too narrow," Baney recalled, "but it was better than nothing."[9]

Senter was it silent partner; Baney ran the show. Because he would have had to pay taxes on a dollar admission, he made it a penny less and "didn't have to get involved with the government." He advertised by posting bills around the San Fernando Valley, and Saugus sometimes drew fifteen hundred people, but the average Sunday turnout was only in three figures. C. J. did better than that, even though people in the San Fernando and San Gabriel valleys thought of Santa Ana as a long way to go. Orange County itself had a total population of only 220,000. Where a vast urban village of two million would sprawl by the 1980s, there was then mostly mile after mile of orange groves.[10]

Needless to say, the drags were decidedly small-time. Santa Ana and Saugus usually had about two hundred cars in competition on any given Sunday, the majority nominally stock but with a few dozen that had been

Enthusiasm has been one of drag racing's primary engines of change.

modified, most of which looked pretty rough-hewn. Each strip had a system of classes, with stockers the slowest and fuel-burning roadsters the fastest. There were time trials before noon and elimination rounds after the lunch break, with trophies for class winners. At Santa Ana there was no prize money per se, although a winner who preferred cash could sell his trophy back to C. J. for its wholesale cost, $7. Baney offered a $25 war bond for the racer who could best the entire field, or $18.75 cash, which is what a bond cost. Occasionally, he would offer a $100 bond, or $75 cash. The racers always took the cash. "I don't think we ever actually gave away a war bond," Baney remarked.[11]

Later, in the mid-1950s, Baney campaigned a Cadillac-powered dragster that ran speeds in the 150s and won some big events. Then he got deeply involved in the automobile business with Bob Yeakel, a classmate from Manual Arts High School, and he was away from the racing scene for several years. When he returned in the 1960s, he recalled, "the cars were going a whole lot faster," and a lot of other things had changed as well: "I almost didn't recognize it."[12] Drag racing had become a spectator sport; there were thousands of people in the grandstands. And often as not there would be a thousand dollars posted for the day's "top eliminator." . . . [H]owever, the shock would have been mild compared to what it would have been for someone who was absent for an extended period and then attended an event that was part of NHRA's Winston Championship Series.

Forty years from its beginnings at Santa Ana and Saugus, Salinas and New Jerusalem, the drags would be transformed into a lavish spectacle with full-blown television coverage, plush suites for sponsors, and multimillion-dollar gates at a nationwide series of four- and five-day events. It would have produced a stunning theater of machines, quite as ingenious in sum as any technology ever contrived in isolation from government patronage. Drag racing would have superstars, prophets, and a genius or two, with a few old-timers still on the scene as sages—Pappy Hart, Bob Cress, and Lou Baney among them. Fran Hernandez would have gone on to a big-time career at the Ford Motor Company. Vic Edelbrock, Jr., and Ed Iskenderian's sons would be running large-scale facilities for producing parts for the so-called automotive aftermarket.

Wally Parks first sat down to recount drag racing's history in the 1960s, and it has been related several times since, mostly as a tale of ever better performances (both technologically and theatrically), ever bigger rewards, larger gates, higher levels of "professionalization," a tale of incredible growth. To read *National Dragster* week after week, year after year, is to bathe in a saga of unilinear progress. This is a compelling saga but probably not a great deal different from that of many other activities that became something much more than anyone had anticipated at the outset, including many sporting activities. People like Hart, and like Parks, who founded the National Hot Rod Association in 1951 as a "semi-social car club" and then built it into a position of drag racing dominance that approached absolute, may be forgiven a tendency to muse about never having dreamed "it would get as big as it did." Yet a mere chronicle of growth is less meaningful, and much less interesting, than an analysis of differing concepts of purpose.

We know that there is no intrinsic logic to technological change, that it lacks imperatives of its own, although certainly not its own power. We know that technology is affected by "the politics of design." This provides an extremely valuable conceptual tool, but assigning agency to contests over power is an exercise that readily slips over into economic determinism. As a matter of perspective, we need to keep in mind an observation of Eugene Ferguson's from which I have already quoted a phrase: "To plumb the murky depths of human motivation with measuring rods precisely calibrated in economic terms is to miss the strong romantic and emotional strain in the narrative."[13] Along with everything else, drag racing has always had its romantic and emotional strain. Ferguson has also written that, "if we fail to note the importance of enthusiasm that is evoked by technology, we will have missed a central motivating influence in technological development."[14] Enthusiasm has been one of drag racing's primary engines of change.

Notes

1. On the business firms mentioned, see Les Nehamkin, "The Story of Fuel Injection," *Honk!* Oct. 1953, 18–22; Karen Scott, "Meet the Manufacturer [Hilborn]," *Drag News*, May 10, 1969, 8; "Meet the Manufacturer [Edelbrock]," ibid., Apr. 6, 1968, 16; Dave Wallace, Jr., "Jack Engle Walks Softly, Carries a Big Bumpstick," ibid., Nov. 22, 1975, 16–17; Ed Iskenderian interview, Feb. 6, 1989, DROHA, NMAH; "Interview: Ed Iskenderian, Mickey Thompson, Ray Lavely Discuss Rodding," *Cars*, Dec. 1964, 58–61ff; "Iskenderian Racing Cams," *Drag News*, Mar. 3, 1964, 24–25; Karen Scott, "Meet the Manufacturer [Iskenderian]," ibid., Apr. 12, 1969, 8; Charles Hillinger, "Self-Made Million-aire [Iskenderianl Can't Resist a Bargain," *Los Angeles Times*, July 7, 1971, pt. 2, 1, 3; and "California's Big Wheels [Baney and Edelbrock]," *Best Hot Rods* 1 (1952): 30–33.

2. A brief account of the day's events appeared in Dan Roulston's "Hot Rod Story," 2:22–23. Mike Doherty, editor of *Drag Racing*, gave it the title and published an embellished version in his April 1969 issue (42–45). It stirred so much response that he printed it again in July 1970, and in October 1973 he told another tale, "The First Top Eliminator," which added embroidery. "The Day Drag Racing Began" also appeared a few years later in *Drag News*.

3. Dave Wallace, Jr., "C.J. Pappy Hart," in *Petersen's History of Drag Racing*, ed. Dave Wallace, Jr. (Los Angeles: Petersen Publishing Co. [PPC1, 1981), 20–21; see also Wallace, "The First Dragstrip," ibid., 4–11. In the Wallace Family Archives in Mokelumne Hill, California, there is a file pertinent to Hart's career which includes clippings, correspondence, and a fragment of a family biography begun by Peggy Hart before her death in 1980.

4. H. F. Moorhouse, "The 'Work' Ethic and 'Leisure' Activity: The Hot Rod in Post-War America," in *The Historical Meaning of Work*, ed. Patrick Joyce (Cambridge: Cambridge University Press, 1987), 243.

5. Gene Balsley, "The Hot Rod Culture," *American Quarterly* 2 (Winter 1950): 353.

6. One needs to keep this in mind when considering that long afterward, with sanctioned drag strips from coast to coast, there was still a thriving street racing subculture around most big cities. For suggestive material on the persis-tence of street racing in the Los Angeles area in the 1960s, see Rob Ross, "The Subterranean World of Los Angeles Street Racing," *UCLA Daily Bruin*, Dec. 15, 1965, 7, 10; and "Big Willie . . . King of the Street," *Drag Racing*, Dec. 1968, 42–47.

7. Wallace, "First Dragstrip," 5.

8. On the early days at Santa Ana, see: "Santa Ana: A History of Drag Racing, 1950–1959," *Drag News*, Mar. 28, 1959, 8–9ff; "Meet the Manufacturer: Chet

Herbert Cams," ibid., Apr. 16, 1960; Dick Day, "Our Point of View," *Car Craft*, Oct. 1966, 10; W. A. Huggins, "Hot Shots for Safety," *Best Hot Rods* 1 (1952): 62–63ff; Don Montgomery, "Drag It Out," *Street Rodder*, Feb. 1987, 78–83; *Hot Rods as They Were* (Fallbrook, Calif.: Author, 1989), 146–57; Wally Parks, Editor's Column, *Hot Rod*, June 1959, 3. In July and August 1965 *Drag Sport* ran a series titled "Santa Ana Relived," which included photos from the collection of Don Tuttle, who had been the Santa Ana announcer. In the archival holdings of the National Hot Rod Association in Glendora, California, there is a typescript history, apparently derived from the same source as the *Drag Sport* series, which discusses a nearby military field at which racing had previously been permitted for a short time.

9. "Yeakel 426 Club, or Lou Baney Rides Again," *Drag News*, July 6, 1963, 12. Ostensibly an interview by *DN*'s Al Caldwell, this is actually a lengthy (and extremely informative) monologue by Baney.

10. See Rob Kling, Spencer Olin, and Mark Poster, eds., *Postsuburban California: The Transformation of Orange County since World War II* (Berkeley: University of California Press, 1991); see also Greg Klerkx, "Drag Strips to Runways: JWA's Seen It All," *Orange Coast Daily Pilot*, Jan. 29, 1989, A1–2.

11. Lou Baney, "Drag Racing: Bean Fields to Big Bucks," *Hot Rod*, Jan. 1973, 132; see also Louis Kimzey, "Saugus Drags," *Hop Up*, Oct. 1951, 12–15.

12. Baney, "Drag Racing," 132. Yeakel, who later ran for mayor of Los Angeles and still later died when his plane crashed on an L.A. freeway, had made local news in 1947 when he mounted a "jet engine" (it may actually have been some kind of rocket) on a '36 Ford chassis and tested it at Rosamond, a dry lake near Muroc (Los Angeles *Daily News*, Jan. 4, 1947, qtd. in Spencer Murray, "The First Jet Car," *Rod and Custom*, June 1953, 18–21ff).

13. Eugene S. Ferguson, "The American-ness of American Technology," *Technology and Culture* 20 (Jan. 1979): 3.

14. Ferguson, "Toward a Discipline of the History of Technology," 21.

The Drag Racing Rage

Hot-rodders' numbers grow but road to respectability is a rough one

Anonymous

※

Life Magazine, April 1957

Drag racing started as a postwar teen-age infatuation with souped-up cars in which speed-crazy kids raced surreptitiously at 80 or 90 mph over lonely roads, scaring ordinary drivers to death. Now in many places in the U.S. it has come out into the open as a respectable—and controlled—sport. An event like that shown below is no longer uncommon—a drag meet at Santa Ana, Calif. where 3,000 spectators and 328 contestants turned out for races held with the blessing of the local police.

Official drag races—the name apparently stems from the need to "drag" or stay in low gears as long as possible—are held on quarter-mile strips in cars that are often a conglomerate of old chassis, high-powered engines and multiple carburetors. Today there are two national hot-rod organizations, the National Hot Rod Association and the Automobile Timing Association of America, and 130 legal strips in 40 states. Last year some 2.5 million spectators swarmed to the strips to watch the nation's 100,000 hot rods in races that usually last little more than 10 seconds each.

But as the sport grows, so does the controversy over it. Safety groups and some police officials feel that the glorification of speed on the strips infects the teen-agers with a fatal spirit of derring-do on the highways. The young drivers are finding the road to respectability a rough one.

Acceleration in Legal Meets

The first drag races were pickup affairs on city streets, which often started at stop lights and lasted to the next light or the wail of a siren. The key to victory was fast pickup and today, on the strips, the race is still a straight-away acceleration test. It is really won in the first 500 feet by the driver who can lay on maximum power without causing his rear wheels to spin or the rear end to "fishtail," that is, swing back and forth. The driver must also shift gears skillfully to keep constant acceleration. . . .

Cars race in classes based on weight, fuel, cylinder displacement and body styling. Since weight is crucial, many hot-rodders have eliminated "superfluous gadgets." In a race they are waved off in pairs from a standing start for a quarter-mile whoosh to the finish line. Over that distance most of the better hot rods will break 100 mph—the record is 166.97. Winners race against each other in elimination heats until the fastest of the day rolls off with the big trophy. N.H.R.A. and A.T.A.A. handed out nearly 17,000 trophies last year. Then the boys tow or truck the cars home since most hot rods are built only for racing, not transportation.

Surreptitious Races in the Center of the City

Illegal drag racing, the bane both of police and of reputable hot-rodders concerned for the good name of dragging, is prevalent in places like New Orleans which have no legal racing strips. But even in the Los Angeles area, which has six strips, sometimes hot-rodders race illegally at night, when the strips are closed. One of their favorite nighttime courses is the bed of the Los Angeles River. Except in flood times, the river is confined to a narrow strip in the middle of the bed, leaving high and dry a wide, flat pavement that is ideal for drag races. "Dragging there is great till the fuzz arrives," says a hot-rodder, in language explained [below]. "Then the badge bandits break things up and everybody bugs out."

Clubs and Hangouts for Hot-Rodders

No serious-minded hot-rodder can get along without belonging to a club whose name he wears emblazoned on shirt, overalls or jacket. Some clubs pour all their money into one car which they race together. Others are made up of individual owners.

The primary activity of the country's 15,000 clubs is the repair and improvement of cars. Hot-rodders, who never consider a car finished, put a couple of years' labor and from $500 to $8,000 into a prizewinning car.

[The] second most important club activity is public relations. They have to work on civic projects to gain support from groups who can help finance strips, and to placate police and motorists who sometimes blame hot-rod clubs for teen-age recklessness. They also set up a disciplinary system that forces members to drive carefully and avoid bad publicity.

Rising Arguments on National Scale

Until recently the controversy over drag racing has been at a local level. Some police departments made peace with hot-rod clubs, found them strips and got along fine with the hot-rodders and their racing. Other cities have had nothing to do with either. But in September of last year

the International Association of Police Chiefs raised the controversy to a national level. At a convention in Chicago the chiefs condemned hot-rod club speed competition which, they felt, inspired participants and spectators to drive recklessly on the highways. Then the National Safety Council also came out against drag racing. Recently, Socony-Vacuum and Mobilgas, which had supported a hot-rod safety tour, bowed out and left hot-rodders to shift for themselves.

Drag supporters like N.H.R.A. President Wally Parks argues that police who have been in contact with sanctioned drag racing longest are usually its strongest supporters. One of these is Ralph Parker, police chief at Pomona, Calif. He has stated that although Pomona has grown more than a third since it opened its drag strip in 1950, the accident rate for the under-20 group there has decreased 6%. In all California it has gone up 45%. To this authorities like Bernard R. Caldwell, commissioner of the California Highway Patrol, reply that California, Holy Land of dragging, also led the nation last year in highway deaths and injuries.

In spite of the attacks hot-rod clubs continue to gain 1,500 new members a month, and Americans, who seem destined to hear a lot more about dragging, may as well learn to dig drag jargon (*below*).

A Dictionary of Drag Racing Jargon

A-bomb	Modified Model A Ford
Batch out	Take off from dead stop
Badge bandits	Cops
Beast	Exceptionally fast car
Bug out	Get out fast
Choose off	Challenge somebody to drag
Chopped top	Hot-rod with roof lowered
Dragster	Car built only for dragging
Fuzz	See badge bandits
Goodies	Hot-rod accessories
Gutted	Car with interior stripped
Nerf	To push another car
Pot out	Engine failure
Prune	Beat another car
Rails	Hot-rod frame
Rake	Forward list to a car
Squirrel	Dangerous, careless driver
T-bone	Model T Ford
Top eliminator	Best car at a meet
Twin pot	Dual carburetor

Drive-Ins, Dry Lakes, and Drag Racing

We did it all, and we'll never see times like these again

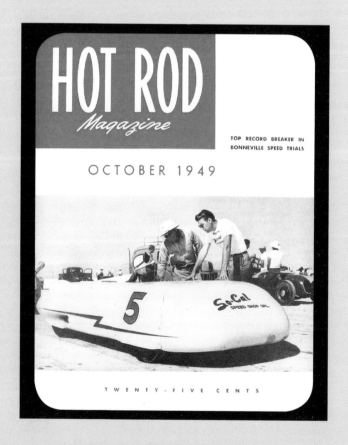

HOT ROD
Magazine

TOP RECORD BREAKER IN
BONNEVILLE SPEED TRIALS

OCTOBER 1949

So-Cal
SPEED SHOP SPL.

5

T W E N T Y - F I V E   C E N T S

By Dean Batchelor

The American Hot Rod, 1995

May 7, 1950. The last thing I remember on that Sunday afternoon at El Mirage dry lake was starting my return record run in the So-Cal streamliner. We (Alex Xydias and I) were running a Ford V-8 60 for power, and I had qualified for a record run the day before by clocking 152.28 mph.

I don't know how fast I was running on this return run, but inasmuch as the existing record, which I had set the previous July, was 138.74, I was trying to do about 140. We were trying to move the record up about 2 mph at each successive lakes meet so we could gain enough points to win the season championship. Having already turned a 152, I thought this would be an easy way to get the needed points.

Unfortunately, when we turned the car around at the east end of the course to start back on the second leg of the record run, a cross-wind had come up and was blowing from my left at about 45 degrees to my path of travel. Because the streamliner was so light (a little more than 1,300 lbs. with driver, fuel, and water) with about 65 percent of the weight on the rear wheels, it wasn't stable in a cross-wind.

I got a good start from the push car, and the little "60" was pulling well, but I had a premonition that something was wrong. I didn't know what, but it bothered me, and I considered aborting the run. I should have paid attention to my premonition.

I was correcting for the quartering wind by steering a bit to the left. Suddenly the wind let off and the car took a dive to the left. In spite of my frantic steering correction to the right, it was too late and the car went completely sideways, skating up the lakebed full broadside to the course until the right wheels dug in, and the car did a complete barrel roll in the middle of the time traps.

I am only here to write about this because the car landed on its wheels. We had a good safety belt and an onboard fire extinguisher, but that was it for the safety equipment. We had no roll bar. If the car had landed on its top instead of its wheels, my head would have been ground off to my shoulders.

Further, we had no floorboards, relying on the streamlined body's bellypan to serve that purpose. When the car went over, the riveted-on pan came off like a tossed frisbee. By losing the bellypan/floorboards, my feet could have fallen through that gaping hole when the car came down and I could have lost both legs.

Additionally, our throttle control was a device used with outboard motors for trolling: When you squeezed it you could move it, but letting go of it locked it in place. When the car went over and the wheels were in the air, rpm picked up from 6,200 to more than 8,000 and it came down running wide open and headed for the crowd at the finish line.

Several things happened at that point, none of which I had control over as I had been knocked unconscious when my head hit the steering wheel, gashing my forehead above my right eye.

The impact with the ground broke the front engine mounts, which dropped the front of the engine about two inches, shearing the Kong ignition from the front of the engine when it hit a piece of angle iron which supported the tach drive. The engine quit running at that point, thus stopping the car.

The next thing I remember is regaining consciousness in Jack Purdy's ambulance which was going flat out down Cajon Pass toward San Bernardino. Purdy had guaranteed the SCTA that he would transport injured parties from El Mirage to St. Bernadine's Hospital in San Bernardino in forty-five minutes. It was about fifty-seven miles, as I recall, with the first few miles being a washboard dirt road from the lakebed to the paved road. I'm glad I was unconscious for most of the trip.

My first thought on coming to was where am I, followed by what am I doing here? The ambulance attendant explained that I had been in an accident, and they were taking me to the hospital. Then I thought, oh shit, the car is damaged, and we won't be able to run at the next meet. It's strange how one's priorities rearrange themselves in situations like this.

I should have been thinking about my eyesight (it all worked out, but there was a serious question for awhile about how much of it I would regain), and here I was worrying about running the car again.

As it turned out, I never drove the car again—by choice. Alex had a friend, Bill Dailey, who wanted to drive the car, and I had a friend, Ray Charbonneau, who also wanted to drive. We arranged to have them take turns, which worked out okay, but kept both out of the 200 MPH Club when it was formed two years later. While both had driven the 'liner over the 200 mph mark several times, neither had made a two-way run at that speed to qualify for club membership.

A few weeks after my accident, we took the car apart in Alex's Speed Shop and found that both front spindles were broken, and the front axle was split from the right kingpin inward about eighteen inches. The rear axles had each made a full 360-degree twist before shearing the axle keys. All these pieces were replaced, magnafluxed, and installed as before, retaining the ball-bearing races for wheel hubs, carrier and pinion bearings. The frame, a pair of Model T Ford rails, came through unscathed, and Valley Custom, in Burbank, which had built the body, repaired the body damage.

Looking back on all of this I wonder how I could have been so smart and so dumb at the same time; smart, because I was instrumental in creating a car that was about 30 mph faster than anything in its class (and actually faster than any car on the dry lakes or at Bonneville—making it the fastest car in America at the time), and dumb, not to build more safety features into the car.

The SCTA technical committee, in its infinite wisdom, passed a rule that prohibited lock-on throttle controls, but didn't pass a rule requiring separate floorboards in addition to the underbody panel. Had they done this in 1950 (it was made a requirement later) it would probably have saved Fred Carrillo's foot at Bonneville in 1953 when the fiberglass body of his streamliner disintegrated during his accident there. Unfortunately, I think I was on the technical committee at the time so I can't blame someone else for the oversight.

Heartache
on the Lake

By Ken Gross

The Rodder's Journal, Winter 2002

El Mirage Dry Lake, Sunday, May 22, 1949

It's early in the morning at El Mirage, about 125 miles north of Los Angeles, at the edge of the Mojave Desert. The high desert morning fog is lifting; it's windy and getting hot. There's a persistent cloud of overhanging dust from previous hot rods making high speed runs.

Twenty-one-year old Rulon O. McGregor, a new member of the SCTA Road Runners hot rod club, hunkers down in his Class "C" lakester, ready for a return run across El Mirage. His car is powered by a lusty 276-cid '42 Mercury flathead. Well-equipped for the era with top-line speed equipment, his engine sports Evans heads, an Edelbrock manifold, a Clay Smith cam and Potvin ignition. Starting his return run, he's moving much too quickly as he accelerates down the course. Perhaps he wanted to retest something? Whatever the case, instead of a leisurely return, he's going surprisingly fast.

Crouching low behind the steering wheel, McGregor deliberately keeps his head down to minimize wind resistance. He tries to watch his tach while he simultaneously peers over the T's cowl to sight down the course ahead. His wide-open full-race flathead, thundering through straight pipes, sounds even louder as the bellow from its open headers echoes across the flats. McGregor nails the throttle; overcoming some wheel spin as his tires scrabble for grip on the hard alkali-laced lakebed surface. Quickly gathering speed, he roars ahead. His mouth is swept open in a wind-induced grin.

He will be dead in less than 20 seconds.

On the other side of the course, almost perpendicular to Rulon McGregor, and driving a '40 Ford business coupe as a patrol car, Gents car club member Robert Fadave, 22, has stopped to pick up his two friends, Jackson R. Pendleton, 21, and John Cuthbert, 18. Glancing quickly across the vast lakebed, he fails to see that McGregor has begun his return. Rulon's lowslung lakester is partially obscured by a combination of wind, lake dust and morning fog. Up ahead, Fadave doesn't see or hear the fast-moving McGregor accelerating back toward the starting line. He decides to take a fatal short cut, angling right across the race course.

Rulon McGregor, whose peripheral vision is limited by his concentration, doesn't see the '40 Ford coupe until a split second before they collide with a horrendous crash. The still-accelerating lakester T-bones the coupe squarely in the drivers' side, bounces off the '40 into the air, hangs for a moment, rolls over, sheds its flimsy body shell and comes to rest on its wire wheels. The hard-hit coupe flips, rolls, slides a few feet, and comes to rest on its side with nearly every panel damaged. The horrific force of the sudden impact kills Rulon McGregor and coupe passenger Jackson Pendleton immediately. Mortally injured, coupe driver Robert Fadave succumbs from his injuries in the ambulance en route to San Bernardino hospital, 57 miles away through the Cajon Pass. Fadave's other passenger, John Cuthbert, was first taken to that hospital, then transferred to Queen of Angels Hospital. Whether he survived is unknown.

After the sickening crunch of the crash, many spectators and racers, at first stunned, immediately run toward the scene of the accident. The lakebed erupts with shouts, screams, and a siren as a big Buick ambulance, on call for just this type of occurrence, roars over and parks alongside the two horribly wrecked cars. It's a scene of carnage with car parts and bodies strewn about. Realizing that two men are still barely alive, rescue workers extricate them and place them into the ambulance for the long run to the hospital. A few spectators pull out cameras and begin taking pictures. Bell Timing Association officials and others try to wrest the cameras away and destroy the film.

El Mirage was shared during May 1949 by the SCTA, RTA, and the Bell and Mojave Timing associations. *Hot Rod* magazine carried dry lakes racing schedules so we know the smaller Bell Timing Association was the sanctioning body on that fateful day. Hot rodding was still something of an outlaw sport in 1949, and no group wanted the bad publicity a tragic incident like this would generate. It could have meant an end to dry lakes racing.

Lynn Yakel, a frequent Russetta Timing Association competitor in the '50s, and the owner of one of the coolest chopped and channeled '32 five-windows ever, actually saw the accident happen. "I was driving onto the lake with Frank Leonard and Connie Weidell in a '36 Ford coupe," he told me. "The race car was coming back right next to the course and this '40 coupe was cutting across. We all looked over and somebody said, 'What's that asshole doing?' There was a crash and a huge pile of dust. A few seconds later, a wheel came rolling out of the dust cloud.

"People were trying to take pictures," Yakel recalled. "I saw a few cameras smashed. They didn't want pictures of that stuff happening. A lot of time was spent cleaning things up. Then," he said laconically, "after a few hours, they resumed racing."

Richard "Dick" Saillant was also a spectator that day. He snapped a few photographs of the carnage, then tried to aid the victims. Remembering back 50 years, he recalls, " . . . it was already hotter than hell." He also wondered " . . . how could this happen . . . why was the coupe cutting across the course?" He remembers that the area " . . . wasn't definitely designated. They lacked monitoring equipment," he says. "I didn't know any of those guys, but like nearly everyone else, I ran to the scene immediately after it (the accident) occurred."

Trying hard to remember an event that happened 52 years ago, Lee Hammock, another eyewitness from Santa Barbara, told me, "As near as I can recall, the coupe was angling across the course. The race car hit it on the driver's side. The guy in the coupe had stopped to pick up two friends. Cars could drive alongside the course in those days.

"I was sitting near the ambulance," Hammock recalls, "and I remember thinking, they're gonna hit! (After the accident) I was one of the first people there. It was three-quarters of the way down the track. I had my camera because I just loved taking pictures. It was just an impulse. After I took a few pictures, I threw the camera back in the car and tried to help. But there wasn't much anyone could do. When I got to the scene, one of those guys was lying on the ground, obviously alive, but screaming in pain. As far as the guys inside the lakester and the coupe, there was no question.

"I wasn't proud of the fact that I took these pictures; I even took them out of my album," Hammock says today. "A guy I knew worked for the newspapers. I told him about the accident. He said he'd develop the film fast. In those days it usually took about a week. Then I saw what I thought was my picture in the *L.A. Times* or the *Examiner*, but it could have been someone else taking pictures from the same angle. That really upset me." Lee confirms that after a few people took pictures of the wreck, photography was discouraged by the authorities and concerned spectators.

Bill Burke, the first hot rodder to build a belly tank, remembers the tragic scene all too well. "I built that lime 'T' for Rulon," he says sadly. "It was a '23 or '24, with a 'T' grille. It had a Model 'T' frame and wire wheels. The engine was a modified flathead. He was returning to the start when the guy in the coupe cut across in front of him. Rulon was moving pretty strong. He was well down the course when it happened. Accidents took place, but ones like that were rare. In the early days," Burke continued, "they didn't have the restrictions they did later. People would drive all over the course."

On the following Monday, May 23, 1949, the *L.A. Times* quoted Deputy San Bernardino County Coroner Edward P. Doyle, who said that the information given to him was that the two cars were traveling between 60 and 90 miles per hour when they hit. The front page headline reads; "Crash of Hot-Rod (sic) Racers Kills Three, Injures One." (Not surprisingly, no mention of the fatal wreck occurred in subsequent SCTA or RTA publications or, for that matter, in *Hot Rod*.)

"Accidents took place, but ones like that were rare. In the early days, they didn't have the restrictions they did later."

Back in Los Angeles, after his son's funeral, Rulon McGregor's father, Orel T. McGregor, is understandably distraught. Following the service, he and his wife make a curious decision. Young Rulon McGregor also owned a custom '39 Mercury convertible. It was mildly dechromed and fitted with a genuine Glen Hauser chopped padded top from the famed Carson Top Shop at 4910 South Vermont Avenue in Los Angeles. The elder McGregor decides he will keep Rulon's Mercury indefinitely. He apparently can't bear to part with this last poignant reminder of his son and the young life that's been prematurely snuffed out. So McGregor stores his son's convertible in a rickety garage, alongside a '34 Auburn Salon coupe, and he never drives it. It's destined to remain there for thirty years. Periodically, people attempt to buy the low-mileage custom, but McGregor won't sell it.

In the early '80s, Jim Fuller of Santa Barbara talks with a man about custom cars. The fellow lives in Monterey Park. "That's where all the old custom cars were," Fuller says, "but they're all gone." His contact replies, "There's one left," and he tells Fuller about the McGregor car. Fuller pays $300 for a tip to learn where the chopped Mercury is located. Although he is able to see the car, Mr. and Mrs. McGregor remain adamantly opposed to selling it.

But Jim Fuller is persistent. "I hired a 'professional' to come with me," he recalls, "my friend, Robert Morris. We brought all the money in a paper sack. Robert handed Mrs. McGregor the bag of money and told her to count it. The old man still didn't want to sell the car, but she told me, 'I've been signing things for him for years.' She gave Robert the pink slip and we took the car."

When found, the Mercury had a stock engine in it with dual exhausts. "It had a hopped-up motor," says Fuller, "but supposedly McGregor put that in a lakester." The original interior was stock maroon leather, worn and dried out from years of storage. The Carson top needed recovering and the paint was in rough shape.

Fuller contracted Fran Busey to recover the Carson top with the correct pebbled grain white fabric. Then he repainted the Mercury a similar shade of dark red. Fuller also installed the present engine, a Mercury with a four-inch crank, a Winfield SU-1A camshaft, twin carbs and high-compression heads. He kept the car for about fifteen years, using it very sparingly. "Every time I'd take it out," he says, "it would stop. The gas tank was filled with crud from sitting so long. We finally took it out and cleaned it."

Walter F. Larson, chairman of Larson International, Inc., Plainview, Texas, arranged to buy the Mercury from Jim Fuller. "I had heard about the car in the 1980s," said Larson. "I saw a picture of it. But Fuller wasn't ready to sell. Still, we kept in touch through the years."

Finally, Fuller agreed to sell the Mercury. "First, the price was too high." Walter Larson told me, "and then it got higher. But we made a deal in the fall of 1999, and I bought the car."

When the Mercury arrived in Texas, Larson quickly decided it was just not what he wanted. "I thought I was getting a show car," he explains. "Even with the car's interesting history, which I learned, I was disappointed." In the summer of 1999, Walter then placed an ad for the chopped Mercury in *Hemmings Motor News*.

When I read that ad in *Hemmings*, I was the Executive Director of the Petersen Automotive Museum in Los Angeles. I thought the Rulon McGregor Mercury would make a good exhibit car for the Museum. After all, it had been California owned and customized the right way for the period. It seemed to be in largely original shape except for the engine, top and paint freshening. We struck a deal with Walter Larson that September, and the Mercury became the property of Robert E. Petersen. It's now at the Petersen Automotive Museum. When it's not on display, it rests quietly in the Petersen's basement garage, better known as "the Vault," with many other great cars.

I didn't know all the details about Rulon McGregor and his death. Those came out after we purchased the car and I examined the materials that came with it, including copies of the grisly accident photos. I made up my mind that some day I'd find out more about him and try to piece together what happened. It's been quite a task, but with the help of many who are mentioned in this story, I think we know the sad tale now.

Rulon McGregor's old Mercury is a great example of a typical custom, before they started chopping big bulbous Mercs and spelling custom with a "K." Sitting inside, you can still see the small black Carson Top Shop plaque on the top header, just to the left of the windshield split. The Mercury's overall condition, while solid, reflects its age, so the car still looks very much the way Rulon McGregor built it. It sits on a dropped axle in front and it's been lowered slightly in back. Some chrome has been removed and the holes are filled. The interior is finished nicely in period-style matching red and white tuck and roll. The engine, as previously noted, is mildly modified. It's likely that McGregor had more plans for the car. We'll never know.

Just who was Rulon McGregor? One thing is certain: 52 years after his death, he's still elusive. He was very active as a Lakes racer in the months just before he was killed. His name (misspelled as "Rulan") appears in results we've found from a September 12, 1948, Russetta meet at El Mirage. Driving for the Stockholders Car Club in a "E" roadster, at that meet he clocked a mid-pack 118.57 mph, beating such notables as Phil Weiand by nearly 2 mph. Dean Moon (of the Hutters Club and later the founder of Moon Equipment) ran 125.00 mph that day. Doug Hartelt, a member of the high-flying Lancers of Los Angeles, had the top time in the class with a 137.19 mph run.

We know Rulon McGregor ran again at a Russetta Timing Association meet on November 7, 1948, turning 114.35 in the "C" roadster (250–300-cid) class. Top class speed in that meet was Drifter Club member Bob Riese's roadster with a 138.88 mph run.

In January 1949, McGregor is pictured (although this time his name is spelled "Rulor") at the National Guard Armory in Los Angeles at the Second Annual SCTA-sponsored ten-day-long Hot Rod Exposition. If you look in *Hot Rod* for March 1949, on page 10 you'll see photos of several Road Runners Club members assembling one of two giveaway '32 roadsters. A pair of lucky ticket holders that year each got to take home a completed deuce as the ultimate door prize. That ensured great attendance on the last day of the ten-day show.

In the *HRM* photograph, three Road Runners members—Rulon McGregor, Bill Burke, and Harvey Haller—are working on the giveaway car. Their names are printed on a sign adjacent to the '32 on the stage. The roadster is equipped with Kinmont disc brakes, a converted Kurten or Spaulding Lincoln Zephyr distributor, high compression heads and a trick dual manifold. Selected teams of hot rodders would build a well-detailed car like this right on stage and it would be given away at the end of the event. This particular deuce was known as the "Burple" roadster, reflecting the unusual paint color developed by Bill Burke, who's also credited with building the first belly tank. That roadster was won by a Long Beach lady, Mrs. F. C. Bailey. Wonder where it is now? (Harvey Haller was also killed in a Lakes accident.)

Bill Burke remembers, "Rulon was a nice young fella, really delightful. He had a lady friend and I think they were planning to get married. I was in charge of building the show roadster so I used him in my crew. We'd worked together at a steel company." I wondered if McGregor was a good mechanic? "He was quite handy," Burke replied.

McGregor's name also appears on the official SCTA entry list for the May 7–8, 1949, speed trials at El Mirage. He was getting quicker, with a top time on Saturday of 134.32 mph in car number 121, listed as a T lakester, in that meet. For 1949, rods based on Model Ts were redesignated as Lakesters by the SCTA, not roadsters, because they were considered smaller and more aerodynamic by the owners of bigger, bulkier '29s and '32s. According to *HRM*, Marvin Lee's Wayne Chevy-powered streamliner had the overall top speed at that meet with a 156.79 one-way run. Gusty winds and a "loose course" reportedly forced a cancellation of that Sunday's racing.

McGregor had just two weeks more to live. It's likely he wanted more racing experience, so he elected to try again in a Bell Timing Association sanctioned event. It may not have been as well-organized as the SCTA or Russetta groups. Old-timers have said that guys were frequently making fast blasts out in the desert, alongside the course, to tune up their cars or test something new before actually racing. In those early days, dry lakes discipline was undoubtedly a bit lax. So accidents could happen and they did so with depressing regularity.

As a postscript to all this, I searched for some mention of Rulon McGregor's tragic accident in magazines and dry lakes meet programs, but found nothing. But in *Hot Rod* magazine for July 1949, there's an article by Charles Camp about the Russetta Timing Association meet at El Mirage that took place on May 29, 1949, just a week after McGregor and the others were killed. Apparently it was very windy that weekend, the course was "loose" and " . . . roadster drivers said they were suffering slippage of up to 15 percent." Possibly similar rough conditions had existed the week before. Interestingly, Camp concluded his article saying, "Other items under consideration are the tightening of patrols and general meet organization." We can't help but wonder if that was a reaction to the McGregor crash.

By 1950, as the number of drag strips increased, lakes attendance began to fall off. Accidents were still prevalent. The dry lakes courses were becoming loose and rutted. As speeds increased, lakes racing became even more dangerous. Wind, dust, and poor conditions necessitated frequent cancellations. Bonneville, located some 450 miles farther northeast, had begun in the summer of 1949. The longer, wider salt flats were safer, and their relatively smooth surface permitted cars to go even faster. Bonneville soon became the preferred high-speed destination for hot rodders. Sadly, it all happened too late for young Rulon McGregor.

Those Early Years

By Tom Madigan

※

The Loner: Story of a Drag Racer, 1974

The era that was "early hot rodding" is gone forever, but its memory is the foundation on which the sport of drag racing is built.

It all started in California, long before the coughing, choking monster smog had raised its ugly head. Skies were blue, and the Chamber of Commerce promised this "holy land" to those who would leave the ice and snow of the east and midwest and, as Horace Greeley advised, "Go west, young man." Times were peaceful. World War II had been settled and, unfortunately, so had the west. So the pioneer instincts within young men of the times looked for new horizons to conquer.

All young men during the late forties and early fifties were fascinated by the automobile. It was not only transportation but the way to a girl's heart. It was a status symbol or, as we say today, the "in" thing. And, as more and more cars were being produced and the general populace had more money to spend, the automobile became even more interesting. The public became motorized.

The natural offspring of this fascination for cars was motor racing and it provided a focal point for the energy of young Americans. However something was different about the young members of this new breed of auto enthusiast.

The old structure of auto racing—dirt track, Indy, stock car, etc.—had restrictions. Age was one; the problem, "who do you know, not what do you know?" was another. If you didn't know someone in the business, or you didn't have a fat money belt to build the particular type of car needed, or if you weren't over the voting age (21 years old in those days)—you didn't race. With more and more under-twenty-one-year-old men driving, and the urge to compete growing stronger, the result was obvious.

Somewhere on a forgotten, lonely road, two cars stopped. The drivers looked at one another. A new phrase was struck: "Do you wanta drag?" Thus began the era of drag racing. At first drag racing was crude. There were no set distances; sometimes a half-mile, sometimes less. It really didn't matter. It was competition. Drag racing was easy too: just pull up to a stop sign or slow down to a crawl and then let 'er rip. Besides anyone could drag race—you didn't need a competition license or to be of a certain age. All you needed was a car, and the quiet sprawling roads of California provided all the space necessary to compete. Drag racing was born; progress and the availability of an automobile were its parents.

As is the case in any endeavor, survival depends on acceptance and growth. Where was drag racing going? It definitely would not get the slightest support from those who engaged in established professional racing endeavors, although many of these pros began as hot rodders. They were enjoying a postwar boom, the greatest revival ever to hit their segment of the sport. People had extra money and they were in the mood for entertainment. Drag racing faced the additional hindrance of being very popular in its "street" version, a practice that is against the law.

There were the dry lake racers, although some consider them second-cousins to drag racers. However a large portion of those who participated in dry lake events—the two most famous were El Mirage and Muroc, the former becoming Edwards Air Force Base in later years—also participated in the street-racing activities.

Most of the cars that ran the lakes in the early days were roadsters and were street driven. It was not uncommon to see magnificently restored '29 and '32 Ford roadsters on the streets during the early forties and fifties. So it would have been too much to assume that these cars would not be involved in the everyday form of stop-and-go racing. As natural as it was, it was nevertheless doomed. Law-enforcement personnel, as good-natured as they were, could no longer allow a pair of hopped-up roadsters to square off for a little "go" any time they had the urge. Drag racing had to have a place of its own.

Tony Nancy, now 41 years old, was one of the young advocates of both dry lake racing and this new sport of drag racing. As he begins his story, his eyes have a reminiscent depth to them, and a smile crosses his face.

Obviously I had no aspirations to become a fuel dragster driver as a child, for the simple reason that dragsters were an unknown commodity. They were still far in the future. Actually my interest in the automobile and, subsequently, things mechanical, began with models; airplane models to be exact. My parents were divorced when I was two years old. My mother, aunt, and grandmother moved to California to start a new life.

Because my mother worked to support us, there was little time to spend together, and my grandmother was the only full-time guardian I knew for a number of years. The only male guidance I received in my pre-teen years was from an uncle who would appear when a stern hand was needed, and in this calling he excelled! After the necessary steps had been taken to insure my obedience to the Golden Rule, he would slip back into his own world.

It could have been this lack of adult male companionship that triggered my need for self-reliance. Regardless of the facts, I spent a great many hours building models. I seemed to take particular pride in finishing each one, be it plane, boat, or car, and no matter how painstaking the task, each finished product had to be perfect down to the smallest detail. In this segment of my life my grandmother played an important part. She was a constant source of encouragement and always urged me to take pride in my work.

As time passed my interest grew in the direction of the automobile. This was the case for most young boys in those years, but money—or rather the lack of money—prevented most kids, including myself, from doing anything other than dreaming. So for the time being I stayed content with baseball, school, and building models. Still the desire to learn about the automobile was there.

Some time after the seeds of curiosity were planted, a neighbor, who was at least twelve to fourteen years my senior, invited me to tag along on a trip to the dry lakes. Now to a kid in those days who was fully engrossed by the automobile, the thought of going to see real racing cars in action was almost too much to comprehend.

The lakes were flat pieces of the California desert that probably abounded with sea life during prehistoric times. Two of the most famous, Muroc and El Mirage, were where most of the activity took place. Cars of all descriptions ran from a standing start for a mile or better.

My neighbor, Greg Fisher, participated in dry lake racing with a 1932 Ford highboy roadster. He probably asked me to go with him in an effort to ease my pestering as he worked on his car. He was interested both in cars and model building. It seemed that model building was much more popular then than it is today. Whenever I finished a project I would take it down to Greg and wait for his approval. Then on weekends I was down at his shop, behind his house, hounding him for facts about his car and breaking down his resistance to taking a kid to the dry lakes.

Well I must have been plenty persistent because one bright, sunny Saturday morning I found myself in the back of a pickup truck on my way to El Mirage. I didn't know quite what to expect. I had only seen pictures in magazines of stripped-down roadsters trekking across those old lake bottoms, with rooster tails of sand flying in the air. But now I was on my way to complete those pictures with sounds and feelings.

This was one of the most important days of my life. It could have been the reason the sun was a little warmer and the air a little sweeter. It was quite an experience. I was hoisted into the back of that old pickup with Greg's '32 roadster in tow behind. For a kid who had little in the way of fatherly companionship, the chance to partake in a real man's game added to the excitement.

El Mirage has long since been taken over by the Government's never-ending policy of growth for the good of man and was turned into an Air Force base, but back then it was just a dry lake bed that had been acquired (by virtue of "squatter's rights") by hot rodders and their dry lake organization, the Southern California Timing Association. The sand that once formed the bottom of a lake was now cracked and parched by the desert sun.

We arrived early, and the first sound that penetrated my ears was a harsh, rather rasping sound of unmuffled old flathead Ford engines. I had arrived; at least in my way of thinking, I had. It was Paradise for a car lover. The sandy pit area was filled with high boy roadsters of '29, '32 and '34 vintage. There were coupes and stripped-down cars of all descriptions. Some of the braver souls had converted aircraft wing fuel tanks into what were called "lakesters" or belly tankers. Others had chopped tops and channeled bodies. This was the practice for dry lake racing; to cut down the height of the top by cutting down the window post. Channeling was accomplished by setting the body lower onto the car's frame rails. In some cases custom body panels replaced original components. Regardless of the types the cars were all very fascinating to a boy there for the first time. I knew little of the men who drove these creations, but the men who would become the foundation of the sport of drag racing were there: Ak Miller, Robert E. "Pete" Petersen (who turned his race programs into the first drag racing-oriented enthusiasts' monthly, *Hot Rod* magazine), Wally Parks, Vic Edelbrock, Sr., Howard Johansen, Eddie Hulse, Tony Capana, Lou Baney,

Bill Burke, Don Francisco, Joaquin Arnette and Andy Ortega (better known as the "Bean Bandits"), Ed Iskenderian, Dean Batchelor, Paul Schiefer, and so many others that it would take a separate chapter to list them all! They pulled to a standing-start position in their "run what you brung" vehicles, then off they would go, accelerating for a full mile toward a timing device that would record the run. Speeds of over 145 mph were recorded. I just couldn't imagine a car going at such speeds. I was hooked; the automobile had entered my bloodstream, and there was no getting it out!

It was nearly four years before I could afford my first car. In the period of waiting I mowed lawns, washed windows, cleaned yards—all of the odd jobs possible for a kid to handle after school.

Finally the day came when I had enough to purchase my first car. I think that for a boy who is struggling to overcome the throes of adolescence, the act of buying that first car helps to bridge the gap between boy and man. Mine wasn't much of a car, just a stock 1929 Ford coupe, and I couldn't drive it because you had to be sixteen years old to get a license, and at the time I had just turned fifteen. But when you're young, and a car is the center of your life, it matters very little if the vehicle you possess is running or not or if you can drive or not. The whole meaning is that it's *yours*.

To pass the time while I was waiting for my sixteenth birthday, I decided to retire from the model-building business for a time and find out firsthand what made an automobile tick. Once disassembled there were constant trips to the public library to check out every tech manual available. Dyke's *Encyclopedia of Cars* was one of my favorites.

After months of trial and error I somehow managed to repair the broken pieces, rebuild the four-cylinder engine, grind the valves, obtain new bearings, and clean everything that could be cleaned. I repainted the car, and to go one step further, I stumbled through the first-ever Tony Nancy upholstery job. When the job was completed it wasn't the fastest car in town and it wasn't the most detailed, but it was all mine. I had accomplished what I considered a difficult job, and I had done it *by myself*. The peculiar feeling I experienced at having done it alone is one that has stayed with me from that point on. As my knowledge grew so did a need to accomplish more. Whenever the opportunity was right (and my funds were adequate), it was back to the lakes to watch. Then simply watching was not enough to turn back the flow of energy. I had to participate in the action. After running across a 1929 roadster body, my decision was not long in coming.

I discarded the coupe and mounted the roadster body on the waiting rails of my coupe. After mounting the body the old "four banger" was replaced by a stock flathead. As in the case of the first engine, all of the work was done in my spare time with no outside help. The hard work was worth it all because by my own hand, presto, I was transformed from a spectator to a participant!

Now I could run in a street roadster class at the lakes. Remembering back, there was a fellow by the name of Randy Shin, sort of the Don Garlits of that era. Randy was my idol. He had the fastest and cleanest roadster that you could ever imagine, and just to run with him as equal was a great honor for me. Unfortunately his speed of nearly 132 mph left my sub-100 mph runs with a lot to be desired. But still this was a wonderful period of my life. I was sixteen years old with my own car, something to work for, and very few worries . . . very few worries with the exception of the fact that I found myself withdrawing. I enjoyed doing things *my way*. This strong will of mine resulted in many disagreements that, in turn, resulted in bloody noses, cut lips, and a few hard feelings. Again the fact that I was without the hand of a father, and the pressure of being the man of the house no doubt played on my mind.

Suddenly my life was caught up in the wave of mass hysteria called World War II. Until this point in my life nothing was important to me except things that interested children, but as I made the transition from toys to cars, there was the war and its responsibilities staring me right in the face. A few more incidents due to a short temper and I found myself out of school and fighting in the final stages of the war on a Pacific island in the uniform of the Marine Corps. At age 16 the automobile would have to wait; the days of sunshine and flying sand were set aside for three years while a period of my life that I don't even like to talk about ran its course.

Art Was My Copilot

279.50 mph in 5.92 seconds!

By Ralph Guldahl Jr.

※

Hot Rod Magazine, December 1971

Time and time again *Hot Rod* publisher Dick Day drives it into our heads: "Get involved . . . get involved." Hmmm, how to get involved, I think to myself over a cup of hot coffee as the early-a.m. staff meeting gets under way. The answer came sooner than expected.

Dick sifted through a pile of papers on his desk, then briefly held up a letter for all to see. "As you may or may not know," he said, "Art Arfons has a new Cyclops Two jet car. It has a passenger seat, and he's offering a ride to a *Hot Rod* staff member. Anyone care to get involved?"

"Cyclops Two, huh?" queried Don Evans. "That's what bothers me. What ever happened to Cyclops One?" Silence reigned.

Somehow, suddenly, I was at York, Pennsylvania's U.S. 30 Dragway and the AHRA Summernationals, roaming the pits looking for the flash of green that would be Arfons' Super Cyclops Green Monster, and then maneuvering to break through the wall of fans ringing the Super Cyclops pit. I approached the former Land Speed Record holder. "I'm Ralph Guldahl from *Hot Rod*."

"So you're my man, huh?" replied Arfons. We talked of the old Allison-powered Green monster days, and somewhere along the line Art caught me directing a furtive glance or two at the awesome Cyclops. Partly in humor, but also to check, Art asked, "Still want to go?"

"Yep!"

Art, with a grin a mile wide, went on: "Ralph, you'll never believe this, but already I've had three or four guys pestering me to start a 'stand-by' passenger list because they know that guy from *Hot Rod* is gonna chicken out!"

For the last time Art shot me the question: "You still want to go?"

In the interchange, I remember saying something like, "Let's beat Tom Ivo's passenger record." Art calculated how much it'd take to edge the Arfons-Ivo 272-mph mark, "You know, we lose up to ten mph in this hot (91-degree) weather, so I'll have to drive it deeper into the lights than usual."

I nodded okay, even though I had heard that the effect of the top-end Gs was "like putting a vacuum cleaner in front of your mouth."

Now round one of top fuel and funny car is about wrapped up, and the last cacophony of sound plays echo bounce-tag off the hills. Super Cyclops is pulled to a ready position "for the ride of a lifetime." I spot an old friend, top fuel shoe Gary Cochran. So many times I've been there with notebook or camera when Gary straps into his digger. The positions are reversed now, and Gary's arm pointing and "Aha! Now it's your turn!" is a piece of good-natured fun. Ted Austin hands me a pair of clear goggles. These go on first, then the helmet. No flame suit, only a nylon jacket. Art wears a World War II Dennis Morgan Flying Tigers jacket right out of the movie "God Way My Co-Pilot." I've got one foot in the cockpit when Art yells, "Wait, wait! I forgot something. C'mon over to the truck." Art produces a paper from the glove box. "You don't mind signing this, do you?"

It reads: "I, the undersigned, do absolve Art Arfons of all liability, etc., etc." My pen makes wooden motions across the dotted line.

"By the way, I didn't ask you before . . . but are you married? Got any kids?"

I don't recall stepping into the cockpit, but Ted sees to the tight-tighter adjustment of lap and shoulder belts. The driver's "pod" is on the opposite side of the car, and a tall portion of J-79 engine effectively "walls out" driver-passenger communications; however, Art does have a side-view mirror affixed to the top of the engine. "The mirror's to glance at him (the rider) to make sure he's still there before I leave the line. About the time the engine 'lights up' a nervous partner might 'light out'!" explains Art.

Ted is in the pushtruck. He has plugged in the APU (auxiliary power unit), and as the engine begins to "windmill" at seven percent, my hearing picks up a faint stir of life inside the J-79. Art presses the ignition switch, then advances the throttle to the idle detent. The APU keeps on cranking until the engine gets to 25 percent. The familiar whine is compressor noise. We now have a "light," so Ted pulls the power cable. The engine continues to accelerate to 67 percent. (6000 Rs) Hey Art, now you've gone and done it—we're moving! Arfons' alternate pumping of the brakes up to 2000 pounds line pressure and the all-the time—increasing rpm causes a faintly unsettling side-to-side rocking sensation.

Where's my head now? Scared? No. The enormity of what is about to happen—the curiosity of what it'll be like—transcends everything else. None of those "ofergoodnessakes, what've I talked my way into now?"–type thoughts. The view down the strip is a clear and true perspective: the converging yellow lines, the timing lights, and a very close-looking Highway 30. I laugh inside at how bitchin' it is going to be to get there, way down there, by the short count of six. A motion by photog Jim Kelly for more peace signs readjusts my head back into the environment of the car, and what it is doing. We're staged. The engine is accelerating to 95 percent, the maximum that wheel brakes can hold. Art nods to the starter "for a 'Tree" and slips the J-79 into "burner fuel." This triggers a purging of all the lines and—from the crowd—a few oohs and aahs at the intensity of the burner smoke streaming out.

Instant green and Art hits the "hotstreak" button, lighting the fuel that's flowing in the burner pipe; in the same motion he's advanced the throttle and released the brakes. From the stands the sound of a lighting after-burner is boom! But sitting inches from the engine (and about amidships) I hear this horrendous hum. Ever ridden a streetcar? That electric motor sound when the driver/conductor gets on it . . . times fifty!

At launch, the Gs are punishing enough to force both eyelids shut, and will peel the corners of your mouth clear back to (it seems) your ear lobes. I recall flashing a self-assuring thought like "Pretty close to what I expected—Long Beach Pike Cyclone Racer (roller coaster) stuff." Get those eyes open, man! A very loud turbine whir is coming through the helmet now, and the pavement just ahead appears to be melting before our charge. The feeling of speed is pure, and is unencumbered by vibration. I see us move toward the yellow center line and think: Hey now, why this? Later Art told of walking the strip, finding a dip in the right side of the right lane, and just as planned, he is now steering around it! At about the eighth the green machine seems to gather itself up (the jet's really rammin' air into the intake at 200 mph) and just plain march. It pulls so hard I think I am going to be driven right through the seat back. I feel squeezed down to midget size. The track surface unexplainably rises up to eye level; peripherally, I see the traps explode by. We're at 3 Gs all the way until . . . Art triggers the twin Deist chutes . . . wham! There's this unbelievable wrench and my mind drops to the floorboards. Jim Deist says the deceleration is 9 Gs for just a split second. The chutes have dropped the car to 80 mph. Now Art is leaning heavy on the triple-spot Airheart brakes. The pavement is rolling by—slowly—like the scenes projected through a train window as it pulls into the station. We steer a graceful 45-degree onto the turn-off road. Suddenly Art Arfans' head and shoulder pop into view above the engine. "You all right?" he pipes. Residual tailpipe smoke blows back over us. Art hustles to get the chutes off the hot tailpipe. The aftermath is a feeling of exhilaration, not owing to the realization that you're still alive, but from the speed itself. I dig the car for what it has done for me (5.92 e.t., 279.50 mph). I don't want to get out of the cockpit; no way, man. I'll just sit here for a while and let my mind dwell on that fantastic six seconds worth of fast.

Wally Parks

By Dave Wallace

※

Petersen's History of Drag Racing, 1981

For all you can tell from the bleachers, the National Hot Rod Association pays this tall, distinguished-looking gentleman just to ride around in pace cars at all the big meets, waving and smiling to spectators who sometimes respond with shouted demands for Miss Golden Shifter. Later in the day he hangs around to help out with photos and trophies, pressing flesh, and posing with the winners after everyone else has gone home. Not a bad job, if a little boring.

Of course what the casual observer fails to realize from his seat in the stands (or in front of a television set) is the fact that without that guy in the coat and tie, this country's hottest hot rods might yet be found on the streets, as they were in the Forties, instead of racing down dragstrips (and across TV screens). Besides being the single most powerful force in the sport of drag racing, Wally Parks, founder and only president of the National Hot Rod Association, is the best friend a hot rodder ever had.

Like the speed equipment industry and the hot rod itself, the man is a gift from the California dry lakes. Self-described as a nonspectacular contestant, he gravitated instead toward the organizational end of things. In 1937 Parks helped form the Southern California Timing Association, of which he later became both president (1946) and general manager (1947). As the only full-time SCTA employee, it was only natural that Wally Parks would be answering the phone the day that Robert E. Petersen called.

The year was 1947, and the first of Wally's big public battles on behalf of the hot rod was born with that call from young "Pete" Petersen, representing a group called Hollywood Publicity Associates. "There was a movement afoot at the time that would have made it illegal to use any type of hot rod equipment on the public highways," explains Parks. "Consequently, when Pete Petersen learned about that, he called me at the SCTA office and suggested a meeting.

"We talked about this problem, and his suggestion was that their organization could probably be of some service to the SCTA and the small (speed equipment) business it represented at that time, either in lobbying for or trying in some way to influence the other side of the picture. As a result of that initial meeting, we collectively came up with the idea of raising funds, because our organization didn't have any money to hire their services.

"I suggested the possibility of producing a hot rod show here, which had never been done in California at that time—or anywhere, that I know of. I said that we had the vehicles and the personnel to produce the show, but we needed the publicity, promotion, and the personalities from the entertainment industry that could help make it a success. We felt we could serve a couple of purposes. We could paint our own picture of the types of cars and people we were to the public that attended and also raise some funds that would make it possible for us to put an active publicity campaign in effect to try to offset this proposed legislation."

The 1947 Los Angeles Hot Rod Exposition proved successful on both counts. Moreover, it was during the production of the show that Petersen came up with a plan to publish "a hot rod magazine," which of course appeared in January, 1948, as *Hot Rod* magazine. One year later, Parks quit SCTA to become Petersen's full-time editor, and in 1951 the magazine announced the formation of the National Hot Rod Association, with Editor Parks to double as NHRA president. Using the magazine to spread the message, Wally spent the next 12 years simultaneously steering both to success. He built *Hot Rod* into the country's largest automotive magazine, and NHRA into the biggest auto racing organization in the world. It wasn't until 1963 that Parks, by then editorial director for all Petersen publications, finally quit the publishing business to concentrate full-time on NHRA (whose pending projects at the time included sending Don Garlits and the U.S. Drag Racing Team to England).

"We didn't invent drag racing," stresses Parks today. "NHRA was formed as a semi-social car club organization; racing was not its aim or ambition." Meanwhile dragstrips were popping up as far away as Manassas, Virginia, but the organization continued to focus instead on club activities: show displays, reliability runs, safety campaigns.

"Prior to that time, I had been part of a group that conducted some experimental quarter-mile acceleration tests down in Ramona, at an abandoned airport. It was done as a combined project of *Motor Trend* Magazine staff. We took some new (1949-model) cars down, and as part of the regular *Motor Trend* road test, we ran these experimental runs. The purpose of the thing was to find out just how far you could race the average car before you had to start getting stopped. We had a runway down there that I think was 4700 feet long. We had probably 20 different cars running, of all types, including some dry lakes cars; and we found that if we extended the acceleration distance more than a quarter-mile, some of them couldn't get stopped at the other end. It was on that basis that we (later) established the quarter-mile as the official (NHRA) competition distance."

In his excellent hard-cover book *Drag Racing Yesterday and Today* (1966, Trident Press), Wally added about that day in Ramona, California, in 1949: "Fred Davies, a San Diego automobile dealer, showed up with a brand-new Olds 88, leading to some interesting two-car match races before the day ended. A dozen or so miscellaneous cars finally ended up running against the clocks, and each other, in what was probably the fore-runner of fully timed, two-car drag racing events." The following summer saw C.J. "Pappy" Hart hatch the first commercial quarter-mile, and news of the instantly successful Santa Ana Drags blazed up and down the West Coast. By the fall of 1950, the great dragstrip building boom was on.

But it wasn't until 1953 that NHRA, whose members were becoming increasingly attracted to the drags, finally produced a racing event of its own: the Southern California Championship Drags, conducted at the Pomona Fairgrounds, that later gave birth to the NHRA Winternationals. "We were running on the fairgrounds parking lot," Parks recalls. "We had seats for 200, and we drew 15,000! It was successful because it established drag racing as an event that could draw spectators." And even at 50 cents a head, the first NHRA drag meet also demonstrated the infant sport's fund-raising potential. Virtually from that day forward, drag racing has been the sole official activity and the main source of revenue of NHRA, a California nonprofit organization. And prexy Parks has never, never missed a major NHRA event in 25 years.

"It's not that they need me there to run the race, because they don't; I long ago was able to set this thing up so that whether I'm there or not really doesn't make any difference. The best thing I've been able to accomplish, I think, is being able to collect a lot of capable and reliable people. I get the credit and take the bows for a lot of things that we collectively accomplish."

These days the collective accomplishments include the direct produc-tion and promotion of 44 NHRA/Winston World Championship Series events a year; production of several one-hour TV specials for national syndication; publication of *National Dragster*, the sport's sole surviving weekly newspaper; and formation of the new NHRA Street Division, among other things. So when will Wally Parks finally retire? "When I can find something that I want to do more than what I'm doing now; that's when I'll think about retiring. But right now, I really enjoy what I'm doing."

Asked his list of NHRA milestones through the years, Parks, who was born in Goltry, Oklahoma, points with pride to the Safety Safaris that toured the nation between 1954 and '56, educating the general public, civic leaders, and hot rodders alike about these quarter-mile acceleration contests; establishment of a true national showdown for drag racers, the NHRA Nationals (1955); the dawn of network television exposure for drag racing events (1963); NHRA's expansion from California into seven geographical divisions covering the entire U.S.A. (1958); and acceptance into the prestigious ACCUS-FIA international racing association (1965). More recently, his 30-year-old organization has attracted and successfully retained major series sponsors, like Winston Cigarettes and the W.R. Grace Company, confirming in cold cash what the president of the National Hot Rod Association has been preaching since the Thirties: the hot rod is okay, and hot rodders are here to stay.

So the next time Wally rolls by in that convertible, smiling and waving the way he does, give the old boy a hand. After all, our many gifts from Wally Parks include lovely Linda Vaughn, the ever-amazing Miss Hurst Golden Shifter.

Hot Rodders
at Indianapolis

By Wally Parks

※

Hot Rod Magazine, August 1951

This year's Memorial Day "500," at the famed Indianapolis Speedway, pointed out with undeniable emphasis that the hot rods *do* provide the "basic training" for a majority of the big time personalities who contribute to the success of this annual classic.

Anyone familiar with the names of the drivers, mechanics and car owners can readily identify an impressive array of men who have emerged from the ranks of the hot rods. Some have come from the various hot rod track associations, others have been active participants at the dry lake meets of the West, still others have owned their own hot rods, street jobs from which they gained much beneficial knowledge in the art of keeping their equipment in top running condition.

Although hot rods and their interests have been much frowned upon in the past, and are still sadly misunderstood in many instances, there can be no denying the fact that the initial education gained through tinkering with these mechanical guinea pigs has proven advantageous to many of today's top-notchers—men who are responsible for the development of America's production superiority.

Most outstanding among the notables at the racetrack are the drivers, men like Johnny Parsons and Sam Hanks who once drove around town in their own trim little hot rod cars. Jack McGrath and Manny Ayulo used to run their '32 roadsters at the SCTA dry lake meets, then later toured the country with a pair of track roadsters before entering into the magic circle of AAA championship car racing. Countless drivers in this big time event came up from hot rod tracks of the Eastern circuits, all of them gaining much valuable preparation for their present part in the responsibility of keeping championship car racing at its present high level of safety.

Aside from the better known names among the drivers, the pit crew members are equally important and they, too, contain a high percentage of hot rod alumni. Passing through the garage area at the Speedway this year, we ran across scores of old buddies of earlier dry lakes days, also a good number of current day dry lakes enthusiasts.

The main difference that is immediately noticeable between the Indianapolis event and a well organized lake meet is the expensive calibre of the equipment being run. Actually, as far as the personnel is concerned there is little contrast between the two types of activity. Each crew is bent upon putting its entry in the best possible condition and it is here that experience and know-how pay off. Men who are familiar with tools, tune-up procedure, and maintenance are the ones most valuable to the car and driver.

As to the drivers themselves, the ones with a few seasons of competition to back them up are the ones most likely to succeed. With many young new recruits coming into the ranks of the Classic contenders each season, it has been a boon to the old timers, and newcomers as well, that we have the hot rods, the "sandlot leagues" of auto racing, to familiarize man with machine.

Although there are still a few die-hards who are reluctant to admit that there is a connecting link between the hot rods and big time championship racing, it takes only a pair of open eyes and a vague familiarity with the sport to determine, definitely, that the nation's hot rods *do* have a part to play in the success story of the world's greatest auto racing event, and they are playing it more and more successfully each year.

5

Long Haul in a Hot Rod

6,000 Miles
in a Custom

"Oh My Achin' Back"

By Spencer Murray

(as told to Robert Dearborn)

Hop Up, September 1952

Like all the big time writers—before I get started I would like to extend my sincerest thanks

To Bob Frame, for giving up his room in Provo, Utah . . . so we could sleep in comfort.

To Chuck Nestander of Omaha, Nebraska, for the wonderful dinner.

To Mr. and Mrs. C. E. Westell, for their Indianapolis hospitality.

To Keith and Lois Troutwine of Richmond, Indiana, for their friendliness.

To the wonderful "Hoodlifters" of Dayton, Ohio, for just being wonderful.

To Bob Hampke of the Indianapolis "Modockers" for assisting us with our mileage problems.

To Al Reddington of Marysville, Kansas, for the interview.

To Hop Up *photographer Ralph Poole, for putting up uncomplainingly with a bumpy 2,714 mile ride.*

I've made quite a few changes in my Chevy custom since you read about it in the June *Hop Up*; things like kicking up the frame over the rear axle and altering the trunk floor-board and torque-tube tunnel.

I also thought some re-upholstering was necessary if I was going to enter it in the 3rd Annual Indianapolis Custom Auto Show this year, as I had planned. While that work was going on, I took the opportunity of altering the dashboard, lowering the steering column three inches, and re-painting the car silver-blue-organic.

Then in preparation for the show (I had been planning on it for at least six months) I removed the 3 inch lowering blocks and replaced them with 5 inchers. This, plus the inch and a half I added to the bottom of the rear fenders gave me exactly four inches of ground clearance—which sort of explains the sub-title of this story: "Oh! My Achin' Back!"

Even with the heavy duty swivel castors which I added to the rear bumper the trip East was in some ways a nightmare. Even though I wouldn't take a million dollars for my experience, I think we discovered every bump in the road from Los Angeles to Indianapolis. (Every time anybody offers me $1,000,000 I politely refuse.)

When I first talked about my plans to drive to Indiana in time for the famous 500 mile race, *Hop Up* Editor Dean Batchelor told me that Ralph Poole was going too, to cover the race. Dean suggested that Ralph ride along with me and make a picture story out of the whole deal.

And it would have made a wonderful picture story if we had called it "The Snake Pit." It was the craziest trip I ever took over dry land. I figure we were lucky to get home in one piece.

Fred Beindorff and I drove out to Downey (a Los Angeles suberb) [*sic*] and picked up Ralph (our favorite custom photographer) on the evening of May 16, 1952, and headed East . . . with high hopes of a wonderful trip. We had everything planned right down to a gnats [*sic*] eyebrow. How much money we would spend, how many miles we would cover in a day, how long we would be gone, how many prizes we would win with the car at the show, and so on. We even started the trip at night so the desert crossing would be cooler and easier.

Believe me, our hearts were young and gay . . . for the first fifty miles, that is. And then our troubles began.

Loading Ralph Poole in the back seat and all his photographic equipment and luggage in the rear deck, caused the tires to start rubbing against the wheel wells on curves. Even though we drove carefully and much slower than we had intended, we still sensed a rather interesting odor of burning rubber from time to time.

We stopped the car and shifted all the luggage and equipment into the rear seat. Fred and I made room for Ralph in the front seat with us. That helped a lot inasmuch as the highway was as smooth as glass. We drove with hardly an interruption the rest of the night.

I say hardly an interruption. Actually something happened which scared me right out of my wits.

You know, how it is, driving along at night. You imagine you see things . . . animals, and stuff like that. I've had that happen to be [*sic*] before but never on quite such a large scale.

I had been driving along for miles. Ralph and Fred were sawing wood beside me. The miles were clicking off in a very relaxed fashion. All of a sudden I looked up and saw an elephant in front of me. I started to flick the wheel to skid around the big beast, when I realized I must be seeing things. Too long a stretch at the wheel, I thought. Maybe I'd wake Ralph and Fred up before I closed my eyes completely.

As I nudged the other two Rover boys awake I realized that I could still see this big Indian elephant! Right above the hood ornament, if the Chevy had had a hood ornament. Ralph and Fred looked over the hood and both yelled "What in the—?" I backed off on the throttle a little. Here was this great fat elephant with flapping ears and waving trunk floating along ahead of us in mid-air. Then all three of us saw what it was. What a relief! It really was an elephant! Riding on the back of a truck! I put my foot to the floorboard and swung around the truck before the big animal got a chance to break the small rope which held him in, fall out of the truck and smash in the front of the car. Once past the truck we relaxed again and drove on into Las Vegas for breakfast, a little behind schedule.

After chow, everything continued fine until we got to the Nevada–Arizona State Line. The car bottomed right on the state line where the two state's highway crews had met, or almost met. We kept right on bottoming as we ran over chuck-hole after chuck-hole. And every time the tires hit the fender wells it was as if the emergency brake had been applied. It was awful. We stopped the car and put our raising blocks (short lengths of 2x4) between the black of the rear springs and the frame.

From then on the situation improved a little and we were able to increase our worms [sic] pace a mph or so. However, the right real wheel kept on rubbing on the more severe bumps. We stopped for what seemed the millionth time and investigated. The right real wheel-well was found to have a deep dent in it. I don't know how it got there but it was the cause of the trouble so we hammered it out. We spent the night in Provo, Utah, and the next morning we pulled the raising blocks out (because a local "expert" said the road to Denver was in good shape) . . . and we drove on.

Before long we had to stop and put the raising blocks in again. The road was perfect alright, just like the man said. But the part that bothered us was where there wasn't any road at all. Heavy rains had washed the road completely away in spots and we had to come to a near-stop many times. Even with the blocks in place, we spent the whole day getting across Utah.

Conditions improved in Colorado, much to our surprise. The roads were excellent, though we still played it safe with our raising blocks.

We go through Colorado in due time, except for being mildly snowed-in in Berthoud Pass, and we rolled on into Omaha where we found we had covered 1,735 miles. And we finally got our second night's sleep—in a real bed. The next morning we had the car washed while we were eating breakfast and an interesting thing happened. The genius who undertook the job jacked up the car in order to get at the rear wheels which were covered with tar from a freshly surfaced road driven on the night before.

That was very thoughtful and sweet of him, only he put the jack under the gas tank and succeeded in putting a four gallon dent in it. The result: Now we had a 12 gallon tank . . . instead of 16. Not only that, but (we found out later, out in the middle of nowhere) the jack had also bent the pickup tube inside the tank. So we could only actually use 8 or 9 of the remaining 12 gallons. That, plus the fact that the jack had also jarred loose the accumulated scale inside the tank, (which choked up the fuel-filter bowl ever few miles) causes us to spend much of our remaining time in gas stations.

This trip was turning out beautifully.

Seriously, though, we heard some encouraging news in Omaha. One of the Police Officers, named Marchesi, had decided to help out the local speed enthusiasts—who were much frowned upon in town. As a result, things were moving ahead fast and Omaha will probably have a drag strip before it knows it.

All along the way we stopped and talked to people and the reaction to a customized car was very interesting. First of all, they rarely picked the car as a Chevy. Mostly it was mistaken for a Pontiac, then an Oldsmobile, with Mercury, Ford and Hudson following in close order.

We stopped by several high schools too, and were amazed that the kids showed so much knowledge of customizing. However, a lot of them had never seen a custom—only pictures. (We met a lot of *Hop Up* readers, Dean.) They showed real interest. Of course the weather in the Middle West and East is not conducive to customizing, but in some towns we saw cars that would rival anything found in California.

I remember several in Des Moines, for instance, when we stopped by at North High School. The students ganged around the car and as usual began to ask questions.

"How fast will it go?"

"Are the tail pipes real?"

"How do you drive with it so low?" (A *very* good question!)

And of course "What kind of car is it?"

The trouble wasn't over. Not by a long shot.

I might get in my licks right here for universal marking of the roads across country. Some of the states have good signs and some bad. There are a few places where there are none at all. Seems to me there is no excuse for that in this day and age. Another thing that bothered us.[sic] Even in the states where signs where plentiful, very few towns had adequate markings to indicate the route through town. Just because some local commissioner knows the way thru Podunk that's no sign that everyone else does.

There's some advice I'd like to give too—to the speed equipment manufacturers. Many time [sic] we talked to car owners who wanted cams, manifolds, or something of that nature. But there was no place to buy speed equipment in their region. True, these things are available by mail, but the kids—most of them—couldn't be bothered sending for what they wanted. It was too much trouble. Speed shops should be set up all over the country. There's a terrific market for speed products.

Anyway, to get back to our trip. The trouble wasn't over. Not by a long shot. Outside of Des Moines, we ran into a gorgeous rain storm. If you're thinking of customizing your car, don't cut the windshield down too low. Not if you live in a rainy section of the country. If you do, you'll be sorry. A cut-down windshield lacks visability.

And then the highway signs. While picking our way through the ruts of a small town, we took a wrong turn and drove for hours. Finally we came across a sign which said "Des Moines, 18 miles." After a service station attendant had confirmed our fears we headed back in the right direction. But not until Ralph and I had appointed Fred official navigator and made him responsible for our fate from then on.

We got through the night O.K. and the next morning at eleven we rolled into Indianapolis. After dropping Ralph at the 500 mile oval we washed up and began looking for the promoter of the big auto show—Ralph Potter. We found him at this Hollywood Muffler Shop and invited him outside . . . to look at the car. You could tell by the look on his face that he wondered about putting the car on display, but when we told how we were going to clean it up, he very kindly directed us to a local garage where we at once got to work.

After pulling out the raising blocks and carefully preserving them for the trip home (we were no fools), we began removing some of the dirt. I noticed that flying rocks from the road had done considerable damage to the paint in some places. But that didn't worry *us* a bit. *We* were too smart to be caught unprepared. *We* had brought paint along with us! So we got to work and began feather-edging all of the knicks made by the stones. Then we applied a primer coat. I went around and opened the rear deck to get out extra silver-blue-organic paint I had so carefully brought all the way from California. As I rummaged through the luggage compartment, I suddenly (in a blinding flash) remembered that I had left the paint on my back porch, over 2555 miles away.

There was only one thing to do and that was put through an S.O.S. to California and have the paint rushed by rocket, carrier pigeon, plane or whatever was handy. Then we bearded Mr. Potter in his den and got him to allow us to enter the car on a temporary basis . . . until the paint got there.

Meanwhile, we tried all over town but the Indianapolis paint mongers gave us the fish-eye when we asked for the ingredients for silver-blue-organic. Nobody in town stocked the basic tinting colors. So we actually saw the big show through with the car looking like a leopard . . . covered with primer spots, because by the time the paint we sent for had winged its way across the Continent there wasn't time to apply it.

The cars in the show, incidentally, caused this Californian to open his eyes wide. They had some real beauties. I remember one very interesting car which belonged to Keith Garber of New Lebanon, Ohio. It is particularly impressed in my memory because, not only had it been owned by Rex Mays at one time, but I got to drive it for a day . . . and it was sensational! It looked very innocent from the outside, but under the hood it sported a full-race engine . . . bored, stroked, and the "works."

During the show, we discovered the same thing to be true as we had found throughout the rest of the country. Everybody was interested in top performance of their cars, but there was no drag strips anywhere. Everyone was really enthusiastic, but they all had to be content with reliability runs and tours around the countryside . . .

Before the show was over Mr. Roe Miller of Farmland, Indiana, gave me a wonderful ride in his Rauch and Lang Electric. Miller got in after me, removed the steering tiller from a clip on the door post, stuck it in a socket in front of him and we were off. No noise, no smell, no vibration. Nothing but clean, silent motion.

Finally with the show over, our pocketbooks said "Go West young man, go West." After seeing the exciting Indianapolis Race we turned our eyes homeward. And the trip West was as fraught with hazards as the trip East.

Chicago. What a town! Big! Bustling! Frightening! We drove around, but the one way streets and traffic scared us off . . . we didn't like leaving the car while we ate . . . there were no inside garages . . . left there right away.

One of my ambitions on this trip East was to pick up a really rare car. I had heard the woods were full of them in the Middle West. What I wanted was either an antique, a veteran, or a body for a long dreamed of "T" roadster—and these bodies are really rare on the Pacific Coast. Before we left Indiana, we scoured the countryside, but all we managed to find was a very fine 1907 Chase truck. It was in showroom condition, but the owner wanted the price of a new Mercury for it.

Westward again . . .

La Grange, Illinois . . . Home of the Diesel engine. We talked our way into one of the big General Motors plants and found to our amazement that the big Diesel railroad engines are made on a production line, just like automobiles. First the chassis, then the engine and wheels. And they are test run around the plant on special tracks.

Meanwhile we were plagued with "bottoming" again through [sic] not as bad as on the trip East. Railroad tracks were a big nuisance. The castors under the rear bumper hit the ground on each bump and clanked over the rails. It was like climbing a stairway.

Marysville, Nebraska . . . We were interviewed by the local newspaper reporter . . . a very nice fellow who gave us two dollars for our pains.

As we wended our precarious way West we were still on the lookout for antique cars or what have you. Along the highway we passed a big wrecking yard which turned out to be the graveyard of every model "T" for miles around. Trying to conceal our greed, lest the proprietor jack up the prices, we paid a very low price for a particularly fine "T" touring body. As we counted bills into the dealer's grimy hand, we noticed two excellent "T" roadsters. We hungrily bought them, too. Who should pass up a bargain?

Then we hunted up another wrecking yard and bought a '36 Lincoln rear end, complete which wheels and tires, and went back after the three bodies. By this time our enthusiasm had cooled a bit and we realized one body was all we could haul to California. Reluctantly we left the touring and one roadster body behind.

After welding the Lincoln rear-end onto the roadster body and fabricating a trailer hitch, we started West once more. But all was not well. The weld broke loose after a few miles and the body began shifting around and causing consternation among drivers of following cars. They thought the body was going to fall off and wreck them. So did we. After trying several times to secure our precious parcel with rope, we had to admit defeat and give up our dream. We stripped off the doors, deck-lid, hardware, etc., and sold the remains to a junk dealer along the way. This sale was further encouraged by the police who suggested that they wouldn't be completely happy until we bought a trailer license for our contraption. Then too, our gas milage [sic] was down to practically nothing. With the price of gas what it is through the Western States we were already reduced to a diet of peanut butter sandwiches and clear, cold water.

Albuquerque, New Mexico . . . Along the Santa Fe Trail . . . that bang we heard wasn't the rifle of a maurauding [*sic*] cattle rustler. It was the snapping of one of our rear springs. Examined damage. Spring was broken alright but the raising block (which caused the spring to break) held the leaf in position so that the car didn't sag. But we were on pins and needles every time we went around a corner. The spring on the other side had to take all the side stress on corners. We managed to get through without breaking that one, however.

Gallup, New Mexico . . . To ease the discomfort of the terrific heat, we soaked our shirts in water. As fast as they'd dry we'd soak them again.

At 8:00 A.M. June 10th we rolled in front of my house, 25 days and 6,037 miles after we had left. Resolved: Crossing the country in a custom car is fine provided you have seven inches ground clearance.

The Summer Saga of the J-Kamp Roadster

There is another world out there. Every now and then you have to get out of your home town and drive across the country. But when you're driving in a channeled '29 A Roadster with a full belly pan and a race-car nose, you're likely to run into some memorable experiences.

By Tom Senter

⁊⁊

Street Rod Quarterly, Fall 1971

It's somewhere between Midland and Abilene, Texas, at two in the afternoon. It's 110° outside the car and 145° inside. I'm absolutely barbecued, with nothing between me and the blazing desert sun but a polka dot hat, and I'm asking myself: "What the hell am I doing here?"

I don't want to suggest that it was uncomfortably hot or anything, but have you ever *poured* the contents out of a tube of toothpaste?

Not for the meek or faint hearted, this Memphis junket. And definitely not for the drive-in bound, Sunday evening cruising machine, either. Two thousand miles, nearly half of it desert, semis by the hundreds, reckless drivers, overzealous hot rod fans, and other hazards, like anti-social Texas Highway Department workers, taxed our endurance nearly to the breaking point.

We rolled into Forrest City, Arkansas, dog tired and smelling like a couple of goats, but none the worse for wear. And the little flathead never missed a beat or gave an ounce of trouble. As it turned out, Jake didn't even need one of those six spare distributor caps.

The NieKamp Roadster did itself right proud, (I'm still trying to shake that Southern lingo) humming along all the way, with not a single malfunction or failure. Warm up a bit—yes. Fail—no. Actually, a good deal of the credit must go to Jake, who thrashed many a morning until 3 AM to put the wretched, channeled, nosed Oakland Winner back into its once-proud '50 Chrysler Blue splendor.

I had often thought that a more appropriate moniker for the fender-less ex-lakes racer would be the J-Kamp Car. 'Long about 40 miles out of Phoenix, for some reason, the name J-Kamp *furnace* kept popping into mind. But no matter, the two-pot coolant cooker never boiled, and that 110° ambient temperature on the desert was enough to warm even the frostiest OHV.

If you think you've really built yourself a hot rod roadster, pull that overhead out and drop in a 24 stud Henry flatmotor. Throw a few bags in the trunk, gas 'er up, and bang off 4000 miles to break her in. Get 20 miles to the gallon while you're at it. And leave the top off so you can get flat *fried* . . . or drenched! And forget the tools, you won't need 'em.

That Jacobs . . . I figured whatever happened to me was going to happen to him too, so I was game when he asked: "Hey, how'd you like to go to Memphis in this thing?" and I said: "Right on, brother," and threw my AWOL bag on the front seat, filled with smokes, camera gear, film, suntan oil, Rolaids, and a Chapstik, and off we went.

And we weren't alone either. Not to be outdone, Bud Bryan and Hugh Teitsworth in the *R&C* '29, and Ron

Weeks and Dick Freeman in the old Dick Kraft T thrashed out the same trip, to prove they were just as bananas as we were. As a matter of fact, because an ice cooler and 336 cans of Coors wouldn't fit in the T (neither do Weeks and Freeman), Weeks pulled a trailer the whole distance.

Three flatheads and three quick-changes singing through the Southwest, an experience not soon forgotten. With any such excursion, the local characters you meet along the way, and their remarks, stick in your mind and find their way into the countless yarns every Memphis participant will spin.

Like the guy in Indio at our first gas stop. It was 12:30 in the morning, and 94°, and this attendant opens with: "Is that thing just fixed up to look like that or does it really go fast? I got a Mustang that'll blow all you guys off." How do you like them apples?

Or the kids in Benson, Arizona who asked, after inspecting the Rods and the California plates: "You don't drive these on the street, do ya?" And after a silence, "I mean, you don't drive 'em in this kind of weather?" (It was raining.)

Then there was the cat in Demming who asked if we were all going to a race, "or sumpthin', because a few hours ago some guys came through here with a bunch of old cars fixed up like roadsters . . . " What a riot.

After witnessing countless blank stares upon learning the car was powered by a flathead—"a what?"—I decided to tell the curious that the engine was a rare old Edelbrock; a racing engine made for a short while in 1942 by a company that later manufactured tank engines for the allied effort.

"Hey, Benjie! Come 'ear. Lookit this. One of them rare old Eddlebrock racin' injuns!"

"Yeah," pointing to Ron's T, "that one's got a Weiand in it," I said. Now *that* they could dig. But a Ford flathead?

"What's a flaphead, buddy?

One chap at a truck-stop outside of Lordsburg, New Mexico, nattily attired in a suit, was "anxious to establish a serious rapport" with us, and "get involved in a discussion of the finer points of these machines." Wild.

Unfortunately for him, he hit us at the wrong time, as we had been driving nearly 14 hours and were in no mood for public relations with the natives. Before he could ask, I said "200 miles an hour and $10,000 . . . it's powered by a jet," and we dragged our feet into the coffee shop, whereupon Weeks wolfed down a couple of tacos at 4:30 AM.

The whole idea of driving three beautiful, fenderless street roadsters 2000 miles to Memphis, Tennessee, from Los Angeles, to wave to a bunch of other street roadsters is preposterous. Yet, after months of preparation, we pulled out of Bryan's driveway at 8:00 PM Friday evening like we were going to an SCTA meeting across town. No big deal . . . Phoenix by morning, right guys?

Quickies singing, grooved Ascots humming mile after mile, under a black dome, punctuated by twinkling stars, bright red Mars, and a sparkling moon, recently the temporary home of our still air-borne astronauts. If they can get to the moon, we can get to Memphis, as Jake runs her right up to 5500 RPM in high gear. Keep on truckin', J-Kamper.

Greeting jackrabbits and other livestock, we rolled into Wickenburg, as the sun slowly lit up the clouds and the beautiful Arizona landscape. Bryan detected a squeak in a home-brewed fan idler and we took advantage of this roadside downtime for his diagnosis and impromptu fix to have a sun-up Coors or three (I think we killed a half a case), and chew the fat with some funny car people headed for a points meet in Phoenix.

"Hey Ron. Pull out your dipstick. I need a little oil to finish this thing up," hollered Bud, and we were on our way. By 8:00 AM it was already 95° and time for breakfast.

"I've got a set of chrome headers that'll bolt right on there," said one of the enthusiasts in the coffee shop parking lot.

"Well," Bryan drawled, "those are custom Hedmans."

"Mine'll bolt right on," he insisted, and we rolled down the street for a swim and a three hour nap at the inn.

Our host in Phoenix was amiable Ron Olmstead, an LA Roadster Associate who tooled up in as fine a Deuce three-window as you'll ever

The whole idea of driving three beautiful, fenderless street roadsters 2000 miles ... to wave to a bunch of other street roadsters is preposterous.

see, original as the day is long (or hot in Arizona), with 21 studder, one barrel carb, stock headlights, and mechanicals.

"You don't see many filled cowl vents around here," Ron answered when I remarked about the heavy 100° heat.

After watching the thrilling Apollo splashdown, and eating a wall-to-wall steak, we topped up the fluid levels, and Olmstead pointed us south to Tucson.

The key to reliability and relative comfort while pounding out a long trip like this is preparation. Take the time to make some of those repairs and improvements that you've been putting off. Balance all four wheels carefully and align the front end. Adjust your headlights properly and be sure your high-beams work. Quartz lamps are really the ticket for night motoring in the desert.

Adjust the brakes and install a loud horn that *works*. Bulb or squeak horns are cute but they won't alert a sleeping driver or some clown who is about to pull out in front of you. Good wipers are an absolute necessity; turn signals are nice, and safer than hand signals.

If you're still building, insulate the firewall with asbestos or fiberglass, soften up that suspension for the hundreds of miles you'll spend on less than ideal pavement.

In short, the conditions out on that endless ribbon of open Interstate are a far cry from the smooth main drag in your town. Preparations for a long trip amount to little more than good safety sense. If there is some little annoyance in your car, or a small discomfort, multiply it by a thousand and you can appreciate the gravity of the situation at the end of your trip.

The Nationals have opened up a whole new ball game for street machines. Many Memphis participants featured air conditioners, stereo tapes, closed cars, automatics, and ultra smooth, modern suspensions. The new name of the game is comfort and endurance.

All things considered, the J-Kamper was as roadworthy as the best—certainly as reliable—simple and unsophisticated as it is. Being essentially a channeled car, leg room is somewhat reduced, and my 6' 3" frame found itself contorted into some curious shapes as the trip progressed. I deduced, as we rolled into Forrest City, Arkansas, that Bill NieKamp is a three-foot tall dwarf with rattlesnake blood in his veins. Other than that, he's perfectly normal.

Down Highway 80 we careened, Bud blowing gum-bubbles, Weeks and Freeman in that outrageous bright red trailer rig, and Jake the Snake dodging jack rabbits and demonstrating the quick steering, and how sure-footed the Roadster is at 75.

I pulled out my camera for a few shots and looked up the road a few miles . . . uh, oh . . . dust storm! Back goes the lens cover, stuff the camera back in the bag, and get ready. We decided to put her to the floor and drive through it. An interesting experience with little lasting effects, except a sandblasted right arm and face.

We logged the miles well into the night, until Weeks—who has impeccable taste when it comes to food and lodging—noticed, a few miles this side of gorgeous Las Cruces, New Mexico, the palm tree–laden Las Cruces Hilton . . . nothing but the finest accommodations.

After another short snooze of four hours, the manager noticed the odd trio of road dusters and politely suggested we get the hell out of there before he charges us for the ground space.

Rise and shine, grab a breakfast and on to the city of Marty Robbins, some 45 miles to the south, hard by picturesque Juarez, Mexico. We cruised into the United States of Texas, blithely oblivious to the fact that it would take two whole days to cross her. For those of you who haven't had the pleasure to cross the Continent of Texas at the widest point, let me advise you to bring your lunch . . . bring a bunch of lunches. It's 11,000 miles wide, and hot (110°) and when it rains in Texas . . . well, how about nine inches of rain in a twelve hour period?

You don't drive through Texas, you endure it. After a while, the car seems to stand still and the road rushes under you like a treadmill. We wondered what it must have been like on horseback, or in a creaking wagon, poking along for miles; months of desert, sagebrush, Indians, and treacherous weather. This AIN'T Marlboro Country!

A shower and a bed in Odessa, Sunday night, provided the necessary elixir for the continuation of our journey, although Jake was disappointed that not one establishment near the motel could satisfy his urge for a dish of sherbet.

Next morning which was Monday (I think) Jake and I went to town to visit the local haberdashery, where we purchased a matched pair of Odessa crash helmets—blue polka-dot hats.

On to Sweetwater, where we were to encounter a nerve rattling experience on the Interstate. A disgruntled Texas Highway Department worker threw a surveying pole, javelin style, at the flawless J-Kamper and put a good sized dent in her flank, narrowly missing the side of Jake's melon. It's an involved story, so let it suffice to say that we were innocent of any wrongdoing. Those people are hostile!

After about two hours of travel, Ron Weeks' right arm suffers from a spasmodic bending of the elbow, his right hand closing in a circle, jerking toward his mouth. The only thing that will relieve this infliction is to put a can of cold beer in the affected hand. This doesn't really eliminate the ailment, but it does slow it down some. We pulled into a comfortable location, marked by the friendly "REST STOP, NO FACILITIES" sign, somewhere in East Texas, and lifted the lids off 24 cans of Denver's Best. Bud took advantage of the stop to change rearend gears to a lower number, while the rest of us bench raced and Jake took all his clothes off just for fun.

"We'll stop in Dallas tonight shower maybe hit a lounge, get some good sleep, and roll into Forrest City tomorrow. How does that sound?"

"Sounds good to me."

"We'll stop when we stop."

"Gimme a beer."

"Look at Jake!"

"Senter, get the camera!"

Many hours later that night, a long way past Dallas, somewhere near who knows where—Saltillo or Omaha, Texas—we dragged to a halt at 3:00 AM for a snack in a charming tar-paper coffee shop in which everything was out of order: the phone, cigarette machine, stamp machine, the john, and the cook who was out cold on the counter, probably the victim of one of his own meals.

"We been driving 16 hours today and we're *still* in Texas."

"We should'a stopped in Dallas."

"We can make Texarkana tonight."

"You're crazy, it's three o'clock!"

"Hey man, I'm dead."

"Honey," to the waitress, "who ate this hamburger before I got it?"

"Check that dude in the Can't-Bust-Ems."

"That's the cook."

"Let's go back to that Holiday Inn we passed."

"We'll be in Texarkana in a couple of hours."

"We'll be in a coma in a couple minutes."

"Look at this dump."

"We shoulda stopped in Big D."

"If the Board of Health walks in here we'll all be picked up as a public hazard."

"The Board of Health should put the torch to this place."

We walked out to the parking lot as seven hippy chicks and one bearded cat pulled out of a wreck of a VW camper.

We drove a few miles until Freeman and Weeks (who seemed to be acting as our travel guides, what with the beer, tools, spare parts and tires in their trailer) spotted one of the nicest mosquito infested swamps in East Texas, conveniently laid out not 40 feet from semi alley. Four minutes later, the entire party is flaked out, sleeping cozily in the midst of a veritable zoo of crawling things, two roosters, a cow in heat, a pack of wild dogs, a slew of roaches who were pulling the tires off the J-Kamper, and a six-pack of dead skunks smashed flat on the highway . . . all except me. I was so full of coffee and aspirin, my eyeballs were jacked open about a foot, so I started counting semis and swatting mosquitoes. I pulled out my can of repellent and a flock of them snatched it out of my hand and drank it.

115 semis roared past before I gave up. 115 semis at 80 MPH, 40 feet away. All I could do was wait until dawn. Nice place you picked, Weeks!

Tuesday morning, it was off to Forrest City, where all the California cars were to meet for the final leg into Memphis on Thursday. We stopped for breakfast and gas in Texarkana and decided to roll non-stop all the way across Arkansas. At 3:00 PM in the afternoon, we shut her off (the reserve tank nearly empty) after having endured a refreshing Arkansas cloud burst around noon. I never thought a Holiday Inn could look so good.

Forrest City at last. Final resting place for a day and a half, before the Highway Patrol led caravan rolled into Memphis, Thursday noon.

Wednesday was devoted to removing all traces of the arduous journey so the machinery would sparkle come Thursday. Everyone worked madly all Wednesday, which was a beautiful hot and sunny Arkansas day . . . except Jake and I: we swam.

The Holiday Inn was transformed into an exhibition of the sharpest wheels the West Coast has to offer, 35 of California's finest; every one driven the entire distance.

Brizio's entourage rolled in Wednesday morn' and the ranks were filled. The air was thick with the odors of wax, chrome cleaner, solvents, Glass Wax, and other spirits.

"Y'all gwine t'Meemfis?" asked the passersby,

"Y'all gwine t'Meemfis?" asked the waitress.

"Y'all with them carrs?" asked the custodian.

"No, we're not all with them cars, just most of us."

The J-Kamper remained in the same spot it had occupied since Tuesday afternoon, right where Jake shut her off, while all were busy as frenetic beavers preparing for the glittering parade the following day. Weeks even adjusted his valves. Orv' Elgie's wife outdid herself in a spectacular display of fine auto detailing ability, while Orv' spun yarns about Peoria. Bud and Hugh shined the Highboy like she's never been shined before . . . and we swam.

Flawless machines went up on frame stands, mag wheels were removed and polished to a high lustre; last minute detailing of brass and aluminum was attended to . . . and about 4:00 PM. the sky turned dark.

Chins dropped as the pleasant breeze became a rather strong wind. It was headed in our direction, no question about it. Tools were tossed into boxes, chemicals were grabbed and capped in a frenzy of activity as it became painfully obvious that we were in for a first class Arky thunder shower.

Within minutes, the rain was dumping down in torrents, the sky was completely black, and the winds had reached gusts of 50 MPH So much for the day's work. The shine and wax festival degenerated into a roaring inclement weather party, lasting well into the night, leaving some with unpleasant memories. Cold Duck replaced chrome cleaner, VO was swapped for Meguires, and a pint of Cutty sneaked in there somewhere.

After the rain subsided, Jake and I dry-towelled off the roadster in about ten minutes and we were ready for

Freddy.

Thursday morning, we touched up the chrome, gathered the goods and joined the group for the short 50-mile trek to the Mighty Mississippi to our long awaited destination.

After a brief stop to meet the congenial Mayor, we finally settled down at the Brooks Road Holiday Inn (all the Holiday Inns are hereby highly recommended for travelers) for four of the most memorable days in the history of street rodding.

My compliments to the Memphis Street Rods, the NSRA, the *Rod 'n Custom* staff, and all the other folks who worked so hard to make the Nationals a reality. The City of Memphis is to be congratulated for offering such a warm welcome and full cooperation . . . it was an event which will be long remembered. Elsewhere you will find extensive coverage of what happened at the Nationals. I thought you might like to know what it was like getting there.

Old Roadsters Never Die

Looking Forward to Another Twenty Years

By Jim "Jake" Jacobs

※

Street Rod Quarterly, Winter 1971

By this time you've no doubt read Tom Senter's play-by-play account of our trek across the open plain to the Memphis based Nationals in the NieKamp roadster (Fall *SRQ*) and how the mighty flathead up front never missed a single beat throughout the three day/ twenty-one hundred mile jaunt. Well, every word is truth. That forty-year-old coolant cooker ran like a top. Tom and I . . . that's a different story. Man, even before California's state line had flashed 'neath the rig's blue belly we both were in need of a rebuild. Just to even the odds though, and since there wasn't even a smidgen of covering over our heads, a few miles the other side of Phoenix we popped the hood into Week's trailer and with carbs unfiltered, ran headlong through an Arizona dust storm so dense that we had to turn on the headlights (still losing sight of each other) and then flushed a couple of Texas downpours right out the exhaust pipes. Talk about reliability—all that flathead had to say about our double dose of foul weather was "you guys wouldn't get so wet if you'd go faster;" the speedo laid on 70 mph through both rams and flinched not one iota!

I wasn't unprepared for the worst; an extra set of points and SIX new spare distributor caps shared the cramped luggage compartment with emergency flares, tire changing equipment, and tools. Heck, six pillows and a tube of Preparation "H" would've been more appropriate baggage. But only two days prior to leaving, the yet unproven 12-volt system taxed my troubleshooting experience to the limit with a faulty distributor cap. "Great, the car isn't even ready and now this!" The distributor quickly came apart, but not finding a thing wrong, it went back together unchanged. There was no apparent failure except for the cap—which had numerous hairline cracks running from each of the terminals. I replaced that cap with a new one and sixty miles later it too became junk. What now? Maybe this thing's trying to tell me it doesn't want to go to Memphis. "No way, baby! I've worked too long and hard to make this trip to be whipped by a lousy flathead ignition." Disgusted, to say the least, I stormed down to Long Beach and checked out the same 12-volt setup on Joe Mac's Ford Obsolete A-bone coupe, then returned home with the half-dozen new caps to install a voltage-drop to a 6-volt coil, swapped distributors with an engine that hadn't turned an inch in eight years, popped a new cap in place and roared all the way across the mighty Mississippi without an incident.

What was it? That's something I may never know. It might have been too hot a spark and too much advance causing the spark to jump ahead of the terminals, or it could've been a worn bushing that allowed the rotor to nick the leads at high rpm shattering the plastic. To be quite truthful about the matter, as long as it doesn't happen again I could care less. That distributor unit is definitely not going on another one of my motors!

What I knew about Henry's flatmotor up to that time wasn't any more than the general basics (eight cylinders, sixteen valves, etc.) and my only real encounter with its personalities was some years back with my older brother's stock '50 Ford tudor work car I had happened to borrow on two different occasions. The first time it ran out of gas, and the next time a dead battery found me hustling a push on Pacific Coast Highway with an unimpressed girlfriend.

So when it came time to put an engine in the roadster—my stand on the restoration theme determined that a flathead it must be—I merely rustled up a good recyclable 24-stud engine and had someone who knew pistons and crankshafts do the number. It's for sure I didn't want to end up stranded in the middle of Texas with a spun bearing or a lunched rod . . . "No thanks." My only regret now in having someone else do the work is not being able to take the credit for the beautiful performance rendered by that outdated mill . . . Then too, maybe it's just as well I didn't touch it.

The motor I started with was in exceptionally fine condition to begin with. As a matter of fact, right up to the time I got it, it was seeing daily service in a sweetheart '46 Ford tudor sedan that parked only a few blocks from my home. The car itself showed no signs of owner abuse and was immaculately original throughout . . . except for one thing. A speeding drunk had completely destroyed the passenger side, moving the cowl, door, and rear quarter panel inwards about ten inches. The elderly gent who owned it from the day it was new hated to part with the wreck but $65 was more than the auto junky would give him . . . and I wheeled home a raft of gennie parts. The motor was stock as a stove and purred like a kitten; I wouldn't have been the least bit afraid to drive her across country to Memphis just like she stood. Nonetheless, the engine came out and was hauled straight to Jerry Kugel's garage in Whittier, without even taking time to drain the crankcase oil. "Nothin' trick, Jerry, just a good solid lower end with enough oats to pull a slippery roadster."

Jerry's own roadster, you'll remember as *R&C*'s Project '27 lowboy, has turned a very respectable 230 mph at Bonneville with a 427-inch cam'r Ford. I had no ill feeling about his wrenching capabilities, to say the least.

With the heads lifted the block was found to have absolutely no cracks in the valve seat area, and about the usual amount of cylinder ridge for an engine its age. It also contained something which I was very glad to see: a factory relieve job. "Outasight!" This factory relieve, though not as deep or smooth as that in Bud Bryan's modern flathead (*R&C* Feb. '70), would save the trouble and resulting expense for a custom tailored job and for moderate street use was felt to be quite sufficient. Following teardown the barrels were taken out to .040 over stock and the lifter bosses were drilled to accept Johnson adjustables.

The stage was now set for a mild street motor; boring kept to a minimum cleanup job was off-set by installing a Merc crank which lengthened the stroke 1/4-inch and upped the total cubic inches in the neighborhood of 260. With this in mind the next step then was to secure a cam suitable for the engine's needs. To do so, we contacted Sir Harry Weber of Weber Speed Equipment, Santa Ana, California. The engine dimensions, intended use, and other pertinent information was related by phone and from this Harry whipped up a stump-puller street grind with performance and torque right out of the gate. Something would ultimately be needed to get this new power to the rear so Weber also fixed us up with one of his latest aluminum flywheels and matching clutch pieces.

Compression was to be kept on the mild side to ensure maximum life from bearings and related parts and for overall dependability . . . an important thing to remember, especially when building a street flathead. For instance, a heavy sedan should have no more than 8 to 1, a street roadster can get by with 8.5 or 9 to 1, while higher compressions should

Why have a keen roadster if it can't be driven, especially when the weather warms up?

be applied only to a gutted drag roadster or a guy who has plenty of spare time and engine parts. For the NieKamp it was established that 8.5 to 1 would do just fine. The heads chosen for the job are Edelbrock items, and because I didn't want to step into someone else's headache (leaky gaskets and such) they are new. Well, basically that's it. Everything that turns in a circular motion is fully balanced; Kugel carefully assembled each piece checking clearances and waving his professional wand. All I had to do was bring it home and screw it into place. No muss, no fuss.

There was enough to do without getting involved in building motors. Much work had to be concentrated on the car itself before it would be roadable and the time before Memphis was fast disappearing.

In the last report (*R&C* June '71) we got as far as restoring the once butchered '27 Essex frame rails. The kicked-up rear portion was repaired to perfection using sections of '36 Willys' frame and the pedal assembly and steering mounts fabricated to fit. I briefly mentioned that the steering position had moved down and slightly to the rear of the car. So let's take it from there.

Originally the car had for motivation one of Ford's famous flatheads, probably most famous for its inherent heating problem or so I'm told. For a radiator, it had a 3 1/2-inch thick unit with a total 17 inches of core height and 17 inches wide which sat behind the tube front cross member and directly above the steering tie rod when positioned in the frame. The radiator and engine compartment's only source of incoming air is through the small oval opening in the nose, and just to complicate matters, there was absolutely no provision for any kind of fan. Anyone who drives in traffic knows what it can be like with no fan, but until you try cooling a flatmotor that's tightly sealed under a hood with no louvers and with an air flow that is metered to an impractical minimum upon entering, and forced to exit through the bottom of a belly pan . . . Buddy, you don't know the half of it!

What about the overhead idea? Well, although the overhead itself is by nature of design a cooler operating motor, the installation of the Chevy small block and eventually the Buick into the tight confines of the hooded roadster only made the situation worse. Simply, the larger outside dimensions of the engine put up a wall from side to side, top to bottom, further blocking what little air passage there was. With these transplants also came louvers, large openings in the hood sides, and external headers— but no solution. Had I not taken the machine in this condition on a run for myself, maybe my feelings about the flathead being the right motor for the car would not be as strong as they are. That run was the '70 Roadster Roundup held in Visalia, mid-way between L.A. and San Francisco in the warm San Joaquin Valley. A mere 175 miles from my home and it took me just a little over nine hours to get there! No, we weren't out sightseeing. Actually most of the time was spent filling up the radiator, every six to seven miles to be exact. Just about the time we'd get comfortable (if that was possible) that Buick motor would reach a boil, flushing half its coolant overboard; and this was running without a hood.

In question I discussed the cooling problem with Custom T Radiator man, Jim Babb of Paramount, California, and he came up with an interesting theory. That is, without some type of fan pushing the air out of the engine compartment thus forming a vacuum behind the radiator, the aerodynamic shape of the front could at certain speeds cause the airflow moving around the outside of the nose to suck air forward through the grille, bringing the airflow through the radiator to a standstill. Remember, this nose was designed for short sprint races, not cross-country enduros.

To restore the car back to its original condition of having no fan, to be at all practical, would be utterly insane. Why have a keen roadster if it can't be driven, especially when the weather warms up? The only alternative then was to get a fan in front of the motor and if possible more radiator. It seemed that the Buick installation had already opened the door for such an addition.

In order to fit the lengthy Buick engine and transmission into the roadster chassis the previous owner found it necessary to shorten the driveshaft and fabricate a new firewall. He did so with no hesitation. Approximately four inches was removed from the torque tube and shaft. Tin snips were used to cut the stock firewall to within 1/4-inch of the cowl, leaving no interference for the huge overhead.

Putting the flathead back in the classic is now much easier. With the driveshaft already shortened and no reason (like firewall clearance) to reposition the motor in stock NieKamp location, setting the motor back seems the obvious solution to fan room and the logical thing to do. Besides giving us an opportunity to use a fan, this 4-inch setback also means the radiator can move back behind the tie rod, thus allowing a taller, thicker cooling core.

It was time for a new radiator anyhow and so once again Jim Babb was called into action, this time for one of his brass masterpieces. Maximum cooling being the idea, of course, Jim fitted the flatmotor with as much radiator as would possibly fit within the limits of the nose. The new radiator is thicker than the retired unit by 1/2-inch, which equals an extra row of cooling tubes, and has 22 inches of core height . . . 5 inches more than the old core. This amounts to 1/3 again as much radiator as the roadster originally had, plus it is backed with a heavy duty flathead aluminum six-blade fan. There's no question that this is a great improvement over previous conditions.

The new firewall mounts flush with the '29 cowl and is recessed 3 inches leaving a good 1 inch space between it and the engine block, allowing plenty of airflow over and around the motor en route to the opening in the belly pan. It is made from 1/2-inch plywood and covered with fiberglass cloth and resin on both sides, and can be easily removed at any time by loosening four carriage bolts that hold it firmly to the cowl and lifting straight up and forward. Throttle linkage is the only thing fastened to it, keeping the engine compartment sanitary and uncluttered.

The reason then for the relocated steering is this engine setback. Instead of protruding through the frame rail as it originally did, it now sits below the rail and comes out through a notch in the belly pan, directly behind the wishbone mounting bracket: such an insignificant change that it does nothing to disturb the cars originality.

That does it then, no more alterations. From here on it's no different than restoring any older vintage car, just a matter of putting it back together. And for this reason I think it unnecessary to go into complete detail. Anyone who's ever built a car knows it well and for those not yet acquainted with the assembling of early iron, the *R&C* Highboy project reports by Bud Bryan answer just about anything you need know concerning traditional hardware.

At this point I would like to dwell on the visual impact of the car. We talked considerably about the flathead, its dependability, its performance, and its importance as a traditional piece of the restoration of the NieKamp roadster. This is all well and good. I know for certain that the selected power is appropriate to the rig's classic look, and there's no argument as to the fun one can have with the old Ford mill. But there's more to early era hot rodding than inline 97s and axle keys.

The cars themselves had a whole different look from the street rod that we know today. Generally speaking, they were low, sleek, and somewhat sneaky looking. Coupes and sedans, for example were for the most part hammered (chopped), and channeled where fenders were absent. Dago'd axles front and Z'd rails rear, hung highboys low in the saddle, while the abbreviated silhouette of a channeled roadster was commonplace. Solid hoods, louvered deck lids, chopped windshields with forward slanting Carson-type roadster tops, filled grille-shells and vents, nerf bars . . . all were in vogue in that by-gone era.

It was only too obvious what factor influenced the early look; lakes racing and "speed" was the thing. For this, bodies were trimmed of excess internal hardware. Plain, uncluttered exteriors became finely groomed wind-splitting shapes. The rounded race car nose, the full belly pan, contoured streamlining, to mention a few, came into practice on dual purpose lakes/street rods. Ornamental bulb horns, awkward "T" cowl lamps and tall "kookie" tops were unheard of, and unwanted. By the 1950s the average flathead-powered hot rod was topping 120 mph, with many going much faster, and yet it was not uncommon to see these cars driving both ways to and from the lakes meets.

Such was the case with the '29, "America's Most Beautiful Roadster, 1950." Although it was in every sense a legal street driven roadster, Bill NieKamp's nosed modified consistently ran in excess of 130 mph and ultimately reached a top speed of 142.40, at which time the car was retired from lakes duties.

The NieKamp car is like no other I have ever had the pleasure to ride in or drive; I take allowance in making this statement as having no personal acclaim to the building of it (only the restoration). It is a street machine, an all-out race car, and a go-kart all in one. With its smooth nose cutting through the wind like a hot knife, the panned roadster body accelerates from 65 to 90 mph and above in a matter of seconds. It maneuvers through freeway traffic like an enraged shark. Hang it in the sharpest curves at any speed with total control; handling is with precise accuracy. Like a sprint car, you can throw its weight into a corner then ride the throttle to the very limit of tire traction. It's wild. The firm but flexible transverse leaf suspension and low center of gravity hold the body in a fixed level position while the tires lose their grip. This car actually *needs* Indy hydes (up front) . . . yet with what it has it is glued-in like you wouldn't believe.

Driving the NieKamp is an experience I relish quite frequently and mostly late at night. In the hours around midnight, the city's people have turned-in; rolling this low slung machine from the garage, I find myself hurling down the empty Long Beach freeway before the flathead's water has had time to warm. One mile down you exit to the right, then make a hard left as the roadster streaks up and across a high-banked two-lane overpass some sixty feet above the freeway. Controlling with both steering and throttle the car whirls you through the tight curve like it's on rails. Then it starts to drift; the body remains flat giving you no warning, but the tires make a ripping sound as they slid sideways across the asphalt. You correct, only for a moment though, getting a fresh bite on the road . . . then back into the turn. You're in the front seat of a roller coaster doing 75 mph off the ramp as you swing right and down onto the Artesia freeway taking three of its four lanes to pull out.

By this time, the water temp is up and my head is taching 5000 rpm. Every part of the car has become a nerve; I feel the road's very surface.

The churning quick change rings in my ears sending harmonic vibration through my entire soul. I am united with the machine as the dark, sleeping world passes by. It's a trip, that's what it is . . . an honest to goodness trip. Every turn you make, seems like you've made it a thousand times before. Each new and different stretch of road is as familiar as my own driveway. The roadster goes where I want it—quickly, precisely, without hesitation. I can handle anything, any situation.

It's a grand old roadster. Unique in design, simple and subdued in appearance, impressive in performance and road handling capabilities, and rich in early era hot rodding heritage . . . the only one of its kind. That, my friends, is the NieKamp!

Brooklyn or Bust

Miami to New York
in a Hammered '49 Merc

By Terry Cook

※

Car Craft Street Freaks No. 5, 1981

As I look back at it now, I recall it as one of those weird experiences in life that is a strange combination of pleasure and pain. The fact of the matter is that I had flown to Miami from New York in January with every intention of jetting back home in a few hours. But when my pal, Coney Island Ralph, suddenly decided to buy this full-tilt custom, a chopped '49 Merc two-door sedan, I was automatically drafted to serve as co-driver on the return trip to the Big Apple. The car was a choice example of the breed with a 3-inch top chop, rounded hood corners, tube grille, V'd windshield, '59 Caddy taillights (tunneled, no less), skirts, electric doors and Mercury (?)[sic] flipper hubcaps. It had almost late Chevy power (a 327) backed by a trusty 2-speed Powerglide. I looked upon the return trip as an adventure. Little did I realize that cars built in Hawaii usually never come equipped with heaters, and on the second half of the trip we would be traveling in 10-degree weather.

The car first appeared to us on Sunday morning when the prospective seller drove it into the parking lot of an incredible 18-story condo we were staying in for the weekend. As I peered over the edge of one of the three balconies of the penthouse apartment in Fort Lauderdale, there was no mistaking the Merc. It was the brightest orange you ever saw—a genuine eye magnet. I grabbed my camera and headed for the elevator and lobby, only to spend another 15 minutes trying to find my way out of the maximum security high-rise onto the street. After the usual road test and haggling, a friend of Coney Island Ralph's appeared with a large bundle of $100 bills wrapped suspiciously in newspaper and the deal went down. Scrap the airplane ride home; it was Brooklyn or bust in this chopped Merc lowrider.

We decided to opt for a Monday a.m. departure rather than trying to jump in the sled and head out for New York non-stop immediately following the NFL playoff games that had just transpired on TV. This did not preclude a tour of the town, however, which included such adolescent behavior as a good deal of shouting at passers-by and a simulated abduction, where one member of our entourage was actually tossed into the trunk of the car for the ride back to the high-rise immediately following a first-rate Chinese dinner.

Monday morning dawned and it was off to New York with Coney Island Ralph himself at the wheel, me riding "shotgun," and the indomitable Sheldon slumped in the back seat. Since Sheldon had a reputation for driving in what could best be described as an erratic manner, Ralph wasn't about to trust his newest chopped Merc to his lifelong buddy. Ralph and I resigned ourselves to trading off at the wheel, driving the 1000-odd mile trip straight through—in the interest of adventure. This was the same Coney Island Ralph who had a long lineage of NHRA record-holding gas coupes from the '60s and early '70s. When he did a triple endo and rolled his Anglia up in a ball at the end of the dragstrip because some neophyte "racers" pulled out on the track past the lights just as he was making a pass, he wisely decided to end his career as a racing car driver. Since that time Ralph has gotten into Mercedes-Benzes, fast Porsches and immaculate street rods. Presently he owns a sharp Chevy-powered '40 Ford coupe, a '33 Ford three-window that will knock your eyes out, a full-fendered Ford-powered '32 four-door, three and a half other '49–'50 Mercs (one chopped) besides this one, and some other cars that I don't even know about.

Ralph is an excellent mechanic, but apparently wasn't watching the gas gauge as he ran the tank dry on the interstate about 200 miles north of Miami. I made a GAS sign as quick as a bunny and had hitched a ride up the road before the sixth car had passed. I was back with the can of gas inside of 15 minutes and Sheldon and I good-naturedly ribbed Ralph about his faux pas with the fuel gauge. We filled up at the nearest gas station and pointed the bulbous custom northward once again. Florida is a long state from one end to the other, so long in fact that we managed to run out of gas a second time before we reached the state line. This time it wasn't quite so funny, despite the fact that Ralph managed to coast to an offramp and we pushed him into the station, downhill.

Needless to say, I took the next shift behind the wheel and motored the Merc through Georgia and South Carolina, stopping for a gas fill and dinner just past Savannah with a quarter tank to spare. I was taking no chances.

Out on the open highway, the Merc is really an experience to drive. Unlike street rods, which are traditionally high-center-of-gravity early

Fords with sometimes skittish suspensions, the Merc was more of a boat, with an ultra-low center of gravity and a decent ride. Features like doors that close tight with windows that roll up along with the six-way Caddy power seat made it quite comfortable. Front, side and rear-view mirror vision was excellent despite the mail slot windows. The thing was definitely a car, although it did have a few of the standard hot-rodder type inconveniences. Aside from the lack of a heater, the speedometer didn't work and there was no tach, so you had to drive by the flow of the traffic and the seat of your pants. A rattle in the dash and right door along with a minor drivetrain vibration that let its presence be known when you backed off the throttle were the only other notable flaws, aside from the slack in the steering box which constantly kept you awake. The brakes didn't present any unpleasant surprises, the headlights and wipers worked well, and the AM/FM radio picked up nothing but Country & Western stations. I was trying to stretch it to South of the Border when I managed to run out of gas. Now I could see why Ralph had problems— the needle on the gas gauge fell like an anvil on the last quarter tank. I managed to coast to an offramp, and an open gas station was in sight of the spot where the lead sled came to rest.

It was my turn to stretch out in the back seat and catch some Z's while Ralph took on North Carolina. When I awoke we were off the interstate, out in the middle of nowhere, and out of gas for the fourth time. It was about 10 degrees outside and I didn't believe this was happening to me. By priming the secondaries we managed to sputter into a closed gas station at 4 a.m., where Sheldon and I rustled up a piece of hose and siphoned enough gas out of a wrecked Toyota to put a couple gallons in the Merc. Who could believe that three grown men could run out of gas four times out of five tankfuls?

After fueling up near Dismal Swamp, North Carolina, I took control of the ship and pushed on to Virginia while Ralph sulked in the back seat. By now it was rather nippy outside and we were bundled up in every article of clothing we had brought for the trip. A bit of foot stomping was needed to occasionally get the circulation going, but the temperature inside the car was tolerable due to the heat that seeped through the firewall. Unfortunately that wasn't all that came through, as the aroma of slow-cooking sludge also permeated the atmosphere. It was another factor that helped keep the driver awake. Ralph and Sheldon were on the nod so I decided to open this baby up and see what she'd do. The sweep second hand on my trusty wristwatch, illuminated by the dashboard light versus the roadside mile markers, produced a 53-second one-mile clocking, which translates to 68 mph.

Dawn finally broke, and I opted for more slumber time in the back seat as Ralph skirted Washington, D.C., and made it through the Harbor Tunnel in Baltimore. We stopped for gas and breakfast before pushing on to the Delaware Memorial Bridge and the Jersey Turnpike. No matter where we were, the car drew stares from everyone. Cars passed us very slowly as they checked it out. Gas station attendants freaked out. We just played it cool, which wasn't hard to do with no heater. About noon we rolled into my driveway and the adventure, for me at least, was over. I didn't envy Ralph's impending experience with the patched and potholed pavement of Brooklyn, where he lives, as it has got to rank among the worst roads in the United States, with the possible exception of Alaska.

As the screaming orange Merc drove out of sight I was thankful that my life had been enriched by this experience. The chopped '49 is one of those classic cars that will forever represent cruisin', the custom car era of my youth, and good times. Then I ran for my house and warmth.

Kross Kountry in a Kustom

Mile After Mile in
My Modified Mercillac

By Bob Hirohata
(as told to *R & C* editor)

%

Rod & Custom, August 1953

The first part of my story goes back to September 1952. That was the month that *Hop Up* magazine published an article entitled "6,000 Miles in a Custom" and told the hazards and perils of driving a radically customized car to the East from California.

I laughed at the time—things like that couldn't happen in real life. The story made good reading, though, and it has stuck in my mind ever since I read it.

The second part of my story actually goes further back than the first. It goes back, in fact, to the time I spent in the service. One of my buddies and myself used to sit and talk of custom cars and, when we tired of that, we'd talk about the Indianapolis 500 Mile Race. We vowed that someday we'd see the race, but we had no idea that that time would be so soon.

Ever since I can remember I had wanted a real "krazy kustom." Fortune smiled on me when I was released from the Navy and I found myself with a '51 Mercury being restyled at the Barris Kustom Shop.

When I took the car to the shop, Barris and I discussed a few minor changes but I had no indication of what George had in mind for my Merc. Three months later, when I picked up the car, I would have sworn it wasn't the same one that I left there originally! The top was chopped four inches in front and seven in back, the upper door posts had been eliminated so that the car looked like a hard top convertible, the whole car was so close to the ground that you could hardly see under it, the rear fenders had air-scoops built into them and so forth.

My second shock came when I was handed the bill but I took that as a matter of course. I had only to sell everything I owned and put my great aunt in hock to pay for the car—but it was worth it.

About the time I got the car back, the "6,000 Mile" article came to mind so I dug it out of my file and glanced through it. I could see then that at least a part of what the article stated was true—about entering steep driveways, etc. Some of the paragraphs, though, still sounded a little flowery and farfetched to me.

Some time later, with the Speedway race coming closer, I thought it would be great fun to see the race and, at the same time, enter my car in the 4th Annual Indianapolis Custom Show. I sent off an application and within a week had my answer. "Yes," it said.

Being very happy with the acceptance of the car I began making positive plans. After a good many letters back and forth I finally lined up a place to stay in town—quite a feat during the week of the race. Next, I talked my Navy buddy, Azzie Nishi, into going with me and we both made arrangements to get off work for a couple of weeks.

Needless to say the car received a very thorough going over. The stock Mercury engine was getting a little tired so I thought I'd make a few alterations to it. Somebody, don't remember exactly who, jokingly suggested that I put a Cadillac engine in the car—if it would fit. That gave me an idea—why not do it?

I talked to Dick Lyon of Lyon Engineering and he stated quite flatly that the conversion was not only feasible but had been done many times in the past. That cinched it! A quick trip to a Cadillac agency netted a '53 engine, then I took the car out to Lyon so he could begin the switch. That was eight days before we would leave for Indianapolis. The conversion was to take up a week of that. Time, by now, was of the utmost importance if we wanted to make the show opening.

It was Monday when I took the car to the shop and by Friday evening it was ready to go to the muffler shop for headers. Saturday afternoon the job was completed and I drove the Mercillac home from Nates Muffler Shop. The installation was beautiful and the engine ran pretty good but it always takes a little time before the bugs are worked out.

I got the car home, alright, but not until I learned to handle it with the slightly heavy front end. There wasn't enough time remaining to do anything about it, though, there was only three days left and nearly a million things to do before we were to leave.

I checked and rechecked the car, greased it, cross-switched the tires, polished it until it fairly glistened (that was a silly thing to do before such a long trip but how was I to know?), and bought several rolls of masking tape to put over such exposed parts of the car as would be susceptible to damage from rocks and gravel picked up by my tires or the tires of other cars.

I opened the trunk to check the luggage space and found—to my utter horror—that the trunk interior was a mess. When a car has been altered as much as mine, the trunk usually suffers the most. Shops have a habit

Suddenly we realized that we didn't know just how to get to Indiana!

of storing parts in it while the car is being worked on. Moldings and other sharp-edged pieces of metal had played havoc with the interior lining. I suddenly realized that such a thing would never do so I stormed down Lynwood way to Gaylord's Kustom Shop to see if he could fix me up with some trunk upholstery, it sure needed it.

Gaylord threw up his hands when he realized what all had to be done and the short time in which to do it, but, after he started work, he warmed up to the idea and soon everybody in the shop was working on it. They covered the floor with a beautiful green carpet—better than I have in my own house—and they lined the sides with pleated and rolled white leatherette.

I picked up one handy hint from the story in *Hop Up* and that was to carry an extra can of gas. I even went one step further and found an extra can for oil, too. Forewarned is forearmed, they say! The cans looked out of place in the spotless trunk so Barris painted them to match the car and Gaylord whipped up a sort of sack out of leatherette in which they could be kept without danger of tipping over.

At long last all was in readiness—or so we hoped. It was Tuesday, May 19th, and our schedule called for leaving in the late afternoon—we hoped to beat the heat across the California desert by driving at night. About the time we were ready to leave we began checking the car again and found that the brakes needed adjusting. This was done with little trouble but with a loss of time. Then we decided to apply the masking tape instead of doing it later while on the road.

Suddenly we realized that we didn't know just how to get to Indiana! A map was nothing to me but a bunch of lines and my companion, Azzie, didn't know whether we were to head East, West, North or South. A hurried phone call to *R&C*'s office was put through but they must have been just about to meet a deadline—all I could hear was so much jibberish—it was as though the operator had connected me to a chicken ranch at egg laying time. Above the clatter of typewriters, though, I could hear someone yelling out a number—it sounded like 66. I hoped they were referring to Route 66 instead of a page number because that highway ran through my town—Arcadia.

By the time we bought film for the camera, filled the car (and the extra can) with gas and said goodbye to what seemed like the whole town, it was quite late at night. As a matter of fact it was actually early Wednesday morning and the show, which was to start the following Saturday morning, was some 2500 miles away.

We loaded the luggage, spare tools and equipment into the trunk—the car settled down about two inches from the weight. I got in—the car went down another inch. Then, Azzie got in and the car looked as though we had forgotten to put wheels under it. I remember *Hop Up's* article saying that the lowered car in the story started having trouble when it got on the bad roads in Arizona, but I couldn't even get out of my *own driveway*!

After scraping the bottom of the Mercillac from front bumper to rear, we finally were under way. The dream of such a trip was at last a reality!

The Mercillac rolled smoothly through the darkness. (Well, almost smoothly, the car cleared the ground by only an inch or two.) After driving all morning we arrived at Prescott, Arizona. The engine hadn't acted up at all and we were averaging 18.6 miles per gallon. The roads weren't as bad as *Hop Up's* article stated—but we were taking a different route. There were a number of bad sections, however, that caused us to slow up and lose considerable time. This resulted in our driving continuously, night and day, with no stop-overs to sleep. Needless to say we were slightly beat when we rolled (or rubbed) into New Mexico.

The whole trip was working out exactly as the "6,000 Mile" article had said. In fact, we took a copy along with us and used it quite frequently as a reference book.

Gallup, New Mexico, proved to us that you can't park a radical kustom in a strange town and expect people to leave it alone. Not only did people look at it, they crawled all over it, under it and through it. (I neglected to lock the electric door switches.) The only way to protect our luggage and equipment was to park the car in full view when we stopped to eat. This, of course, reduced us to eating in drive-ins so by the time we got into Texas we were not only extremely tired but hungry as well. A sandwich diet isn't the best thing for two growing boys!

Another thing that plagued us was the careless gas attendants. If we didn't watch them they would slam the hood or the trunk lid and chip the paint. In order to save the car, and to save us from sprouting grey hairs, we talked various station attendants into letting us check the car over and fill it with gas. They almost unanimously agreed so they could look the car over!

I remember one station in particular when we stopped for gas in central Oklahoma. It had an unusually steep driveway and, as I maneuvered the car in at an angle so that I wouldn't tear the bottom out from under it, the thoughtful attendant came running up and suggested that we leave the car in the street and he would fix it there. We weren't sure what he was talking about for the gas hoses were, possibly, thirty feet too short to reach. He stared quite hard at the rear of the car then meekly said, "Oh, I thought you had two flat tires."

Not long after we left that station the engine began sputtering and finally quit altogether. No amount of coaxing would get it started again. We looked at our watches, at the calendar, then at each other. Any delay now and we'd be too late for the car show. We looked and looked and eventually discovered that a rock we had passed over a few miles back had crushed a gas line.

The Great Indy & Back Boogie

By Gray Baskerville

Hot Rod Magazine, October 1992

There's a Ton of Difference between Trailer Queens and Road Kings

I can't remember when our trip to Indy—featuring Boyd Coddington's Cosmic Coupe and Dennis Varni's America's Most Beautiful Roadster—was a done deal. It could have been the instant that Andy Brizio, the T-shirt king, challenged those present at a roast during the 1992 Oakland Roadster Show to drive their rods—not trailer them. It might have happened when Varni promised himself that if his totally rebuilt '29 on Deuce-like rails won the Oakland Roadster Show trophy, it would never see a trailer again. But perhaps it was the day that Boyd Coddington—the guy who was supposed to be the last man on earth to subject one of his creations to the travails of interstate travel—told Varni that all bets were covered. It seems that some of the Bay Area Roadster Club yahoos had a wager going that Coddington's rod wouldn't reach Beach Boulevard—a couple of blocks from Boyd's shop—let alone Barstow, California. The agreed-upon destination was Gary "Goodguy" Meadors' Rod and Race Run, which is held near Indianapolis at the National Hot Rod Association's Raceway Park, the home of the NHRA's U.S. Nationals. Eventually, the 4500-mile entourage included Varni, Brizio and his pal Chet Thomas, as well as George Atterbury, Don Tanner, and Bob Grossi, representing the SoCal Roadsters. As for Coddington? He's now counting his winnings.

Saturday, June 6

The plan of action was simple. The team of Baskerville, Coddington, Varni, and crew chief Dave "Grunt" Willey had agreed to meet both the NorCal and SoCal contingent Sunday night in Rawlins, Wyoming. Even though we were slowed by a wheel bearing failure on the chase Suburban, which was fixed in Las Vegas, we were well ahead of schedule when near disaster struck. During a roadster and coupe "chingo" just 10 miles west of St. George, Utah, we were engulfed in a cloud of smoke. An engine compartment fire, later traced to oil dripping on the turbine housing from a weep hole located under the exhaust-side cam tower, threatened to consume Coddington's Cosmic Coupe! Luckily, a passerby in a camper saw our plight and handed us a jug of drinking water that Boyd used to put out the fire. We spent the rest of the day and a portion of the night figuring out how we were going get this thing fixed in time to meet the gang in Rawlins Sunday night.

Sunday, June 7

Coddington's contingent of car-building pals is as big as Boyd himself. Brent Bodily of Syracuse, Utah, happens to be one of them. One phone call and we were handled. Bodily's fully equipped garage was ours for a day, while his wife Connie fed us and his pals at Tom's Auto Parts spent a long Sunday afternoon supplying our rebuild with the needed innards. By 10 o'clock that night we were up, running, and headed east for Rawlins.

Monday, June 8

Now it was Varni's turn to experience a mechanical gremlin. A noisy hydraulic lifter caused some concern and was subsequently adjusted. We also had to keep stopping every so often to eliminate the oil that was building up between the cam towers on the turbocharged four-cylinder Mitsubishi engine that powers Coddington's pearl-yellow speedster. This was all piddily stuff compared to the bad-ass black clouds that were thundering over Laramie, Wyoming. We were soaking up oil on I-80 when a guy in a battered pickup stopped and told us that sleet was falling 10 miles up the highway. "Bitchin," I thought . . . "now I can get some in-coupe running shots of Varni freezing his hiney off." What we didn't count on, as we pulled to the right and slowed down to get off the Interstate, was an 18-wheeler that literally covered and blinded us and Varni with a giant wave of sleet. It remained pucker city until we found a safe haven in a closed auto wash to ride out the cheeks-chilling weather. Ultimately we passed the storm front about 50 miles west of the Wyoming/Nebraska border and were hot on our way to North Platte, Nebraska, where we would finally catch up with the other adventurers. That's when the Mitsu-rod's tranny nearly went south. Evidently the computer, which controls the lock-out portion of the converter, was damaged in the fire, and after we cooled down the smoking torque converter, we were relegated to conventional drive and reverse. So we sort of cooled it the rest of the way and, much to the amazement of the NorCal and SoCal roadster contingents, which had gathered a few hours before in North Platte, we had finally caught them—well before sundown. Naturally, our arrival led to the consumption of a round of liquid loudmouth . . . but the reader will have to ask Coddingtion if this was where he collected those side bets.

Tuesday, June 9 & Wednesday, June 10

The entire crew—sans Roy Brizio who was also playing catch-up after he and roadster owner Bob Lawrence were slowed by a broken rocker arm—was off to Lincoln, Nebraska, to visit Speedway Motors' Bill Smith and his wonderful collection of vintage racing engines, pedal cars, and a brain-boggling assortment of N.O.S. (neat old stuff). After a couple of two-day non-stoppers, Brizio and Lawrence would catch the rest of the low-flying crew in Omaha, but not us. We had to get to Indy, our ultimate destination, by Wednesday night so Coddington could fly out Thursday morning. Dianne Coddington had issued an ultimatum. Hot Dogs would be in hot water if he missed his two sons' graduation ceremonies that were to be held that same day. We got as far as Davenport, Iowa, on Tuesday and arrived at Indy the next day.

Thursday, June 11

The best part after arriving in Indy was seeing the utter disbelief on the faces of the Midwest and East Coast rodders after they took a "queek peek" at Boyd's fried ride followed by a long look at the California contingent's insect-splattered roadsters . . . including Varni's AMBCR—America's Most Bug Covered Roadster. It was on Thursday afternoon that wave-maker Baskerville issued the first in a series of not-so-subtle challenges. "If we can drive our rods to Goodguys' Indy hapz, you Midwesterners can drive your wheels to Meadors' Pleasanton party."

Friday, June 12 to Sunday, June 14

Meadors' "Goodguys' Indy Hot Rod Happening" remains one of the truly unique runs in the Midwest. Not only does it feature the "Indy 500 Cruise," it also combines an open-air car show (limited to pre-'62 models) with a nostalgia drag race. Some 2300 rods made the "hat rad hapz" this year, including more than 250 racers. Although spectators and vendors are more than welcome, one still gets the feeling that this rod happening is really geared to the participants. For us though, the high point of the entire trip was going for a multi-lap putt around Indy's famous Brickyard. And it wouldn't have been an awesome Indy adventure if we hadn't stopped by Bill Spoerie's restoration shop where he and his helper were working on an '08 'Benz racing car, followed by the inevitable run-in with one of the Speedway's many ancient and obnoxious watchmen. Still, the trip to and from Raceway Park in Coddington's Cosmic Coupe produced a number of memories including a triple take from a most amazed reader of HRM.

Monday, June 15

I had a problem with my return to Los Angeles. My camera sack and dirty laundry wouldn't fit in Varni's roadster, so I had to hitch a ride with Pete Peterson, the guy who drives what may be the world's biggest and brightest mobilehome.

You see, Coddington keeps all his car-show stuff in a 40-foot-long red trailer that's towed by a Kenworth tractor. The tractor, in turn, is fitted with a custom-built living compartment that contains a lounge, lavatory, and cooking facility. Although by definition it's a mobilehome that pulls a long trailer, the sight of Boyd's big red machine has two pronounced effects—it really shakes the truckers *and* rattles the highway police as it rolls down the interstates.

For two days we shook, rattled, and rolled until we caught up with the rodley crew in Oklahoma City on June 16.

Wednesday, June 17

I needed a roadster hit, so the 556-mile ride from Oklahoma City to Albuquerque, New Mexico, was a hoot. First, we stopped just west of Amarillo, Texas, to pose in front of that crop of Caddies that are placed nose down in a field next to Interstate 40. Then somewhere between Amarillo and Al"bug"querque we hit a sail coyote at about 100 mph. Bump-bump and Varni's AMCER—America's Most Coyote

Encountering Roadster—added some hair to its fast-growing assortment of grille kill.

Thursday, June 18

The return trip between Albuquerque, New Mexico, and Kingman, Arizona, was getting boring. Aside from Coddington's flaming-and-smoking trans; Brizio the elder's broken alternator bracket; Brizio the younger's broken rocker; Grossi's cracked front main leaf; Atterbury's snapped shock, stoplight switch failure, lunched overdrive, and excessive front tire wear; Tanner's broken windshield plus making road pizza out of one turtle, two birds, one squirrel, and the aforementioned coyote—nothing was happening. So Varni saved the day. What he thought was a trans going away turned out to be far more serious. Both lower-rear radius rods had broken loose from their mounts and threatened the integrity of the drivetrain.

As luck would have it, a muffler shop across old Highway 66 from where we were staying had the wherewithal to make the necessary repairs. One hour and $15 later, Varni and crew were consuming adult beverages and preparing for their victory tour into the Pomona, California, fairground.

Friday, June 19

Almost before we knew it, we were home. More than 4500 miles had passed under the tires of the six remaining roadsters—Roy Brizio and Bob Lawrence had gone on to Florida from Indy. We also figured that during our trip more than 2500 gallons of gas had been burned, but none of us were burned in turn by the smokies. Yet in retrospect, one aspect of this two-week adventure must be discussed. One never knows what their hot rod is all about until he or she spends 14 days in it doing the Indy-and-back boogie. And like we said in the beginning, there are two types of rods—trailer queens and road kings.